THE BRITISH MUSEUM

MASTERPIECES
OF ANCIENT EGYPT

THE BRITISH MUSEUM

MASTERPIECES
OF ANCIENT EGYPT

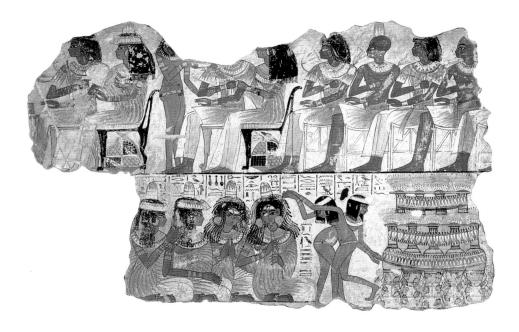

NIGEL STRUDWICK

THE BRITISH MUSEUM PRESS

First published in 2006 by British Museum Press
A division of The British Museum Company Ltd
38 Russell Square, London WC1B 3QQ

ISBN-10:   0-7141-1972-5
ISBN-13:   978-0-7141-1972-4

A catalogue record for this title is available from
the British Library

Original design for the Masterpieces series
by Harry Green
Design by Proof Books
Printed and bound in China

All photographs in this book were taken by the British
Museum Photographic and Imaging Dept and are copyright
the Trustees of the British Museum unless otherwise stated.

Map on page 23 by David Hoxley.
Photographs on pages 8, 9, 19 by Nigel Strudwick.
Photographs on pages 11, 15 by Graham Harrison.

Half title: Lion, page 278.
Frontispiece: Colossal bust of Amenhotep III, pages 152–3.
Title page: Fragment of banquet scene from the tomb of
Nebamun, pages 170–7.

CONTENTS

Preface

THE PURPOSE OF THIS BOOK is to present highlights or masterpieces of all aspects of the British Museum's collection of Egyptian and Sudanese objects, ranging from about 4500 BC to the later fourteenth century AD. Many of these objects have never been illustrated in full colour before, and a number have received no proper publication. The selection criteria for the almost 200 objects is somewhat personal, and beyond the obvious pieces, I know that many readers will regret the omission of this object or wonder why that one does appear. I have tried in the limited space available to present up-to-date information about the original context, discovery, and acquisition of the objects and their history in the museum. A reading list is provided for the general reader, while the specialist will find the essential publications relevant to each object at the end of the book.

It is a pleasure to acknowledge the help of others in the production of this publication. Colleagues in the Department of Ancient Egypt and Sudan have kindly contributed entries on objects which are within their own areas of research or which are of particular interest to them. Thus I thank: Renée Friedman (EA 35502); Marcel Marée (EA 1785); Richard Parkinson (Ramesseum Papyri group); Jeffrey Spencer (EA 35571-2); Neal Spencer (EA 22); John Taylor (EA 6647; EA 15655 and 27735); Derek Welsby (EA 1650). In addition, all my entries in this book have been read over by colleagues in the department, and I am extremely grateful to all of the above and also to Julie Anderson for helpful comments and suggestions, although I bear the responsibility for the conclusions I have drawn. Above all, I would like to thank Vivian Davies for supporting this project through to its conclusion, and also for reading and commenting on many of the entries on sculpture.

It has been possible to obtain new photographs of roughly one-third of the objects. Some had never been photographed in colour before, and the opportunity was also taken to obtain up-to-date images of a number of pieces which were last photographed around 1980. This work has involved a high level of co-operation with the Museum's Department of Photography and Imaging. I appreciate the enthusiastic support of Ivor Kerslake, Studio Manager, for his time and for allocating the time of his photographers to this project. My greatest debt is to Sandra Marshall who has been responsible for most of the new photographs – she has produced a series of superb images, and has been a model of patience and tolerance as the list of objects changed in front of her eyes. Lisa Baylis completed the photography with great efficiency at the beginning of 2006, including a number of awkward objects; Ivor Kerslake himself was able to take the new photograph of EA 26 on a special visit to Houston.

The photographs could not have been made without the help of the Department of Ancient Egypt and Sudan's Museum Assistants (Darrel Day, Evan York, Tony Brandon, Bob Dominey, and Emily Taylor) who made the objects available, which sometimes required a great deal of awkward physical work to remove glass from objects in the galleries. I have constantly pestered the Department's Photographic Officer, Tania Watkins, for information about images, and have benefited from her remarkable memory of what is and is not photographed. Many volunteers in the Department over the course of this project have helped with doing the initial image research, inputting of data, and checking lists and numbers. Without their generous assistance, I could not have completed the entries for the book in the time-scale, and I am very grateful to them all.

The book was originally designed by Harry Green, who sadly passed away when the book was approaching the first proof. His place has been enthusiastically taken by Peter Bailey. At the British Museum Press, my editor Carolyn Jones has guided the work along in her usual quiet and expert way, and has been incredibly tolerant when changes have been enforced on the schedule, whether by the pressure of other museum work or by personal circumstances. I wish to express my profound gratitude to her for the effort she has expended in bringing this publication to print. I also thank all Carolyn's colleagues who have contributed to the finished book, in particular Sarah Levesley.

Nigel Strudwick, 2006

ANCIENT EGYPT

ANCIENT EGYPT is the oldest known African civilization and one of the earliest and greatest in the world. Along the Nile river, the ancient Egyptians built temples, tombs, palaces, and houses. Their concern that their temples and tombs should endure for eternity, combined with the dry desert climate of Egypt, means that an astonishing array of elements of their material culture has survived, to be seen both on the ground in Egypt and in museum collections around the globe.

As in most ancient societies, power and wealth in Egypt belonged to a relatively small elite, in essence the royal family and a circle of powerful and trusted officials. These people were able to command considerable resources for the construction of monuments and statues, and for presenting their view of the world. It is easy to forget the largely anonymous mass of the ancient population, most of whom were farmers, with smaller numbers functioning as priests, labourers, servants, and craftsmen. Their labours were responsible both for creating the wealth of the state, which was then channelled into the production of statues, reliefs, and paintings for temples, and also for constructing the objects and buildings themselves.

The civilization of ancient Egypt lasted thousands of years, surviving many political upheavals and the rise and fall of numerous dynasties. Its history is briefly summarized below

The desert cliffs at Abydos.

(a list of periods and dynasties, with dates, appears on pages 16–17). The Department of Ancient Egypt and Sudan of the British Museum holds objects from every stage of this long history, forming one of the most comprehensive and magnificent collections in the world, surpassed only by the Egyptian Museum in Cairo. This volume is the first to give the interested visitor and reader an illustrated overview of the most important objects in the British Museum's superb collection. The entries in this book are arranged in chronological order, offering an overview of some five thousand years of continuous civilization in the Nile Valley.

THE HISTORY OF ANCIENT EGYPT AND SUDAN

Predynastic Period: The last phase of prehistoric Egypt before the establishment of a unified kingdom, about 5300–3000 BC, is characterized by a series of localized cultures, mostly named after the type-sites at which they were first recorded. The cultures of the north of Egypt were quite different from those of the south, and the close of the Predynastic Period was accompanied by the gradual northward spread of the southern material culture. Type-sites in the north include Merimde, Omari, Maadi, and the cultures of the Faiyum; in the south the main phases are known as Badarian and Naqada I, II, and III. Contemporary with the later phases of the Egyptian Predynastic cultures was the A-Group culture of Nubia. The earliest writing appeared in Egypt in about 3500 BC.

The central Old Kingdom cemetery at Giza, with the pyramid of Khafre.

Early Dynastic Period: Dynasties 1 and 2, *c.* 3000–2686 BC. The Upper Egyptian late Predynastic cultures showed dramatic cultural developments that continued into the historical period. One feature was increased social stratification, leading to the development of a ruling elite, some of whom were buried at Abydos and are known as 'Dynasty 0'. About 3000 BC the Upper Egyptian cultures seem to have taken over the northern ones, leading to the development of a unified state; the identity of the first king is uncertain, but Narmer and Aha are possibilities. In later times this king came to be known as the semi-mythical figure of Menes. Cultural developments were rapid, and many of the basic symbols and characteristics of Egyptian culture emerged. Kings were buried at Abydos and Saqqara. There is evidence of military incursions into Nubia.

Old Kingdom: Dynasties 3–8, *c.* 2686–2125 BC. The first great phase of Egyptian culture is notable for the development of the pyramid as the royal tomb at the beginning of the Third Dynasty. During this period a great centralized power base grew up at Memphis. Kings constructed pyramids north and south of Memphis, and large necropoleis (cemeteries) of officials

Old Kingdom statue of Nenkhefta, page 58.

grew up around some of the pyramids, particularly at Giza and Saqqara. The Egyptian elite tomb developed into the basic form that endured for the next 2,500 years, with a decorated chapel and a subterranean burial chamber; many of the decorative motifs lasted almost as long. The administration of Egypt was highly organized under royal control, with a small group of senior officials overseeing the system; some administrative papyri survive from this period. The first expeditions to the east and north-east of Egypt, to the Sinai, for turquoise, copper, and various types of stone, were apparently made at this time. Late in the Old Kingdom, perhaps about 2200 BC, the monarchy seems to have weakened, a process only visible today as a proliferation of kings with very short reigns (the Seventh and Eighth Dynasties). After about 2150 BC, however, the centralized administration seems to have failed. The reasons for this are not completely clear, but may be a combination of many factors, such as low Nile floods, famines, and weak kings, and there is a general impression of problems and disorder.

First Intermediate Period: Dynasties 9–11, *c.* 2160–2016 BC. With the collapse of central control, the Nile Valley broke into a number of independently ruled districts centred on the different provinces. Predominant among these early on were the rulers of Herakleopolis, the Ninth and Tenth Dynasties. Little is known about them, but they seem to have controlled the country at least as far south as Asyut, whose governors (*nomarchs*) were loyal to them, and they may have received some nominal allegiance in other parts of Upper Egypt early on. However, the provincial rulers in the south fought with each other for control; gradually the rulers of Thebes became the dominant southern power, and began to call themselves kings (Eleventh Dynasty). Fighting between Thebes and Herakleopolis, probably around Abydos, is referred to in several contemporary texts. The Thebans were ultimately victorious, and gradually extended their control over the whole land; this process seems to have been complete by about year 39 of Nebhepetre Mentuhotep II (*c.* 2016 BC). There is little documentation for the later stages of this internal strife, but many Upper Egyptian sources record the earlier stage of the conflict.

Middle Kingdom: Dynasties 11–13, *c.* 2016–1650 BC. The Middle Kingdom began with the unification of Egypt under Mentuhotep II. Following two more kings of the same name, the throne passed to a new family (the Twelfth Dynasty), also apparently from southern Egypt. These kings moved the capital north to Lisht, and were buried at sites between Dahshur and the Faiyum; all (bar the last) were named either Senwosret or Amenemhat (Greek: Sesostris and Ammenemes). Although residing in the north, they made Thebes a religious centre, and were largely responsible for promoting its deity, Amun, to the top of the Egyptian pantheon.

The Middle Kingdom was a period of prosperity and stability. Military expeditions were sent abroad, and Lower Nubia was brought under full control by means of a series of forts south of the Second Cataract; limited forays may also have been made into the Near East.

Considerable numbers of people from Canaan moved into the Eastern Delta during the later Twelfth Dynasty. Internal administrative reforms improved the running of the land, and in the later Middle Kingdom, the Faiyum area was first developed for major settlements and agriculture. This dynasty's artistic products are among the finest in Egypt, and the era is also renowned for its literary output, including many of the greatest written works of ancient Egypt, such as the *Tale of Sinuhe* and the *Teaching of Ptahhotep*.

The last ruler of the Twelfth Dynasty was a woman, Sobekneferu. The following dynasty continued to rule from Lisht, effectively as an extension of the Twelfth, but there is a noticeable decline in the number of monuments and an increase in the number of kings with very short reigns, a sure sign of a less stable era.

The temple of Ramesses II at Abu Simbel.

Second Intermediate Period: Dynasties 13–17, *c.* 1650–1550 BC. The internal history of Egypt at this time is still most unclear. The disintegration of the state was due to several factors, such as administrative decline, famine, and plague, and the establishment of a Canaanite polity in the Delta (Fourteenth Dynasty). It seems that the weakened Thirteenth and Fourteenth Dynasties were overthrown in the north by an invasion from Canaan, doubtless the rulers known now as the Hyksos (based on Egyptian *heqau-khasut*, 'rulers of foreign lands') – the Fifteenth Dynasty. The south of Egypt was under varying control, but in due course another Theban dynasty (Seventeenth) reasserted the area's independence. The later Seventeenth Dynasty, particularly its last two kings, Seqenenre and Kamose, fought to topple the Hyksos rulers. It seems that the Egyptians also had to contend with an invasion in the south from the kingdom of Kush, based at Kerma in the Sudan.

New Kingdom: Dynasties 18–20, *c.* 1550–1069 BC. Ahmose, the first king of the Eighteenth Dynasty, does not seem to have taken up arms against the Hyksos until later in his reign. He laid siege to the Hyksos capital of Avaris in the Eastern Delta (modern Tell ed-Daba) and chased them into Palestine. With this event begins Egypt's great imperial epoch. It was not long before the royal residence and capital were transferred back to Memphis, and Ahmose's

Statue of Amenhotep I, page 126.

successors began both large construction projects at home and military expeditions abroad. Thutmose I expanded Egypt's control into both Nubia and the Near East, reaching at least as far south as the Fourth Cataract in the Sudan and the Euphrates river in Iraq. Thutmose III, probably his grandson, mounted a series of campaigns spreading Egyptian influence further around the Near East. A permanent military presence was established in Nubia, but the Asiatic provinces were governed by vassal governors with a relatively limited Egyptian presence. Considerable international trade built up, and Egypt became more prosperous and aware of its place in the world than ever before.

Much temple-building happened at this time; in particular, the cult centre of Amun at Karnak was rebuilt and expanded dramatically. The kings built temples elsewhere, including mortuary temples for their funerary cults on the West Bank at Thebes, to complement their rock-hewn burial places in the Valley of the Kings. By the reign of Amenhotep III (c.1390–1352 BC), the furious pace of foreign campaigns had ceased, and he lavished considerable wealth on many grandiose temple schemes.

Amenhotep's son, also called Amenhotep, made some very visible changes to the practice of religion after only two or three years on the throne. He changed his name to Akhenaten, concentrated his worship on one god, the solar disc or Aten, and moved his capital to the new site of Akhetaten (modern Amarna) in Middle Egypt. (This part of the dynasty is often called the Amarna Period.) The reasons for this are hotly debated; suffice it to say that his changes barely survived him, and his successor Tutankhamun gradually restored the old ways. Tutankhamun had no heirs, and the throne passed to two of his senior officials, Ay and then Horemheb.

Horemheb seems to have designated his general Ramesses as his successor, and his family is termed the Nineteenth Dynasty. They came from the Eastern Delta, and it was not long before the residence and capital were moved from Memphis to Pi-ramesse (modern Qantir). After Ramesses' short reign, his son Sety I, and particularly his grandson Ramesses II, undertook extensive building projects in Egypt; they also campaigned vigorously in the Near East, where many political changes in the later Eighteenth Dynasty, perhaps coupled with less active interference from Egypt, meant that the empire was smaller than in the time of Amenhotep III. Ramesses II's conflict with the Hittites (Egypt's main enemy) culminated in the famous battle of Qadesh, and led ultimately to a peace treaty. The dynasty ended in disputes about the succession, and Sethnakht, a man from outside the family, seized the throne, beginning what we term the Twentieth Dynasty.

His son, Ramesses III, was the last of the great kings of the New Kingdom. At this time, the so-called 'Sea Peoples', groups who formed part of the great population migrations in the Eastern Mediterranean and Near East in the later first millennium BC, were attempting to settle in Egypt. Ramesses kept these forces at bay, but lost the remnants of the Egyptian empire, other than in the south. This king built temples and made great donations to the cults of Amun, but

Egypt began to decline. He was succeeded by eight further kings also called Ramesses. During this Ramesside Period various economic and political problems became apparent, as recorded by many documents on stone and papyri from the west of Thebes. Workmen went on strike for wages, there were unspecified threats from the desert, and tomb-robbery became common. By the end of the dynasty, the king was ruling primarily in the north, and the religious capital of Thebes had become largely self-governing, ruled by the high priest of Amun.

Third Intermediate Period: Dynasties 21–25, *c.* 1069–664 BC. The division of Egypt remained in force. The new rulers in the north are termed the Twenty-first Dynasty, with their capital at Tanis. Some of the Theban high priests assumed royal titles, but there was contact between the two halves of the land, and one of the Twenty-first Dynasty kings, Psusennes I, was the son of the Theban high priest Panedjem I; Psusennes II, the last king of the dynasty, had previously been high priest in Thebes. Upon his death, the kingship passed to Sheshonq (the biblical Shishak, who attacked Jerusalem), from a family of Libyan descent from Bubastis (Twenty-second Dynasty). This dynasty maintained stronger connections with Thebes, but the Delta became increasingly fragmented, with a number of local rulers, some of whom are possibly the Twenty-third Dynasty; the Twenty-fourth Dynasty consisted of kings in Sais.

In the mid-eighth century BC, southern Egypt came increasingly under attack from Kush, a powerful state based in Upper Nubia (northern Sudan). Various incursions were made, largely shows of strength, with the invaders returning to Nubia, but in 715 BC Shabaka launched a campaign to take over Egypt. He and his successors are known as the Twenty-fifth Dynasty.

Late Period: Dynasties 26–30 and Second Persian Period, *c.* 664–332 BC. With the reunification of the country came something of a renaissance in Egypt. Artistic styles based on older models harked back to the great eras of the past. Periods chosen for inspiration generally depended on the location of the new monuments – thus Old Kingdom models are more common in the north, and Middle and New Kingdom ones in the south.

After almost fifty years, Egypt came under threat from the expanding Assyrian empire. After making several attempts at invasion, the last Kushite king (Taharqa) was driven out in 667 BC, and the Assyrians gained the allegiance of various vassal rulers. Of these, Psamtek of Sais (Psammetichus I), first established himself as pre-eminent and then removed Egypt from Assyrian control; his dynasty, the Twenty-sixth, lasted until the first Persian invasion of 525 BC under Cambyses, continuing the revivals of his predecessors and producing many great works of art.

The First Persian Period (Twenty-seventh Dynasty) was punctuated by a number of

Sarcophagus of Sasobek, page 266.

Egyptian revolts, but the Persians were able to maintain control until their influence was ended by Amrytaios in 404 BC. His Twenty-eighth and the succeeding Twenty-ninth Dynasties have left relatively little material, but with the accession of Nectanebo I (Egyptian: Nakhtnebef, Thirtieth Dynasty) of Sebennytos in 380 BC, perhaps after an internal coup, another artistic renaissance began. He and his successors constructed many temples and set up fine works of art in them; the third king of the dynasty, Nectanebo II (Egyptian: Nakhthorheb) encountered renewed Persian expansion, and Egypt fell to Artaxerxes III of Persia in 343 BC. Egypt was then controlled by foreign powers until the 1952 revolution. This Second Persian Period is occasionally termed the Thirty-first Dynasty, and fell in turn to the imperial expansion of Alexander of Macedon in 332 BC, who was apparently treated by the Egyptians as a liberator.

Ptolemaic Period: 332–30 BC. Egypt's history now largely tracked that of the classical world for the next seven centuries. After Alexander's death in 323 BC, the empire was divided among his Greek generals, and Ptolemy, son of Lagos, took Egypt. His capital was Alexandria, from where his successors – all male and called Ptolemy except for the last, Cleopatra – ruled for nearly 300 years. The Ptolemaic Period is marked by a number of revolts of the native population, and, as well as putting these down, the kings made various attempts to obtain the favour of at least the priestly elites – one attempt resulted in the decree of 196 BC promulgated on the Rosetta Stone. In the arts, interesting mixtures of Hellenistic and traditional Egyptian forms attest the co-existence of the two cultures. In the first century BC, Egypt came increasingly under the influence of Rome, as did the rest of the Mediterranean, and was drawn into some of the internal Roman political conflicts, the last of which resulted in the defeat of Mark Antony and Cleopatra in 30 BC at the battle of Actium, and the addition of Egypt to the Roman empire.

Roman Period: 30 BC–AD 395. With the death of Cleopatra, Egypt was no longer an independent nation but was ruled by the Roman emperor, who appointed a prefect to run the country. Egypt was termed the 'granary of Rome', as it supplied grain for the empire's needs; harsh taxes were often imposed since it was a wealthy land. Various prefects and emperors campaigned on Egypt's southern borders, and there were times when the country was threatened by Syria and Persia. Christianity, by tradition brought to Egypt by St Mark in AD 65, flourished and expanded despite persecutions in the third century AD, culminating in those of the emperor Diocletian (ruled 284–305). In the reign of Constantine (306–337), Christianity became the official religion of the empire.

Coptic/Christian, Late Antique or Byzantine Period: AD 395–642. Egypt was thus largely Christian when the Roman empire split into eastern and western halves in 395, and Egypt came under the rule of Constantinople, the eastern capital. Christianization continued apace,

Roman mummy mask of a woman, page 306.

The monastery of St Antony.

and the development of monastic communities boomed. Various attempts to reunify the empire achieved only minor success, and in the seventh century Egypt was again briefly ruled by the Persians. With the dramatic campaigns by Arab armies led by the successors of Mohamed, it was not long before Egypt fell to Amr ibn el-As in 642.

Arab Conquest: AD 642. The new conquerors established their capital city at Fustat, south of modern Cairo, and of course introduced Islam to Egypt. For the first 250 years of the occupation, there was little persecution of Christians, although they were subject to higher taxes than Muslims; in fact many of the more substantial older Coptic remains in Egypt date from the fifth to ninth centuries. However, gradual Islamicization did take place, and the Copts were reduced to a substantial minority in Egypt.

Kush: Kush is the Egyptian name for the southern part of Nubia. The first kingdom of Kush (*c.* 2500–1500 BC), also known as the Kerma culture after its capital city, came into conflict with Egypt in the later Second Intermediate Period. After a period of Egyptian domination during the New Kingdom, the second kingdom of Kush established itself in the region of Gebel Barkal in the ninth century BC, and in 715 BC took control of Egypt as the Twenty-fifth Dynasty. This period is known as the Napatan phase (ninth–fourth centuries BC) of the kingdom. The Kushite state adopted many Egyptian cultural and artistic characteristics; the Egyptian language was used in monumental inscriptions, though it is unlikely that it was spoken by the people. By 664 BC the Kushites had been expelled from Egypt by the Assyrians; they withdrew to the Middle Nile area, where their culture continued to flourish for another thousand years. In the fourth century BC, the royal residence moved south to Meroe, while Gebel Barkal remained the religious centre. This may reflect a dynastic change. Between the fourth century BC and the fourth century AD, Kushite monuments display a rich mixture of Egyptian, Graeco-Roman, and indigenous African architectural and artistic styles, and the Kushites began to write their own, as yet undeciphered, language, known as Meroitic. This later period is known as the Meroitic phase.

Chronology of Ancient Egypt[1]

Dates before 664 BC are all approximate.

Predynastic Period, c. 5300–3000 BC

Badarian Period	4400–4000
Naqada I (Amratian Period)	4000–3500
Naqada II (Gerzean Period)	3500–3200
Naqada III (Dynasty '0')	3200–3000

Early Dynastic Period, c. 3000–2686 BC

1st Dynasty	3000–2890
2nd Dynasty	2890–2686

Old Kingdom, c. 2686–2125 BC

3rd Dynasty	2686–2613
4th Dynasty	2613–2494
5th Dynasty	2494–2345
6th Dynasty	2345–2181
7th and 8th Dynasties	2181–2160

First Intermediate Period, c. 2160–2016 BC

9th and 10th Dynasties	2160–2025
11th Dynasty (*Thebes only*)	2125–2016

Middle Kingdom, c. 2016–1650 BC

11th Dynasty (*whole of Egypt*)	2016–1985
12th Dynasty	1985–1773
13th Dynasty	1773–after 1650

Second Intermediate Period, c. 1650–1550 BC

14th Dynasty (*minor rulers*)	1773–1650
15th Dynasty (the Hyksos)	1650–1550
16th Dynasty (*in Thebes*)	1650–1580
17th Dynasty	1580–1550

New Kingdom, c. 1550–1069 BC

18th Dynasty	1550–1295

(*The reign of Akhenaten, c. 1352–1336 BC, and his immediate successors is known as the Amarna Period.*)

19th Dynasty	1295–1186
20th Dynasty	1186–1069

(*The 19th and 20th Dynasties are also known as the Ramesside Period.*)

Third Intermediate Period, c. 1069–664 BC

21st Dynasty	1069–945
22nd Dynasty	945–715
23rd Dynasty (*contemporary with later 22nd, 24th and early 25th*)	818–715
24th Dynasty	727–715
25th Dynasty (*southern Egypt*)	747–716
25th Dynasty (*all Egypt*)	716–664

Late Period, 664–332 BC

26th Dynasty	664–525
27th Dynasty (First Persian Period)	525–404
28th Dynasty	404–399
29th Dynasty	399–380
30th Dynasty	380–343
Second Persian Period	343–332

Ptolemaic Period, 332–30 BC

Macedonian Dynasty	332–305
Ptolemaic Dynasty	305–30

Roman Period, 30 BC–AD 395

Coptic/Byzantine Period and Later, AD 395–642

Arab Conquest, AD 642

THE CULTURES OF LOWER AND UPPER NUBIA

A-group	*c.* 3700–2800 BC	
C-group	*c.* 2300–1600 BC	
Ancient Kerma ('Kerma Ancien')	*c.* 2500–2050 BC	} *First kingdom of*
Middle Kerma ('Kerma Moyen')	*c.* 2050–1750 BC	*Kush*
Classic Kerma ('Kerma Classique')	*c.* 1750–1500 BC	
Napatan Period	9th–4th centuries BC	} *Second kingdom of*
Meroitic Period	4th century BC–4th century AD	*Kush*
X-group	4th–6th centuries AD	

THE EGYPTIAN COLLECTIONS OF THE BRITISH MUSEUM

How did the British Museum come to hold its wonderful Egyptian and Sudanese collection? Objects have been acquired by a variety of means, mainly purchase, excavation, and donation. Understanding these different contexts of acquisition sheds a great deal of light on how the practice and philosophy of collecting have changed over the past two centuries.[2]

PURCHASE

The majority of the objects in the British Museum's Egyptian collection were purchased. In the first half of the nineteenth century, many people collected objects in Egypt, either for their own pleasure or with the ultimate aim of financial reward (or a mixture of both), and several of these collections now rest in the Museum. The earliest and most important is the first collection of the British Consul-General Henry Salt,[3] who began to collect objects not long after his appointment in 1815, partly on the understanding that he was acquiring objects for the British Museum. His large first collection was purchased after considerable wrangling by the Trustees in 1823 for the relatively small sum of £2,000, and the huge range of material in it (more than 120 crates) put the Museum's Egyptian collection on a better and more systematic footing. Previously, the representation of Egypt in the Museum consisted basically of the objects taken from the French in 1801 and a variety of miscellaneous donations; while these were of the highest importance in raising awareness of the ancient culture in Britain, the appearance of the Salt material in the galleries in 1823 did much to advance the appreciation of Egyptian objects, particularly sculpture. The collection was considerably expanded by purchases from Europeans such as Joseph Sams (1834), from Salt's estate (1835), and from

Naos (shrine) of Ptolemy VIII, page 300.

Giovanni Anastasi (first in 1839 but also later), and there were many smaller purchases.

Attempts were soon made in Egypt to control the frenetic collecting by foreigners. In 1835 Mohamed Aly, the ruler of Egypt, tried unsuccessfully to ban the export of antiquities; he also planned to set up an Antiquities Service. The Service des Antiquités founded by Auguste Mariette with the blessing of the viceroy Said in 1858 was more successful in reducing or practically eliminating unauthorized excavations by foreigners, although it did little to stop antiquities-hunting by the local population.[4] The mid-nineteenth century was probably the time when antiquities dealing really came into its own, and the purchase of antiquities from a local dealer became the most common way in which foreigners could acquire antiquities in Egypt. The British Museum did not buy directly from Egypt at that time, as the Museum's Egyptologist, Samuel Birch, did not go there; instead he relied primarily on purchasing objects from British travellers such as the Revd Greville Chester[5] or from dealers in Britain.[6]

Ernest Budge (keeper 1894–1924) took a more active approach. He travelled annually to Egypt, starting before he became keeper, and during those visits made numerous acquisitions, often in circumstances which can be most tactfully called questionable, and frequently buying objects from illicit excavations. For example, shortly after purchasing the papyrus of Any (see pages 218–21) in 1887–8, he was involved in a rather difficult intrigue to avoid trouble with Grébaut, the head of the Service des Antiquités, over the purchase of this and other papyri and the Amarna cuneiform tablets.[7] Budge also used other agents in Egypt to help him to acquire antiquities from dealers, such as the Revd Chauncy Murch, an American missionary.[8] In consequence, the collection increased dramatically during Budge's keepership (from about 10,000 objects in 1870 to 57,000 in 1924).[9]

Since that time, the practice of buying from dealers in Egypt has declined, and Egypt has quite rightly made the purchase and export of antiquities illegal. Nowadays the history of a potential acquisition has to be very carefully researched and exhaustive enquiries made. In the course of the 1990s, the Department of Ancient Egypt and Sudan helped to uncover a number of antiquities thefts, and in recent years it has been instrumental in co-operating with the authorities in returning several illegally exported objects to Egypt and the Sudan.

DONATION

Donations have been an important source of objects almost since the foundation of the Museum. For example, the first mummy in the collection came from a bequest of antiquities by William Lethieullier, who died in 1756.[10] Many important pieces in this volume were presented to the Museum – perhaps the most significant donation was a substantial set of sculptures (including the Rosetta Stone, pages 298–9) given by George III in 1802, acquired by the British Nation following the defeat of the French fleet at Abukir. This donation gave the British public their first real taste of Egyptian monumental art, which was strengthened immensely by the gift in 1818 of the colossal bust of Ramesses II (see pages 202–3). Of course, the very nature of donation makes it an unsystematic and unpredictable method of acquisition, and in the twenty-first century, a donation is subject to the same stringent rules applied to purchases; in addition, it is not now usual to accept a donation unless it materially strengthens the collection in some way.

EXCAVATION

A particularly important form of donation is that arising from excavation. Authorized foreign scientific excavations, with proper permits, began in Egypt shortly after 1881. The newly-founded Egypt Exploration Fund (now Society) of London was one of the first organizations to take advantage of this, and from 1883 onwards, objects began to come to the Museum from the Fund's divisions (as the partition of objects between Egypt and the excavating expedition is known). Over the years more than 11,000 objects have come to the Museum from this particular source, including pieces in this volume from Bubastis, Deir el-Bahari, and Amarna. This only stopped with the cessation of divisions in the 1980s,

Early morning excavations of Theban Tomb 99, in 1997.

although divisions still continue in the Sudan. Other organizations from Britain also excavated in Egypt and the Sudan and presented objects to the British Museum; they included Petrie's Egypt Research Account and British School of Archaeology in Egypt, which flourished from the later 1880s until the 1930s. Other donating institutions include the Oxford University Expedition, which excavated at Kawa and Faras in the Sudan. The British Museum has of course also conducted its own excavations in Egypt and the Sudan, and received divisions of objects. Sites investigated include Asyut (1907), Mostagedda and Matmar (late 1920s), and Ashmunein (1980s) in Egypt, and, from the 1990s on, many sites in the Sudan, including Soba, Kawa, and the Northern Dongola Reach.

In very recent years, the collection has been expanded beyond its traditional limits with the donation of a number of important collections from outside the UK, resulting from fieldwork by others in Egypt and the Sudan. Thus a vast collection of material from the work of Fred Wendorf (Southern Methodist University) at prehistoric sites in the deserts has come to the Museum, as has the collection of stone samples taken by Dietrich Klemm and Rosemarie Klemm (University of Munich) during their work on the quarries of Egypt. A study collection of material from the work of William Adams (University of Kentucky) at Kulubnarti in the Sudan is presently being accessioned.

A major problem with many objects is that next to nothing is known about the context of

Early Dynastic statuette of a king,
page 36.

their discovery, particularly those acquired by purchase and donations (excluding those found in excavations, of course). There are several reasons for this, from deliberate misinformation on the part of the seller to keep the authorities off their track, to lack of interest on the part of the purchaser/owner in anything other than the object's aesthetic qualities. Often there is anecdotal evidence about the findspot (see pages 130 and 166), but it is probably no exaggeration to say that more than half of the collection has no good provenance. Examples from better-excavated contexts can help, and providing such a context for similar material is an important justification for certain types of fieldwork, but for most of these objects, their findspot has been lost forever.

SURVIVAL AND DISCOVERY

The likelihood of an object's survival is primarily dictated by a combination of the place where it was laid or abandoned by its ancient owner and the material of which it was made. The Nile in Egypt and the Sudan runs through the eastern part of the Sahara, which is so lacking in precipitation that the development of settled communities is extremely difficult or impossible without modern technology, except in places such as oases. At present there is 25–50 mm of rain annually, and there was little more in ancient times, with the present hyper-arid conditions setting in during the Old Kingdom in the mid-third millennium BC.[11] The Greek historian Herodotos' oft-quoted statement that 'Egypt is the gift of the Nile' is incontrovertible: where the Nile flooded and laid down a thick layer of fertile sediment, it created the right conditions for agriculture and the development of the advanced culture of Egypt. However, where the Nile did not flood, there is just sandy desert. This extraordinarily fertile soil was always at a premium, and from earliest times the southern (Upper Egyptian) cultures, never far from the infertile desert, buried their dead in the desert. It will not have taken long for the inhabitants of the valley to realize that the desert preserved the remains of the dead, which probably gave rise to the remarkable culture of death and burial in the ancient civilizations of the Nile. In the Delta, settlements were mostly far from the desert and burials took place in the alluvial floodplain, usually in areas of little use to agriculture. The inevitable dampness of the environment and its frequent later conversion to agricultural land mean that little organic material has survived, so the archaeological record of funerary practices is very strongly biased in favour of Upper Egyptian material.

Thus in Upper Egyptian tombs, despite external factors such as robbery or unexpected ingress of water, delicate materials such as wood and papyrus are capable of preservation for thousands of years. Robbery took two major forms: ancient destruction of burials in the hope of recycling some of the more valuable materials, such as metals and valuable oils (see the Tomb Robbery Papyri, pages 232–5), and the wholesale ransacking of burials in search of objects for sale to foreigners, which was at its peak in the first half of the nineteenth century AD, as mentioned above.

Most ancient habitation would have been within the cultivated area, often on higher-standing land to avoid the annual Nile floods. It is very likely that the settlement pattern in ancient times was not dramatically different from that seen before the annual inundation was controlled in the course of the twentieth century AD. Moisture was never far away, which made the survival of domestic organic objects less likely; hence objects from the desert – the paraphernalia of death – are bound to be over-represented. To this must be added the contribution of archaeologists. Only in the past half-century have Egyptologists shaken off the inevitable attraction to the more openly promising finds from the deserts, which naturally worked to the detriment of knowledge of settlement sites; archaeologists experienced in working on settlement sites have only recently come to Egypt. In addition, settlement sites are very much less fossilized in time than those in the desert: they were frequently rebuilt in ancient times, and of course many (indeed perhaps most) have continued in use to the modern day, with all the difficulties that this presents to the archaeologist.

Thus, the Egyptian and Sudanese collection of a long-established institution such as the British Museum is inevitably biased towards material from burials and those contexts, such as temples, where the ancient remains have not been built over; the amount of material which relates to settlements and the daily life of the Egyptians is small in comparison. Hence this book is replete with evidence of the funerary customs of these ancient peoples, ranging from the astonishingly well-preserved burial of the man from Gebelein (pages 26–7) through the tomb groups of the Middle Kingdom to the burials of the Roman Period. Temple objects are likewise very prominent, from royal statues of Middle Kingdom temples, through the massive products of the New Kingdom, down to the Late Period resurgence in the construction and embellishment of such edifices, and the maintenance of the pharaonic style in the products of the Meroitic phase of the kingdom of Kush. Objects of daily use are not prominent, and those which exist mostly owe their survival to burial in a tomb or desert temple (for example, the two groups of papyri in this book bearing administrative records, the Abusir Papyri, pages 60-1, and the Tomb Robbery Papyri, pages 232-5).

It is ironic that much of the information used to reconstruct daily life in Egypt is derived from funerary sources. Thus the scenes of agriculture, crafts, and even banqueting in the carved and painted tomb chapels of the Old, Middle, and New Kingdoms are regularly quoted as important evidence of how these activities were carried out. Similarly, items which must have had their origins in burial deposits are frequently used to illustrate the jewellery the living wore, the furniture they used, and so on. This is not to suggest that this is inappropriate, but the reader should not

Cattle from the tomb chapel of
Nebamun, page 170.

simply assume that tomb scenes represent daily reality, or that artefacts in tombs are necessarily objects from life taken into the place of burial.

A further irony is that some of the settlement sites which are also used to illustrate daily life are not themselves typical. The collections of the British Museum contain many objects from excavations at Amarna, the city of the 'heretic pharaoh' Akhenaten, which was used for only ten to fifteen years and was built in the desert and not in the cultivated area. Undoubtedly, the material from Amarna can be used to draw very important conclusions about the functioning of a city,[12] but it should not be assumed to be typical. The same is true for the village of Deir el-Medina in Thebes,[13] home to the workmen who built the royal tombs in the Valley of the Kings, from which the British Museum has a number of mainly inscribed objects (for example, the ostrakon on pages 206–7). The villagers of Deir el-Medina were a privileged group, and the community must be used as a source for daily life with a measure of caution.

Nevertheless, the objects represented in this book offer a vivid and impressive, if necessarily partial, picture of life and death in ancient Egypt. They open a window into a unique and sophisticated culture that lasted for millennia and which retains the power to influence and inspire us to this day.

NOTES

1 The chronology of ancient Egypt is based on I. Shaw (ed.), *The Oxford History of Ancient Egypt*, Oxford, 2000. The dates for Lower and Upper Nubia come from D.A. Welby and J.R. Anderson, *Sudan: Ancient Treasures*, London, 2004; see p. 315 for a table relating the Egyptian and Nubian cultural phases.

2 Several more detailed historical overviews of the history of the collection exist: for example, that by T.G.H. James, in E.R. Russmann, *Eternal Egypt: Masterworks of Ancient Art from the British Museum*, London, Berkeley, Los Angeles, 2001, 46-63. For all persons mentioned in this introduction with no further reference, see the biographical summaries in W.R. Dawson, E.P. Uphill, and M.L. Bierbrier, *Who was Who in Egyptology*, 3rd edn, London, 1995.

3 See D. Manley and P. Rée, *Henry Salt*, London, 2001, for a biography.

4 For a perspective by a non-Egyptologist on the history of collecting in Egypt and controls on it see D.M. Reid, *Whose Pharaohs? Archaeology, Museums and Egyptian National Identity from Napoleon to World War I*, Berkeley, Los Angeles, London, 2002. The foundation of the Service des Antiquités is considered on pp 99–103.

5 1830–1892, a clergyman who travelled frequently to Egypt and who purchased in excess of 6,000 objects which came to the Museum's collection between the 1860s and the 1890s.

6 Harry Cureton (1785–1858) was one of the dealers who purchased from a variety of sources and sold many objects to the Museum.

7 See E.A.W. Budge, *By Nile and Tigris*, London, 1920, I, 138-49.

8 1856–1907; he was involved in the purchase of over 3,000 objects.

9 James, in Russmann, *Eternal Egypt*, 59.

10 See further M.L. Bierbrier, *British Museum Magazine* 43, 2002, 31-3; id., in J. Baines *et al.* (eds), *Pyramid Studies and Other Essays presented to I.E.S. Edwards*, London, 1988, 220-8.

11 Sources: the present, BBC (http://www.bbc.co.uk/weather/world/country_guides/results.shtml?tt=TT000180); ancient, K.W. Butzer, *Early Hydraulic Civilization in Egypt: A Study in Cultural Ecology*, Chicago, 1976, chap. 4.

12 See B.J. Kemp, *Ancient Egypt: Anatomy of a Civilisation*, London, 1989, chap. 7.

13 See M.L. Bierbrier, *The Tomb-Builders of the Pharaohs*, London, 1982.

THE SITES OF ANCIENT EGYPT

There are objects in the British Museum's collections from all the major Egyptian and Sudanese sites. This map shows the locations of the chief sites referred to in this book.

N

0 — 200 km
0 — 120 miles

EGYPT

SINAI

Rosetta
Alexandria
Piramesse
Bubastis
Saft el-Henna
Giza
El Matariya
Abusir
Cairo
Saqqara
Memphis
Dahshur
Meydum
El Rubayat
Hawara
Deshasha
Sedment

Serabit el-Khadim
Wadi Maghara

Nile

Beni Hasan
Deir el-Bersha
Amarna
Asyut
Wadi-Sarga
El-Badari
Akhmim
Sohag
Abydos
El-Amra
Naqada
Gebelein
Thebes (Luxor)

RED SEA

Elephantine
Aswan
First Cataract
Philae

LOWER NUBIA

Faras
Qasr Ibrim
Second Cataract
NUBIA
Semna

Soleb

SUDAN

Third Cataract

Kerma

Gebel Barkal
Fourth Cataract
Kawa

Fifth Cataract

Khartoum

Meroe
Hamadab

Atbara

Blue Nile
White Nile

Thebes inset

Valley of the Kings
Deir el-Bahari
Deir el-Medina
Ramesseum
Medinet Habu

Amun Temple
KARNAK
Mut Temple

LUXOR
Luxor Temple

THEBES

0 — 3 km
0 — 2 miles

Ivory figure of a woman

Predynastic Period, Badarian culture,
c. 4400–4000 BC

From Badari

Gift of the British School of
Archaeology in Egypt in 1929

Hippopotamus ivory

Height: 14 cm

EA 59648

THIS REMARKABLE FIGURE came from a grave at Badari, excavated in the 1920s, and is one of the oldest human-shaped statuettes known from Egypt. The head, nose and eyes are disproportionally large but, like the rest of the figure, have been carefully worked. The arms are separated from the body and rejoin it at the hips, with only the most cursory indications of hands. The breasts and genitalia are very prominent. Like the arms, the legs are clearly separated from each other, and the tiny feet are indicated simply. The whole figure has been made with great care and polished to a fine finish, showing a remarkable degree of technical competence at a very early date in Egypt's history. The nipples and the pupils are marked by drill holes, and may have been intended to be inlaid with some other material.

The function of the figurine is not clear. The very pronounced feminine attributes may suggest that the figure was intended to represent a fertility deity, or indeed as an expression of fertility and (re)birth, but it could also be a servant figure. The excavators, Brunton and Caton-Thompson, found two other figurines in their excavations (which were less accomplished than this example); they are not common, and remain enigmatic.

The tomb in which this figurine was found was otherwise rather uninformative. No bones were located, and the only other finds were a possible polishing pebble and a few beads of steatite and turquoise. Most graves in this cemetery were circular or oval pits. They were, in essence, fairly similar to the much later tomb of the Predynastic man from Gebelein, which has been reconstructed in the British Museum (see pages 26–7). Better-preserved tombs contained pottery, flints, arrowheads, and slate palettes among their grave goods.

The Badarian culture is the earliest of the Upper Egyptian cultures, and was the last to be identified. It was named after the type-site of Badari in Middle Egypt, which Brunton and Caton-Thompson excavated. Subsequent excavations in the 1930s by Caton-Thompson at Hemmamiya brought to light a stratigraphic sequence which confirmed the dating of the cemeteries at Badari to about 4400–4000 BC.

A Predynastic Egyptian

Late Predynastic Period, Naqada II, c. 3400 BC

Said to be from Gebelein

Acquired in 1900

Length of body: 163 cm

EA 32751

UNTIL LATE IN THE PREDYNASTIC PERIOD, the Egyptians buried their dead by placing the bodies in shallow graves, in direct contact with the sand, perhaps covered by a mound of earth. The dryness of the sand frequently acted as a preservative, and there are a number of burials from these early periods in which the body is still in excellent condition. Two of these, a man and a woman, are in the British Museum. The male burial is the better known, thanks to his remarkable state of preservation and, in particular, the remains of his ginger-coloured hair. He was a full-grown adult, but his exact age has not been determined. The body was buried in a contracted, almost foetal, position, which continued to be the principal position for burials until well into the Old Kingdom, when bodies were usually buried fully extended. There may be religious reasons for the change, but it is also very likely that the development of mummification practices showed that it was easier to mummify the body in an extended position. Although this man was not placed in a coffin, the earliest such items were arranged to take a contracted body. Mummification is now known to have been practised during the later stages of the prehistoric period, and parts of bodies showing the use of resin and linen wrappings are known from Hierakonpolis at about 3500 BC.

The body came to the museum without any associated objects, and is now displayed with a selection of typical grave goods of the Naqada II period (c. 3400 BC) from the Museum's collection, arranged in a manner which reflects the practices of the time. The objects include ceramics of three types: the black-topped ware typical of the early Predynastic Period down to about Naqada II, and the plain and painted buff-coloured wares which gradually succeeded it. These would have contained sustenance for the dead. Also included are slate palettes, vessels of hard stone, and flint knives, which were probably indications of status and wealth, and which tend to be found in more elaborate burials. These latter luxury items are most numerous around the beginning of the historical period, and then decline in numbers.

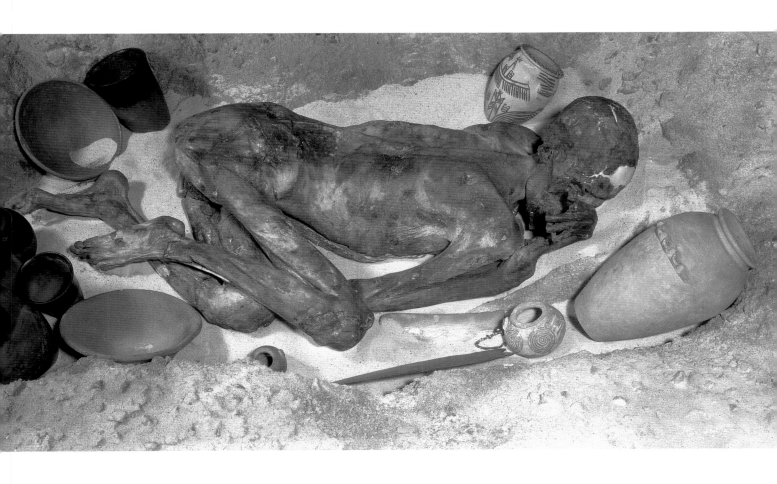

Decorated Predynastic pot

Late Predynastic Period, Naqada IIc,
c. 3300 BC

From el-Amra

Gift of the Egypt Exploration Fund
in 1901

Marl clay

Height: 29.2 cm

EA 35502

DECORATED POTTERY IS RARE and is found mainly in high-status burials. The dark on light style was originally developed to imitate more valuable stone vessels, as shown by the pot's shape and wavy handles.

Light-coloured pots like this, made of marl clay mined from desert wadis and painted with schematic designs in red ochre pigment, are known as Decorated or D-ware. They are characteristic of later Predynastic times (Naqada IIcd, *c.* 3500–3200 BC). The most intriguing Decorated pots are those painted with boats (though other interpretations include ostrich farms, walled villages, or temples on stilts). This pot comes from the tomb of a wealthy young woman, at el-Amra in Middle Egypt, but pots bearing images of boats have been found throughout Egypt and into Nubia. The boats are always strikingly similar, with a curved hull, an exaggerated number of oars, two striped cabins amidships, and a branch on the stern as an ornament or to provide shade for the crew (never shown). The symmetrically-placed boats (usually one on each side) frame a very limited range of ten other motifs. These include rows of stylized ostriches and small bushes, as seen here, reflecting the two main aspects of the Egyptian world: the desert and the river. Combined in regular patterns, these motifs convey a message which we cannot yet fully understand.

Above each boat is a large woman in a tight-fitting gown, her hands raised over her head, evidently engaged in a dance. To one side, her two smaller male companions beat out a rhythm with clappers or castanets.

The female figure is clearly important, perhaps a goddess or priestess, but is essentially passive. It is the men who are active, perhaps serving as mediators who summon the goddess from her sacred boat so that they may imbibe her blessings and power. However, the meaning of these scenes is still debated. Since Decorated ware is found almost exclusively in graves, some scholars suggest it depicts the funeral procession and associated rituals; as similar motifs are also known from desert rock art, the message may be much broader, with motifs forming part of a graphic vocabulary ensuring fertility and rebirth, whether for humans or the cosmos. Such concerns were important throughout Egyptian history.

The lack of variation in style, shape, and motifs of Decorated pottery suggests that these vessels were manufactured at a limited number of workshops; close scrutiny has even identified the work of individual artists. The artist who painted this pot probably made two others found in cemeteries up to 60 km away. The development of a trade and transport system to distribute pottery was one of the critical steps towards the formation of Dynastic civilization.

R.F.F.

Nubian A-Group objects

OSTRICH EGG

c. 3000 BC

From Faras, Grave 31

Gift of the University of Oxford in 1912

Diameter: 12.3 cm; height: 15.4 cm

EA 51157

POT

c. 3000 BC

From Faras, Grave 31

Gift of the University of Oxford in 1912

Ceramic

Diameter at rim: 21.6 cm;
height: 15.4 cm

EA 51168

'NUBIA' DESIGNATES AN AREA of southern Egypt and northern Sudan. The southern boundary of the area changed over time, but in the pharaonic period this usually lay between the Fourth and Fifth Cataracts of the Nile. The term 'A-Group' refers to an indigenous Nubian culture roughly contemporary with the Egyptian Predynastic cultures Naqada I–III to the First Dynasty (*c.* 4000–3000 BC). Most of the remains come from cemeteries, from just north of Aswan to south of the Second Nile Cataract. A non-literate culture, it had a strongly Nubian identity, and perhaps numbered 10,000 persons at most. It probably played an important role as an intermediary between the developing Egyptian cultures and the peoples controlling various sources of raw materials to the south. It maintained close contacts with its northern neighbours, and significant amounts of Egyptian ceramics are found in all its sub-phases, particularly in that contemporary with the First Dynasty. At the very end of the Egyptian Predynastic Period, the culture went into decline, probably largely as a result of Egyptian raids that destroyed contemporary political structures. Inscriptions have been found in the region of the Second Cataract which might belong to late Predynastic Egyptian kings.

Faras lies about 40 km to the north of the Second Cataract, and was first excavated by an expedition from Oxford in 1910–12. As well as these very early finds, the site has produced material from all periods, and is particularly renowned for the wall-paintings in its church, dating from the Christian period. The site was most recently examined during the Nubian rescue campaign of the 1960s, by a mission from Poland.

Both objects described here were found in grave 31 in the A-Group cemetery; this tomb contained a range of pots and other items, almost all of which are in the British Museum. The age and sex of the owner are not known.

Ostrich eggs are common finds in A-Group burials and in contemporary Egyptian graves. These large items were evidently valuable, and could be used, after consumption of the contents, as quite sturdy drinking or liquid storage vessels. They may perhaps also have possessed some symbolic value, as they are not so common in later periods.

The pot is a locally-made bowl with sides expanding from a small, flat base to turn inwards just below the rim; it is restored from fragments. The interior is polished black, and there are red painted lines on the upper part of the exterior, with a solid mass of red beneath.

A flint knife with ivory handle

Late Predynastic Period, Naqada II,
c. 3200 BC

From Sheikh Hamada, Upper Egypt

Acquired in 1974; originally in the
collection of General Pitt-Rivers

Flint and ivory

Length: 24 cm

EA 68512

ONE OF THE GREATEST ACHIEVEMENTS of the Naqada II culture was the production of some of the finest flint knives ever made. They exhibit a remarkable development from the roughly flaked implements produced in the fifth-millennium BC Badarian culture; their quality is such that it is unlikely that the finest examples – such as this – were ever used for anything other than ostentatious display or a 'ceremonial' function. The same is true of the contemporary slate palettes. The blades were prepared by grinding a piece of good-quality flint to the form required. A flat edge was created at the back of the blade to provide a suitable surface from which small flakes of flint could be detached by pressure, a technique employed with such skill that each flake was the same size and shape, creating a rippled pattern along the length of the knife. This pressure flaking was restricted to only one face, the other being left as a smooth ground surface. Finally, the knife's edge was worked into a series of very fine serrations.

The Pitt-Rivers Knife, as it is usually known, has an ivory handle decorated on both sides with rows of birds and wild animals, carved in raised relief. It is not always easy to identify the animals precisely, but they include cranes, elephants, lions, Barbary sheep, hyenas, donkeys, and cattle. All these could probably be seen in Egypt at the time, or were familiar from elsewhere, and some are shown on other carved knife handles and on some slate palettes. The knife handles differ from the palettes in the arrangement of the creatures in orderly rows, probably precursors to the horizontal baseline of the register division so familiar from Dynastic times.

It is difficult to imagine something so delicate and elaborately decorated fulfilling a utilitarian function; it must have been made for an elite group, for some very special purpose. A number of similar items are known, some bearing animal depictions as here, one with boat scenes and others depicting figures in Near Eastern style. The other major carved products of the late Predynastic Period are the ceremonial palettes (see the 'Battle-field' Palette, EA 20791, pages 34–5). The ceremonial palettes seem more likely to have come from temples than tombs, and thus probably had a combined display and ritual function. However, several of these knife handles came from tombs, including two examples excavated in the late Predynastic cemeteries at Abydos in the 1980s and 1990s. It thus seems more likely that they were marks of wealth and status, buried with their owner as a sign of his importance.

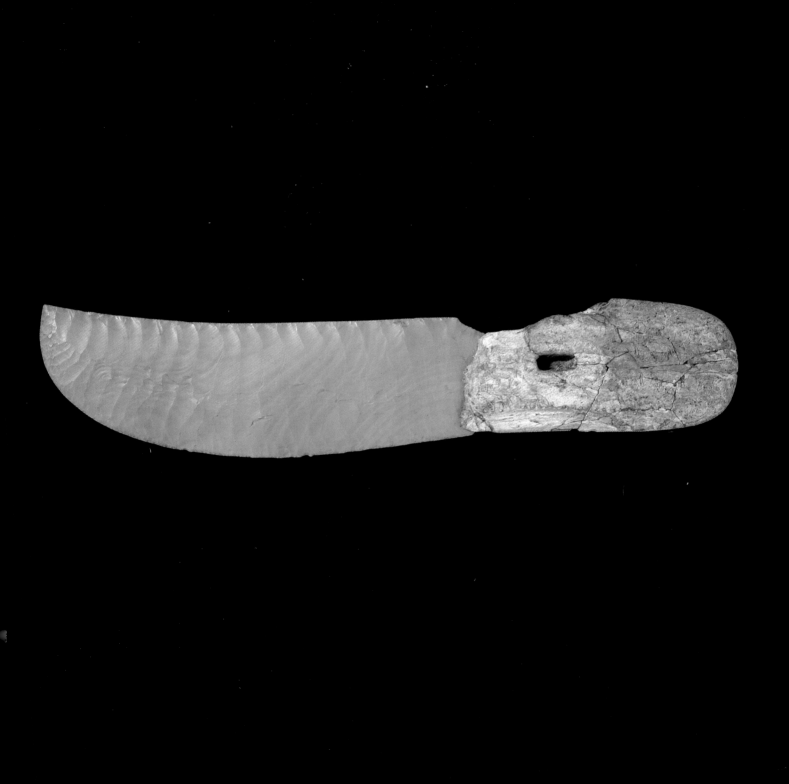

The 'Battlefield' Palette

End of the Predynastic Period,
c. 3100 BC

Provenance uncertain, perhaps Abydos

Acquired in 1888

Mudstone

Height: 19.6 cm; with fragment from
Oxford: 32.8 cm

EA 20791

THIS PALETTE DATES from the very end of the pre-historical period in Egypt. Two more fragments survive: one is in the Ashmolean Museum, Oxford and one is now in the Kofler-Truniger collection in Lucerne. The palette may have come from Abydos.

The reverse (not shown) is decorated with two long-necked giraffes browsing in a date palm. The tree's trunk and branches are highly detailed, contrasting with the simplicity of the rest of this side. Beside and slightly above each animal is a bird with a hooked beak – perhaps a helmeted guinea fowl, although identifications of birds at such an early date can only be tentative.

The better-known side of the palette may depict a stylized battle. In the centre is a circle, usually interpreted as a cosmetic-grinding area, although there is no evidence of such use. Below it is a large lion goring a naked man. His supine position indicates that he is dead, or about to be killed by the lion. Four similar figures lie further down the palette, being picked over by six birds, perhaps crows and vultures. A similar man appears behind the lion, while two bound figures, with divine standards behind them, stand to the left of the central circle (the latter are on the Ashmolean fragment, at the top of which are the legs of more corpses; this side of the Lucerne fragment bears part of another body and a dog or jackal). Dead and bound captives also appear on the Narmer Palette (in the Egyptian Museum, Cairo, JE 32169), which dates to the beginning of the First Dynasty.

The wonderful carving attests the late Predynastic Egyptians' technical ability, but its interpretation is difficult. The lion is usually thought to represent a king attacking his enemies, some being killed while others survive to be paraded as trophies. The reverse side may represent the balance of symmetrical and complementary concepts at the heart of Egyptian kingship. The king's appearance in human form on the Narmer Palette, later a standard scene, suggests the Battlefield Palette is somewhat earlier, from a period when the king's identification with animals was expressed through illustration of animals themselves rather than the later combinations of human and animal aspects.

Such elaborate objects were only available to the highest levels of the elite, probably the kings; they seem to have served as ideological and commemorative displays rather than as burial equipment. Two examples, including the Narmer Palette, came from a temple at Hierakonpolis, and may have played a part in ritual, besides being forerunners of later traditions of relief decoration. One example, however, was found in a cemetery at Minshat Ezzat in the Delta, although it may have played a part in the owner's cult rather than forming part of his burial goods.

Statuette of a king

Early Dynastic Period, perhaps
mid-First Dynasty, *c.* 3000 BC

From the early temple at Abydos

Gift of the Egypt Exploration Fund
in 1903

Ivory

Height: 8.8 cm

EA 37996

THIS FINELY-CARVED STATUETTE is one of the earliest royal depictions known, and certainly the earliest in three dimensions. It shows a standing figure wearing the white crown of Upper Egypt, with both hands held in front and (probably) the left foot forward. The king wears a short enveloping cloak, delicately decorated with a diamond-shaped pattern enclosed by double lines, with distinct borders at the bottom and at the front, where it wraps over the figure. The head juts forward and the ears are very prominent.

The robe is without doubt that worn during the *sed* festival of the renewal of kingship, although there is no diamond pattern on other Early Dynastic depictions of this item of clothing. However, fragments in the early Fourth Dynasty valley temple of Sneferu at Dahshur indicate that similar patterns were present on garments there, although the context is not clear. The *sed* festival could be celebrated at appropriate points in a king's reign – in later periods this seems to have begun at the 30-year mark, but earlier examples are sufficiently irregular to suggest that this was not necessarily the case. Two-dimensional representations of aspects of this festival are known from labels of the First Dynasty (see EA 32650, pages 38–9), and more extensive sets of scenes of the rituals involved are known, the earliest being in the sun temple of Niuserre at Abu Gurob (Fifth Dynasty). A set of structures within the enclosure of the Step Pyramid at Saqqara is thought to have been designed for the enactment of this festival. These First Dynasty representations show that the festival was an established feature of kingship at the very beginning of the historical period.

Doubts have occasionally been expressed about the object's date, but it seems reasonably sure that it was found in a discarded deposit of older temple material from the first two dynasties, even if the deposit itself might have been made later. There is of course no royal sculpture with which to compare it from before the later Second Dynasty, although since it has little in common with the products of the later epochs, it seems fair to assign it to the beginning of the historical period. The forward-jutting neck and head of this statuette point to a stylistic (or technical) feature common to early Egyptian sculptures, which persisted until the Fourth Dynasty (compare the statue of Ankhwa, EA 171, pages 48–9).

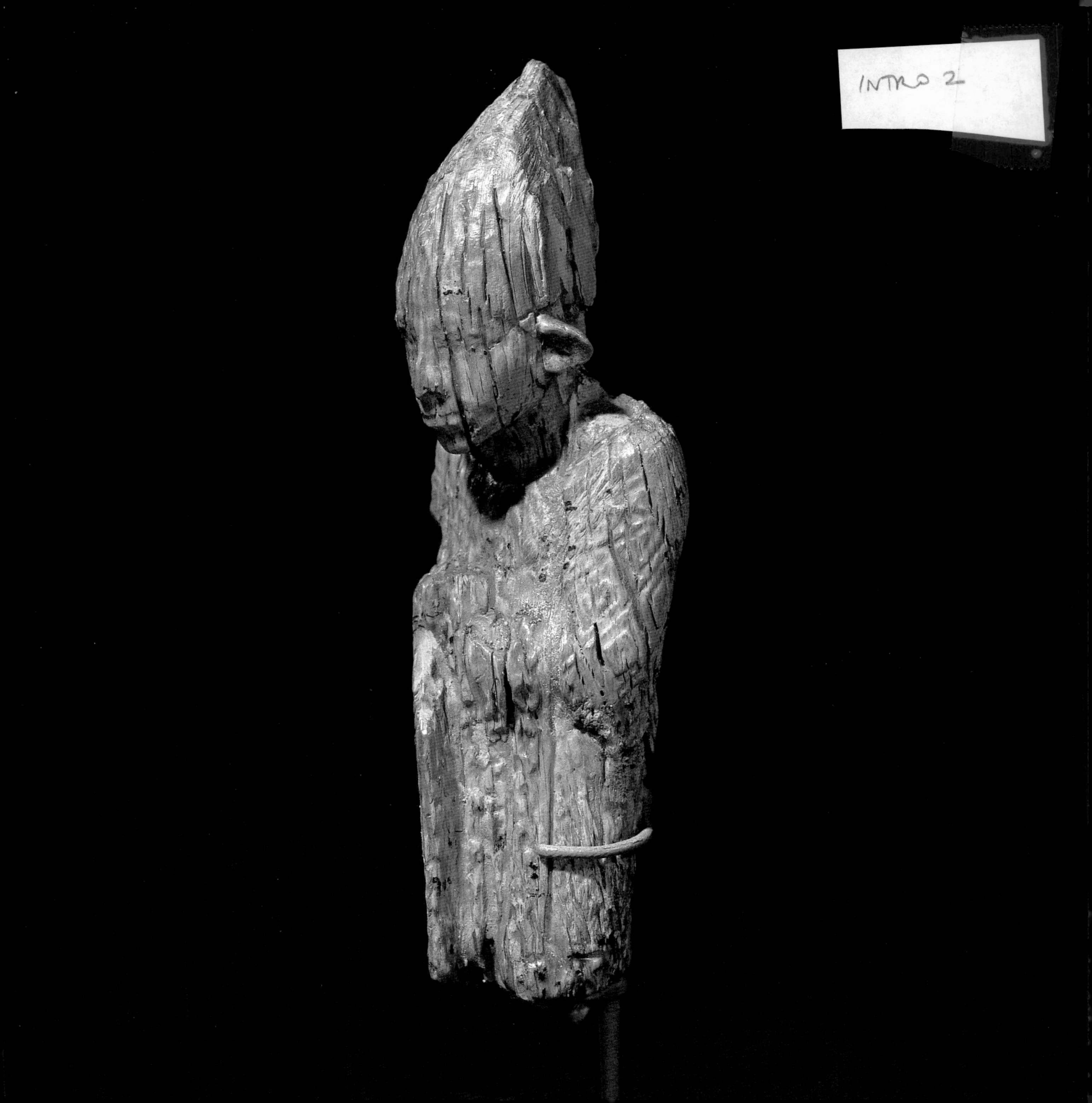

INTRO 2

Label with a scene showing the jubilee of king Den

Early Dynastic Period, First Dynasty,
c. 2950 BC

From Abydos, tomb of king Den

Gift of the Egypt Exploration Fund
in 1900

Ebony

Width: 8 cm

EA 32650

THIS IS PART OF A LABEL for an oil container, restored from two fragments, with a hole for attachment at the top right-hand corner. The front surface bears an incised hieroglyphic inscription, arranged vertically on the left side and in four horizontal registers on the right. The vertical inscriptions give the name of king Den and of the seal-bearer of the king of Lower Egypt, Hemaka, together with the name of another official, Iti-sen. Hemaka is known from the massive Tomb 3035 at Saqqara, which produced a remarkable series of finds now in the Cairo Museum. Next to his name are two signs, of uncertain reading. This official seems to have been associated with the palace and another building, which may have been an oil-press. Beneath the king's name is the designation of the kind of oil to which this label referred, possibly the *setj-heb* oil so prominent in Old Kingdom lists, together with its quantity, although part of the number is missing. On the right of the label, the inscriptions in the four registers are bordered by a large year hieroglyph, indicating that the text records the events of a particular year. The top register bears a scene of the *sed* festival, the celebration of the renewal of royal powers. It shows the king wearing the double crown, running as part of the ritual, and seated on a throne in a booth. It is often asserted that this festival was first performed after 30 years of the king's reign, but there are many exceptions to this 'rule', and it is probably more accurate to suggest that a *sed* festival could take place at almost any time when the king wished to renew his powers (see also the statuette of a king, EA 37996, pages 36–7). The meaning of the lower registers is not entirely clear, but they include references to the destruction of a stronghold and the taking of captives.

Such labels are one of the most important sources of written material of the earliest dynasties. In later periods, it became more common to write on the container in hieratic script. It seems that these early labels performed a more important function than simply indicating the contents; they are probably among the first commemorative objects from ancient Egypt (compare the 'Battlefield' Palette, EA 20791, pages 34–5).

The tomb of Den at Abydos was excavated by Petrie at the end of the nineteenth century. It has recently been re-excavated and restored by the German Archaeological Institute, yielding considerable amounts of new information.

Relief showing two royal figures

Early Dynastic Period, First or Second
Dynasty, 3000–2700 BC

From Tomb 3507 at Saqqara

Gift of the Egypt Exploration Society
in 1969

Limestone

Length: 39.5 cm

EA 67153

TWO KINGS ARE DEPICTED on the right of this slab of limestone; they wear the red crown of Lower Egypt and are dressed in short enveloping robes, a costume associated with the *sed* festival (compare the statuette of a king, EA 37996, pages 36–7). In their left hands, the kings hold what is probably a flail, and in their right a small wand, probably a *hetes* sceptre, or perhaps a stylized lettuce. In front of the royal figures are five fragmentary figures: four birds (including an owl, perhaps an Egyptian vulture, and a falcon) and a baboon seated on a small platform. The object has been dated to the Early Dynastic period, both on the basis of its reused context (see below) and the rather crude style of the work.

The significance of this group of carvings, which might be hieroglyphs, is not clear. The grouping together of two royal figures is most unusual, and it is possible that this stone was actually a sculptor's trial piece, on which he was experimenting with various ideas. However, given that our comprehension of early texts and pictures is minimal, this might be too simple an explanation. On the back of the object is a grid of 1.6 cm squares, incised into the stone; if this is a grid for laying out a scene it would be among the earliest known, and might support the idea of this being a practice slab.

Tomb 3507 is one of the large First Dynasty *mastabas* (bench-shaped tombs) at North Saqqara, dating from the reign of Den. Emery, the excavator, thought it might be the burial place of Queen Herneith, spouse of Den's predecessor Djer. The slab was reused in the casing of a Third Dynasty shaft cut through one of the storage magazines in the superstructure. Assuming that the slab dates from the Early Dynastic period, it is one of the earliest experiments in relief on limestone known and is an important illustration of the progress being made towards the highly-developed work characteristic of the Third Dynasty.

Masterpieces of Ancient Egypt

Stela of king Peribsen

Early Dynastic Period, Second Dynasty,
c. 2720–2710 BC

From the tomb of Peribsen at Abydos

Gift of the Egypt Exploration Fund
in 1901

Gneiss

Height: 113 cm

EA 35597

TWO GRANITE STELAE bearing the king's name were discovered in the sand to the south of the tomb of Peribsen at Abydos, and probably originally stood at the entrance to the tomb. They are of a tall, almost conical, shape, and bear the name Peribsen in a rectangular name-panel (called a *serekh* enclosure) surmounted by a Seth animal. First Dynasty examples show that such stelae, in a variety of shapes, are reliable markers of royal tombs. Second Dynasty rulers before Peribsen seem to have been buried at Saqqara, rather than at Abydos as was the practice during the First Dynasty; Peribsen's return to Abydos was followed by his successor Khasekhemwy.

The design of the *serekh* enclosure may reflect the architectural panelling on the exterior of a mud-brick palace. The *serekh* is usually surmounted by a falcon, the sacred animal of the god Horus. The hieroglyphs it contains are thus termed the 'Horus name' of the king, representing the identification of the living king with the son of Osiris. The intriguing feature of the writing of Peribsen's name here is that, on the *serekh*, the Horus falcon has been replaced by the animal of Seth, the enemy of Osiris; some have suggested that an otherwise little-known Second Dynasty king with the Horus name of Sekhemib could have later adopted the Seth name Peribsen. While we do not know what was at the root of this, it has been speculated that this change from the well-established convention might indicate the existence of some sort of internal conflict in Egypt, and one is reminded of the mythological conflict of the gods Horus and Seth. Peribsen's successor, Khasekhemwy, placed both creatures on top of his *serekh*, which might suggest the reconciliation of any such conflict.

It should be noted that the Seth animal on this stela has been largely erased. It is not known when this occurred; it might have been soon after the burial, when the employment of the image of Seth in this context fell out of favour. However, it could also be later, from a period when the stelae were still visible, or had become so, and it was felt that the presence of an image of Seth in the cult centre of Osiris was improper. For example, in the Abydos temple of the Nineteenth Dynasty king Sety I – whose name includes that of Seth – various devices are employed to avoid using the Seth animal in writing the royal name.

A set of bronze vessels

Early Dynastic Period, Second Dynasty,
c. 2700 BC

From the tomb of Khasekhemwy
at Abydos

Gift of the Egypt Exploration Fund
in 1901

Bronze

Height: 12 cm

EA 35572

Height: 11.4 cm

EA 35571

METAL VESSELS BEGAN to be produced in Egypt at the beginning of the First Dynasty, about 3000 BC. The population's increasing wealth, following the unification of the country under a single king, was doubtless a factor in the adoption of a wider range of materials. Stone and pottery vases had been produced since early Predynastic times, but metal provided a medium for luxury products. Considerable quantities of metal dishes and vases have been found in the burial equipment of First Dynasty tombs, particularly those of high officials at Saqqara. These vessels were manufactured from copper. More durable products and greater ease in casting could be achieved by the use of bronze, an alloy of copper and tin. Bronze, however, does not appear in regular use until the Middle Kingdom, soon after 2000 BC, though these two vessels from a royal tomb at Abydos show that Egyptian metalworkers had mastered bronze technology at a much earlier date.

The two vases form a set for washing the hands. Evidence for this is provided by many representations of similar paired vases on tomb-reliefs, showing one vase standing within the other. Other scenes show the vessels in use, with a servant pouring water from the spouted vessel over his master's hands, and the waste water falling into the basin. A set of these vases, often ceramic, was part of standard funerary equipment in Early Dynastic and Old Kingdom tombs, and even if not physically present, could be provided through the symbolism of images carved on the tomb walls.

The tomb of king Khasekhemwy at Abydos was excavated twice; these vases were only found in the second excavation in 1901, having been hidden under a collapsed wall. Analysis at the British Museum in 1980 showed that their bronze is particularly fine, including 7-9 percent of tin with the addition of one percent of lead. This high-quality alloy must have been deliberately produced, exploiting what was then the latest technology to provide gifts for a royal burial. The larger vase is a simple basin with flared sides and a flat base. The rim's top has been hammered to a flat surface with a sharp outer edge. Traces of linen adhere to the basin's corroded surface, showing that it was deposited in the tomb in a linen bag. The other vase is more elaborate, consisting of a shouldered ewer standing on a flat base, with a spout added at one side. This spout has a double channel, a feature known from other examples of the finest versions of these containers. The hollow spouts had to be manufactured by the process of lost-wax casting, in which a mould is created around a wax prototype. The wax was removed by heating to leave space for the introduction of the molten metal. The spout was then attached to the vessel by a second lost-wax casting. Interestingly, the composition of the spout differed from that of the vessel, being of arsenical copper instead of bronze.

A.J.S.

Rock inscription of king Zanakht

Old Kingdom, Third Dynasty,
c. 2650 BC.

From Wadi Maghara in Sinai

Gift of the Egypt Exploration Fund
in 1905

Red sandstone

Width: 47 cm

EA 691

ZANAKHT WAS A KING of the Third Dynasty at the beginning of the Old Kingdom, the first great phase of Egyptian culture. During the Old Kingdom, a great centralized power base grew up at Memphis. Kings constructed pyramids north and south of Memphis, and large necropoleis (cemeteries) of officials grew up around them, particularly at Giza and Saqqara.

Very little is known about Zanakht. A large mud-brick tomb at Beit Khallaf, north of Abydos, dates from his reign, but may not have been his final resting-place. For many years he was thought to be the predecessor of the more famous Netjerikhet (Djoser), but sealings of the latter have been discovered in the burial of Khasekhemwy, the last king of the Second Dynasty, and seem to argue in favour of Netjerikhet preceding Zanakht. Presumably Zanakht was one of the obscure kings in the middle to late part of the dynasty.

From the Early Dynastic Period onwards the Egyptians were active outside the traditional borders of Egypt. Sinai was particularly attractive for its mineral riches, primarily turquoise and copper. The mines at Wadi Maghara were a source of turquoise at least until the New Kingdom, although the peak periods of exploitation seem to have been during the Old and Middle Kingdoms.

It seems to have been customary, not just in Sinai but in most places during the Old and Middle Kingdoms, for quarrying expeditions sent by the state to leave behind some sort of record on the nearby rocks. This example is one of the earliest of the typical royal inscriptions incised at a quarrying location by an expedition's members; it does not mean that the king himself was present, of course. It shows the king wearing the red crown of Lower Egypt, grasping the hair of an enemy chief (now destroyed) with his left hand and preparing to smite him with his right arm, which is raised behind him. This type of royal representation goes back to at least the First Dynasty (the British Museum possesses a label showing king Den smiting an Easterner, EA 55586), and is more expressive of the standard role of the king in a foreign land than of any individual monarch's actual exploits. Above the king's hand is a rectangular name-panel (serekh), containing his Horus name, Zanakht. The vertical bar to the right originally bore the standard of the god Wepwawet. To the right is part of the earliest example of the Egyptian word for turquoise.

Expedition inscriptions from the Fifth Dynasty onwards include more text and also tend to list the members of the expedition, but this is not the case in these early examples. An inscription such as this would serve not only as a record of the trip, but also as a reminder to the local population of the power that Egypt could exert over them.

Statue of Ankhwa

Old Kingdom, Third Dynasty,
c. 2650 BC

Provenance unknown, but perhaps
from Saqqara

Purchased at the sale of the third Salt
collection in 1835

Pink granite

Height: 65.5 cm

EA 171

SCULPTURE IN THE ROUND is rather rare in Egypt before the Fourth Dynasty, but there are several outstanding examples from the Third Dynasty. This is one of the most important. It shows Ankhwa, also known as Bedjmose. He held the titles of 'royal acquaintance' and 'shipbuilder' and these names and titles are carved on his kilt.

The representation of the body is typical of early sculpture: the figure is slightly squat, with the back curved more than in the traditions of 'classic' Egyptian sculpture, and the head (which is relatively large) jutting slightly forward. The seat is also very characteristic of such early statues, with its inverted 'U'-shaped braces visible on three sides. Ankhwa holds an adze over his left shoulder, another unusual detail. It is doubtless a symbol of his profession, but this feature is very rare throughout most of Egyptian history. This and other Third Dynasty statues have been described as 'pre-canonical', since they show considerable variation in the way in which they represent their subjects, unlike most sculpture from the Old Kingdom. This suggests that these features were very fluid at this point and that craftsmen were experimenting with different arrangements.

The statue shows how adept the Egyptians were at this date at producing sizeable statues in a very hard stone. Despite the fact that Ankhwa was 'only' a shipbuilder, he was nonetheless able to command sufficient wealth and resources to commission a statue of this quality. Ankhwa's other title of 'royal acquaintance' declined in significance during the remainder of the Old Kingdom, but it just might have been of enough importance to permit him access to special resources, such as hard stone, worked in workshops which may have only operated in accordance with the king's orders.

Granite was not often worked at this point in Egyptian history; it was only in the Fourth Dynasty that it began to be cut and moved on a more massive scale. It is thought that most earlier Old Kingdom granite-working used boulders from the Aswan granite-bearing area, rather than conventional quarrying methods.

Fragments of wall paintings from the tomb of Itet at Meydum

Old Kingdom, early Fourth Dynasty,
c. 2600 BC

From the tomb of Nefermaat and Itet
at Meydum

Both paintings were transferred to the
British Museum from the Victoria and
Albert Museum in 1979; they were
originally given to the South
Kensington Museum (which became
the Victoria and Albert Museum in
1899) by W.M.F. Petrie immediately
after his season of 1891–2.

Lime plaster and paint

MAN HOLDING DUCK

Width: 59 cm

EA 69014

MAN FEEDING ANTELOPE

Width: 80 cm

EA 69015

MEYDUM IS THE SOUTHERNMOST of the great cemeteries of the Old Kingdom, used only in the Fourth Dynasty. The most distinctive monument there is a pyramid; its outer casing has collapsed, revealing much of the inner core of what was probably a seven-stepped structure. The king who completed it was Sneferu, the first king of the Fourth Dynasty, and it was begun either by him or by Huni, the little-known last king of the Third Dynasty. A short distance away are a few *mastaba*s of similar date, with a complex history of excavation. Fragments from the *mastaba* chapels of Itet and Rehotep are in the British Museum.

Itet and her husband Nefermaat each possessed a chapel within a large mud-brick *mastaba*, hers at the north end and his at the south. Nefermaat was a vizier in the reign of Sneferu, and perhaps a son of Huni or Sneferu. The tomb was probably completed in Sneferu's reign. Itet was buried in a chamber at the bottom of a shaft in the body of the *mastaba*, to the south-west of her chapel. The remains of her burial were found smashed to pieces – only chips of bone and fragments of pottery had survived.

Nefermaat's chapel contained decoration in a technique never used outside Meydum: the outlines of the figures were deeply cut into stone slabs and filled with paste, and the slabs were then built into the *mastaba*. Itet's chapel used this technique, but also contained some of the earliest painted scenes known from Egypt, including the world-famous geese, now in the Cairo Museum (CG 1742).

The two British Museum painting fragments are also of the highest quality. The upper fragment (EA 69014) shows a small part of the figure of a man holding a carefully painted duck, and another man pulling a rope, which belongs to a clap-net for catching birds. This fragment came from the north wall of the east-west corridor, and can be reconstructed as part of a scene of three men closing a clap-net, watched by (probably) Nefermaat. Below these men were the geese, and below them a ploughing scene. The lower piece bears part of the figure of a man feeding an antelope (EA 69015) and came from the south wall of the east-west corridor in the chapel.

The clarity of the colours and the skill of the draughtsman in both paintings is outstanding, particularly in the details of the duck's feathers. In order to create these paintings, a smoothing coat of mortar was applied to the brick superstructure of the chapel, and then coated with a thin layer of plaster. Once dry, this plaster surface could be painted.

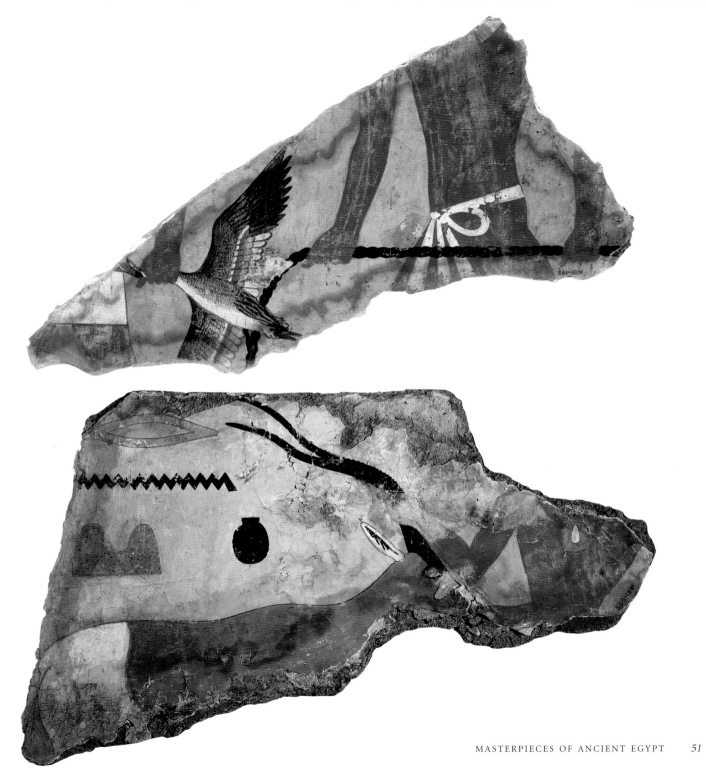

Pair statue of Kaitep and Hetepheres

Old Kingdom, Fourth or Fifth Dynasty
(*c.* 2580–2350 BC)

Perhaps from Giza

Acquired in 1896

Limestone

Height: 47.5 cm

EA 1181

TOMBS, PARTICULARLY THOSE IN THE CEMETERIES of Memphis, tended to have a statue-chamber, known to Egyptologists by the Arabic word *serdab*, which would have contained a statue of the type shown here. The statues functioned as an additional line of defence for keeping the memory and the personality of the deceased persons in existence. If their bodies were destroyed, their spirits would have a recognizable image in which to reside.

Kaitep and his wife Hetepheres are seated on a wide bench with a back. Hetepheres has her left arm around her husband's waist. The couple wear normal dress for men and women, a knee-length kilt for Kaitep and a long sleeveless dress for Hetepheres. Traces of blue and black paint on the legs and arms indicate that Hetepheres was originally shown wearing jewellery; in addition, the white collar areas around her neck and on her husband's shoulders indicate the presence of more decorative jewellery and collars. This group is an excellent example of the basic conventions of male and female depiction in Egypt. Note the distinguishing skin colours – yellow for women, red-brown for men – and Kaitep's heavier build, though he is not shown as being dramatically larger than his wife, a convention known from other statues.

A number of relief fragments have survived from the couple's tomb, some of which are in the British Museum, while others are in the Field Museum in Chicago. The provenance of this statue is not known, and although both Giza and Saqqara have been suggested, Giza seems far more plausible, from the style of the relatively simple statue and the chapel reliefs. Kaitep was a relatively minor priest, but he did hold the title of 'priest of Khufu'; excavations in some of the peripheral cemeteries at Giza have revealed tombs of men with similar titles, and excavations by the University of Alexandria in 1952 brought to light the tomb of another Kaitep who benefited from funerary estates ('pious foundations' for the offering cult) with the same names as those shown in the reliefs of the British Museum's Kaitep. The Giza Kaitep might have been the father of the man in the British Museum statue, which would make it more likely that this statue came from a similar part of the Giza necropolis.

The tombs in these cemeteries are notoriously difficult to date. The simple style of the figures and the curved framing of the faces may indicate the earlier Old Kingdom. The relatively low status of the owner, when compared with the exalted rank of the owners of the great Fourth Dynasty tombs at Giza, suggests that these simpler works might have been made for priests, tomb-builders, and the like, who were buried on the very edge of the necropolis of the Fourth Dynasty kings whom they served.

False door of Ptahshepses

Old Kingdom, middle of the Fifth
Dynasty, c. 2440 BC

From Tomb C 1, north of the Step
Pyramid at Saqqara

Acquired in 1897

Limestone

Height: 366 cm

EA 682

IN THE COURSE OF THE OLD KINGDOM the 'false door' developed from the basic offering niche of the Early Dynastic Period to become a central feature of tombs in the Memphite region. The offering niche, through which the spirits of the dead buried in the tomb were believed to pass, came to be thought of as a 'door', and the jambs on either side were decorated and multiplied in number over the years. This was combined with a panel representing the deceased in front of offerings to produce the classic false door.

Ptahshepses's door consists of two jambs framing the niche; the panel above is missing. The door was set in the west wall of the tomb, with panels bearing columns of text on either side. The panels may imitate the so-called 'palace façade' style of construction, though it is not thought that actual royal palaces were covered with text. Above the missing tops of the door and panels is a long architrave, depicting Ptahshepses and bearing prayers for offerings. These elements are painted red-brown in imitation of a more expensive material, such as granite or wood. On either side are depictions of food offerings.

Although the texts on the panels are incomplete, each column has been plausibly reconstructed as describing a biographical event under each king in whose reign Ptahshepses lived. The name of king Menkaure survives in the rightmost column, followed by that of Shepseskaf in the next, and a block identified in Chicago (OIM 11048) as coming from this tomb bears the names of Userkaf and Sahure in the third and fourth columns. As there are four more columns to the left of the central area of the door, it seems possible that he might have served kings as far into the Fifth Dynasty as Niuserre. In other words, Ptahshepses may have lived from just before the death of Menkaure in c. 2503 BC to about 2445 BC. The events described include growing up with the royal children in the first two reigns and marrying a princess in the time of Userkaf. Ptahshepses' highest title was that of the High Priest of Ptah (in Egyptian, 'the great controller of craftsmen'), but these biographical texts do not mention this or any of his career promotions. Instead they concentrate on recording his importance to the king, for example 'his majesty allowed him to kiss his foot – he did not allow him to kiss the ground'. These are typical 'biographical' statements of the Old Kingdom, emphasizing the tomb-owner's importance, and are not necessarily attempts to record real events. They are particularly significant in Ptahshepses' tomb because they are among the earliest texts of this type, no doubt composed at a time when the genre was still developing. In later tombs of the Sixth Dynasty (such as those of Weni and Harkhuf) these series of unconnected statements grew into lengthy continuous texts.

False door of Kainefer

Old Kingdom, perhaps Fifth Dynasty, *c.* 2500–2300 BC

From Dahshur

Acquired in 1901

Limestone

Height: 258 cm

EA 1324

THE BRITISH MUSEUM possesses the lower parts of the jambs and lintel of the false door niche of Kainefer. The six columns of text on each side record the impressive set of titles held by the owner, and the outermost column indicates that the door was set up for him by his son Kaiwab while his father was 'in the necropolis'; in other words, Kainefer had died before being able to complete his funerary monument. Kaiwab is shown, at a smaller scale, beside the large figures of his father, and six figures appear at the bottom of the jambs: Kaiwab again, two soul-priests, and three men with names compounded with the cartouche of king Sneferu.

This false door niche and its associated offering table were found *in situ* by the French archaeologist Jacques de Morgan in 1894–5. The other parts of the niche, with the exception of the panel of the false door which appears to be lost, are now in the Louvre (E 11286). Its obvious Old Kingdom origin, the title 'king's bodily son', and the proximity to the pyramids of Dahshur led archaeologists to the conclusion that Kainefer was a son of king Sneferu, but the actual date has been much disputed. Relatively few examples of false doors from the early Fourth Dynasty are known, and it has been speculated that the object may actually be later, perhaps from the Fifth Dynasty, although the style of the figures is consistent with a Fourth Dynasty date, as indeed is the massive brick tomb with very small chapels.

Among Kainefer's titles are 'priest of Sneferu', 'overseer of the pyramid of Sneferu', and 'vizier'. There is also a wide range of titles indicative of rank and of involvement with divine cults. The interpretation of the title 'king's son' is much disputed, and is tied into the discussion about the date, since earlier in the Old Kingdom the use of the expression 'king's son of his body' has been taken as meaning a real prince, probably to be contrasted with the plainer 'king's son', a title that could be granted to an individual of non-royal birth as a mark of honour. Such a differentiation was not made so strictly later in the period. The titles held in association with the cult or administration of the Sneferu pyramids have also been used as an argument for dating Kainefer much later than the Fourth Dynasty, as it is known that the royal cults at Sneferu's Dahshur pyramids were still functioning at least in the early Sixth Dynasty. While this is not the place to delve deeply into the arguments, it shows that the complexity of the Old Kingdom title system is still far from understood.

Statue of Nenkheftka

Old Kingdom, mid-Fifth Dynasty,
perhaps *c.* 2450 BC

From Deshasha

Gift of the Egypt Exploration Fund

Limestone

Height: 134 cm

EA 1239

IN 1897 W.M.F. PETRIE EXPLORED the tombs of Deshasha, just south of the Fayum, and excavated some of the cemeteries there. Material spanning a range of dates was found, but the principal tombs are rock-cut examples dating from the Old Kingdom. Petrie also located the remains of the base of a stone-built *mastaba* chapel on a hillside, and discovered a small shaft with a chamber at the bottom filled with fragments of statues. These pieces were reassembled into twelve statues bearing the name Nenkheftka. The British Museum has two statues from this group (the other is EA 29562).

This is probably the finest of the group. Nenkheftka wears the short heavy wig associated particularly with the Fifth Dynasty, a plain white collar, and a white kilt. The red-brown body colour is very well preserved. As usual for standing statues, the left foot is advanced. The face is carefully carved, and even the nose has survived intact. The superb rendering of the facial features and detailing of the wig make this a masterpiece of Egyptian sculpture.

Free-standing limestone statues of this quality are best known in the Fifth Dynasty from the royal court cemeteries around Memphis, in particular at Saqqara. It is thus tempting to date this statue to the mid-Fifth Dynasty on the basis of its style, and to suggest that it was a product of the Memphite workshops, buried with the owner. As nothing is known of Nenkheftka's origins, he may even have been sent out to administer the area from the capital. It is quite unusual for a tomb outside the capital to be constructed as a stone *mastaba*, and this might also suggest that Nenkheftka's burial is earlier than the rock tombs at Deshasha, since the other *mastabas* south of Memphis are from the Fourth or Fifth Dynasty. Petrie suggested that the Nenkheftka of the British Museum statue might have been related to a similarly named individual at Saqqara. This person may have lived in the reign of Sahure or shortly afterwards. While the name might be a convincing case for a link, this remains to be proven.

From the Abusir papyri

Old Kingdom, probably late Fifth
Dynasty, *c.* 2400 BC

From Abusir, temple of Neferirkare

Acquired in 1950 from the estate of
Ludwig Borchardt

EA 10735/7 RECTO

Length: 79 cm; width: 26 cm

EA 10735/10

Length: 39 cm; width 20.5 cm

THE ABUSIR PAPYRI are the most important administrative documents known from the Old Kingdom. Abusir (20 km south-west of Cairo) is the site of the tombs of at least four kings of the Fifth Dynasty. Most of the papyri were discovered in 1893 in illicit excavations and sold to Egyptologists on the antiquities market; they are now in Cairo, Paris and London. Shortly afterwards, the German Egyptologist Ludwig Borchardt identified the findspot as the administrative buildings near the pyramid of Neferirkare (third king of the Fifth Dynasty), and this was subsequently confirmed by his discovery of more fragments in excavations at the temple. The nineteen frames of papyri in the British Museum are the largest and most important group of the documents, and were originally purchased in Egypt by Edouard Naville, then by Borchardt. Czech excavations at Abusir in the 1980s have revealed more papyrus fragments relating to the temple of Khentkaues, a wife of Neferirkare, and of Neferefre, Neferirkare's probable successor.

Most of the papyri seem to date from the later Fifth or early Sixth Dynasty. They reveal important information about royal mortuary establishments during the Old Kingdom, especially their economic organization. The texts include duty rosters for priests, offering lists, temple equipment inventories, letters, and permits. The papyri are damaged and fragmentary; like all administrative documents, they assume that readers are familiar with their background, and often appear quite cryptic. It is clear that the king's pyramid complex was constantly exchanging goods and offerings with state institutions, particularly the (now lost) sun temple of Neferirkare.

EA 10735/7 (opposite, above) is part of a duty roster from the royal temple. The sheet is divided into a ruled grid, with headings at the top of each group of columns. The first column on the right is headed 'those who carry out the rites around the pyramid'; another is 'gate-keepers'; and a third 'those who keep watch at night on top of the temple'. The rows contain individual names, with marks in the appropriate columns indicating their allocation to a particular duty. The more elaborate signs to the left represent three royal statues; the accompanying texts concern priests and officials who dressed, purified, decorated, and censed these statues.

EA 10735/10 (opposite, below) bears two fragmentary texts. At the left, in large hieroglyphs, is the heading, dated in the reign of a king whose name is lost but may be that of Izezi (later Fifth Dynasty). Contemporary dates were expressed as the number of national cattle-counts in the reign, which were usually biennial; as the number here is 14, it might refer to the 28th year of the reign. The hieratic text to the right refers to grain allocations given to two men, Tjezemy and Nefernemtet.

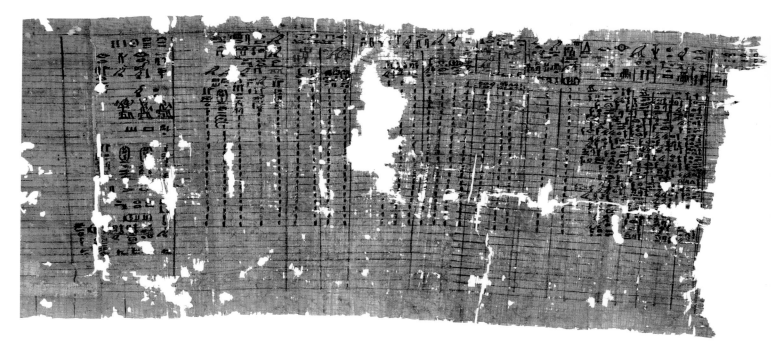

Above: EA 10735/7. Below: EA 10735/10.

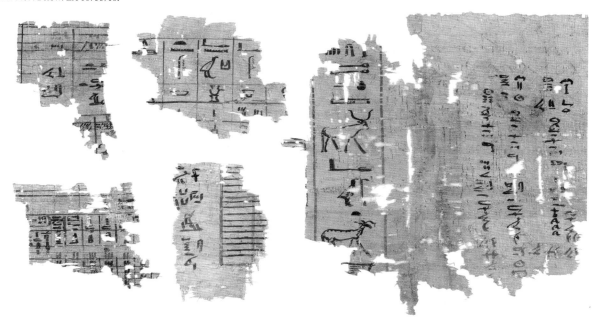

Statue of Meryrehashtef

Old Kingdom, Sixth Dynasty,
c. 2345–2181 BC

From Meryrehashtef's tomb at
Sedment

Purchased with the assistance of the
National Art Collections Fund in 1923.
Excavated by W.M.F. Petrie in 1920–1.

Ebony

Height: 58.1 cm

EA 55722

THIS WOODEN STATUE is one of several found in the tomb of Meryrehashtef, a moderately high-ranking official, an overseer of *khenty-she*, in the provincial town of Sedment, about 105 km south of Cairo on the southern edge of the Faiyum. The word *khenty-she* is not easy to understand, but holders of such titles were usually dependants of particular institutions, especially royal ones. The cemeteries of Sedment date at least from the later Old Kingdom, when the area was the necropolis for the town of Herakleopolis, later to become the home of the northern rulers of Egypt in the Ninth to Tenth Dynasties.

Tombs of wealthy individuals of the late Old Kingdom sometimes contained a group of wooden statues showing the owner in a range of poses and costumes. Three naked statues of Meryrehashtef were found in the tomb (the other two are in Cairo, JE 46992, and Copenhagen, Ny Carlsberg Glyptotek AEI 1560). The British Museum statue is the only one made of ebony, and exhibits a far higher standard of workmanship. Each of the other two statues holds a staff, and one grasps a sceptre as well; perhaps they were intended to show Meryrehashtef enjoying increasing levels of seniority. The nakedness of the statues, however, is intriguing, as this feature appears just in the late Old Kingdom. Normally in Egyptian art, only children are shown naked, and the presently favoured interpretation of these statues is that they express a wish for rejuvenation and rebirth on behalf of the owner by showing him as eternally youthful. Also found in the tomb was a nameless (and very plainly carved) figure of a woman, perhaps a representation of his spouse, or even a concubine figure for the tomb (now EA 55723). Other objects from the burial include a headrest with Meryrehashtef's name and titles, some servant figures, and his wooden coffin, which held the body of a man of mature years.

The quality of carving of this statue has often drawn attention – it is said to have been a particular favourite of the British sculptor Henry Moore. Its slight divergence from the normal angular representation (it faces very slightly left of centre and has a very long stride), is often treated as a mark of the individual skill of the craftsman – but dare one suggest that this is perhaps too modern an interpretation of the piece? It is most unusual in being carved from a single piece of wood, since the arms of most wooden statues were made separately and attached with mortise and tenon joints. Finely-carved wooden statues were probably not considered inferior to stone ones, as wood was a precious commodity in Egypt thanks to its scarcity, and the use of a hard wood which would have been imported from the south (probably Sudan or Ethiopia) would have increased its value.

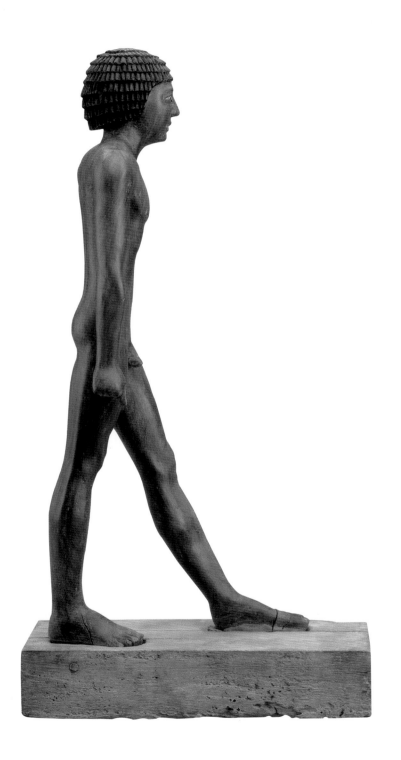

False door of Kaihap

Old Kingdom, Fifth Dynasty, *c.* 2400 BC

From North Saqqara, south chapel of
Tomb 3511

Gift of the Egyptian Government
in 1973

Limestone

Height: 203 cm

EA 1848

THIS RATHER ELABORATE false door was made in two pieces, presumably for ease of manufacture, transport, and installation. It is all that survives of the chapel of Kaihap at Saqqara. The stela is unusual for its date because of the sheer number of people depicted on it, in addition to the inscriptions. The latter are conventional, consisting of a two-line funerary formula at the top, and names and titles elsewhere.

The central aspect of any false door is the central panel of the upper part of the false door. This one shows Kaihap and his wife Meretminu seated at a table, on which are stylized slices or thin loaves of bread; above these is a list of sacred substances. On either side of the couple is a row of five male and five female figures; their relationship to the couple is not specified, though they might be their children. The lower part of the door presents two large standing depictions of the couple, with their names and titles above and in front of them. Behind each depiction are four sub-registers of individuals, male on the right and male and female on the left; these are their grandchildren, six boys and three girls in all. Below the standing figures are ten men carrying offerings, all of whom are soul priests, responsible for the rituals to be performed in the tomb. A considerable amount of colour is preserved on the figures, with red used for males and yellow for females.

It is unusual for quite so many figures to appear on a door, and it seems probable that the entire decoration of the tomb was concentrated on this stela, a compression of the more standard compositions which might put children and priests on adjacent walls. Kaihap was a relatively minor official who would have been close to the bottom of the tomb-owning ladder, and he was probably delighted to have been able to commission a monument of this quality. His two titles on the door are 'royal acquaintance', denoting relatively lowly rank among those important enough to own a decorated tomb at this date, and the unusual 'inspector of those chosen to be in attendance'. Whom Kaihap attended is not clear, but it might have even been the king.

The tomb in which this false door was found was located roughly 100 metres southeast of the South Ibis catacombs, burial places for votive sacred birds in the Late Period and just one group of a number of animal cemeteries in this area, excavated in the 1960s and 1970s by the Egypt Exploration Society. The area had previously served as part of the Old Kingdom North Saqqara necropolis, containing tombs from the Third to the Sixth Dynasties.

The false door was given to Britain in acknowledgement of the country's contribution to the Nubian Rescue Campaign of the 1960s.

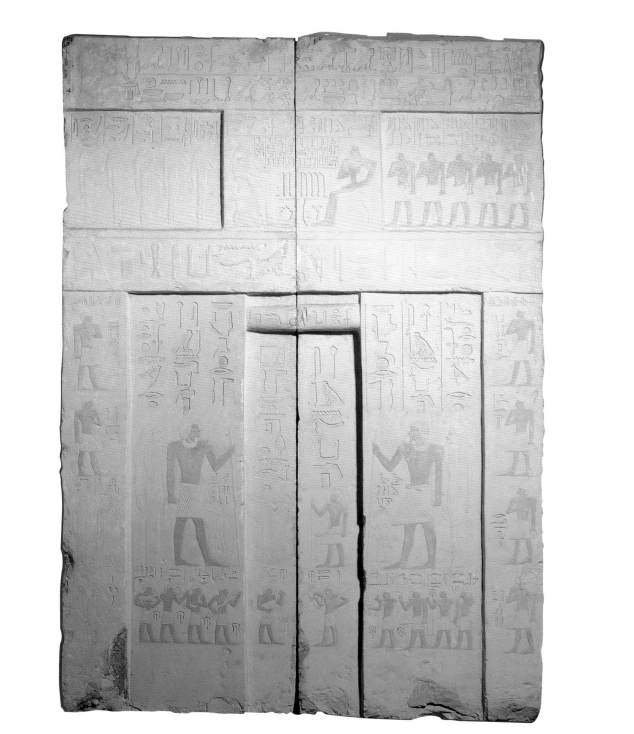

C-Group objects

POT

Classic C-Group, *c.* 1900–1600 BC

From Faras, grave 226

Gift of the University of Oxford in 1912

Ceramic

Diameter: 17 cm; height: 12 cm

EA 51245

MIRROR

Early C-Group, *c.* 2000–1900 BC

From Faras, grave 238

Gift of the University of Oxford in 1912

Copper

Width: 15.5 cm; height: 17.3 cm

EA 51225

STRING OF DISC BEADS

Early C-Group, *c.* 2000–1900 BC

From Faras, grave 238

Gift of the University of Oxford in 1912

Chalcedony

Length: 46.4 cm

EA 51220

THE TERM 'C-GROUP' was originally given to a culture which flourished in areas of Lower Nubia – roughly the same regions as those settled by the A-Group culture, although a long period of abandonment separates the two. These people, who did not use writing, seem to have entered the Nubian part of the Nile Valley at about the beginning of the Sixth Dynasty in Egypt (*c.* 2300 BC). Their earliest traces are found only on the west bank of the river, suggesting that they might have settled in the valley when life in the desert was becoming increasingly harsh, at the end of the Neolithic wet period. Nowadays, however, the term 'C-Group' is used to refer to cultural remains from an area extending further south, which may actually be a northern counterpart to the Kerma culture of southern Nubia.

The C-Group peoples were almost certainly the 'Nubians' with whom the leaders of Egyptian expeditions from Aswan had to deal in the later Sixth Dynasty (*c.* 2300–2200 BC); they acted as intermediaries between the Egyptians and the peoples who controlled various resources to the south, and also served as mercenaries in the Egyptian army. In the Middle Kingdom (*c.* 2016–1650 BC), they were considered enough of a potential nuisance to motivate the Egyptians to conquer Lower Nubia. They were gradually overwhelmed by the rising kingdom of Kush, and seem to have ceased to exist as a separate cultural entity by the beginning of the New Kingdom (*c.* 1550 BC).

Faras lies about 40 km to the north of the Second Cataract, and was first excavated by an expedition from Oxford in 1910–12. As well as these very early finds, the site has produced material from all periods, and is particularly renowned for paintings in its cathedral church from the Christian period. The site was most recently examined by a mission from Poland during the Nubian Rescue Campaign of the 1960s.

The C-Group cemetery consisted of mostly oval graves within circles of stones, and is contemporary with the First Intermediate Period. Some tombs were marked with plain sandstone stelae. Grave goods included mirrors, beads, which were most frequently found in the graves of women and children, and characteristic pottery. C-Group bowls are black, with incised geometric patterns. Early specimens have much in common with the early pottery of the Kerma culture, and the two wares are often found together in graves, at least as far upstream as the Dongola Reach.

Stela of Inyotef

First Intermediate Period, Eleventh Dynasty, early reign of Nebhepetre Mentuhotep, c. 2040 BC

Almost certainly from Thebes

Acquired in 1897

Limestone, with some traces of paint

Length: 101.5 cm

EA 1203

THE STELA OF INYOTEF is perhaps the British Museum's best example of the 'provincial art' of the First Intermediate Period. Old Kingdom artistic styles were remarkably homogenous throughout Egypt, whether around the capital Memphis or in the provinces. Following the collapse of central control at the end of the Eighth Dynasty, styles became very localized – modern scholars can assign provenances and dates to objects purely on the basis of hieroglyph forms. Theban products do not generally exhibit the more extreme features seen elsewhere, such as very narrow waists and divergence from the conventional system of proportions; the distinctive features of this stela are the unsubtle carving, the depth of the relief, and the rather inelegant handling of the heads and shoulders of the figures.

Inyotef is shown standing, receiving an offering from a small man whose position and scale are very characteristic of the First Intermediate Period. Behind Inyotef are three women, all referred to as his wives, named Mery, Iutu, and Iru. This does not prove that Egyptian society accepted polygamy, as it is quite possible that they could have succeeded one another; death in childbirth must have taken many lives, and divorce was not unknown, although it is questionable whether a divorced wife would be shown on a monument.

The stela's principal text is a carefully composed biography, containing offering formulae, narrative sections including important historical information, and phrases describing idealized moral qualities – standard parts of such biographies. The stela's historical importance lies first in the list of three kings served by Inyotef: Wahankh Inyotef, Nakhtnebtepnefer Inyotef, and Sankhibtawy Mentuhotep. The first two are well known and normally referred to as Inyotef II and III of the Eleventh Dynasty; the third king is probably better known as Nebhepetre Mentuhotep, the successor of Inyotef III, though the Horus name Sankhibtawy for this king is not known elsewhere. The text between the two women on the left records that the stela was set up in year 14, the year of the rebellion of Thinis, the nome (province) of Abydos. Fighting here is attested from other texts, notably those of the Asyut nomarchs and the *Instruction for Merykare*. Abydos/Thinis seems to have been the boundary between the warring kingdoms of the First Intermediate Period, so this stela may allow us to date some of the fighting.

Little is known about the earlier part of Nebhepetre Mentuhotep's long reign. He eventually ended the First Intermediate Period and reunited Egypt: the name 'Sankhibtawy' means 'the one who makes the two lands to live'. In his later years he took the name 'Sematawy', 'the uniter of the two lands', indicating that he had completed the process.

The stela of Inyotef is an important monument for both the political and artistic history of Thebes and Egypt.

A bead collar

Later Eleventh Dynasty, *c.* 2050–2000 BC

From Deir el-Bahari, Tomb 4 in the mortuary temple of Nebhepetre Mentuhotep

Gift of the Egypt Exploration Fund in 1905

Faience

Length: 54.3 cm

EA 41668

NECKLACES SUCH AS THIS are usually called 'broad collars' by Egyptologists, reflecting the Egyptian term *wesekh*. As with many items buried in tombs, they could be understood on a number of different levels. Though it is often used for simple adornment, the brilliant blue colour of faience is also highly symbolic of new life and rebirth; collars may also have had a particular ritual significance, as the (later) *Book of the Dead* makes reference to a 'spell for a golden collar to be placed on the throat of the deceased' (Spell 158).

This broad collar is composed of one row of horizontally-strung beads and five vertically-strung rows, two semicircular terminals, and fourteen pendants. The beads are a mixture of colours: bright blue, white, and purple. The terminals, one of which is broken, have six holes in the straight side adjacent to the rest of the beads, and one hole in the rounded side, through which would have been threaded the material which permitted the collar to be hung round the neck. Many terminals from later periods are shaped like falcon heads.

This necklace was found in a subsidiary burial on the north side of the main platform of the mortuary temple/tomb of Nebhepetre Mentuhotep II, the Eleventh Dynasty king who reunified Egypt in about 2020 BC (see also the brewery model from the adjacent Tomb 3, EA 40915, on pages 72–3). The burial was in a simple chamber at the bottom of a shaft, which showed evidence of reuse in the New Kingdom and Third Intermediate Period. No trace has survived of the name of the tomb's occupant, who was buried in a large rectangular limestone sarcophagus, although all other contemporary burials in the area were of women. Remains of more jewellery and some tomb models were also found.

The named female burials were principally on the west side of the platform; each had its own chapel, built during the earliest construction phase of the temple. These women were described as 'king's wives' in their chapel inscriptions but not in their burials, and this has led one scholar to suggest that they were 'cultic' wives of the king when he was fulfilling a particular ritual role, that of the ithyphallic god Min. Hence they might have been a harem for him on earth, and were then buried in his mortuary temple. Although the owner of this necklace was not necessarily one of these women, she must also have been of high status to have received a burial in this highly privileged temple location.

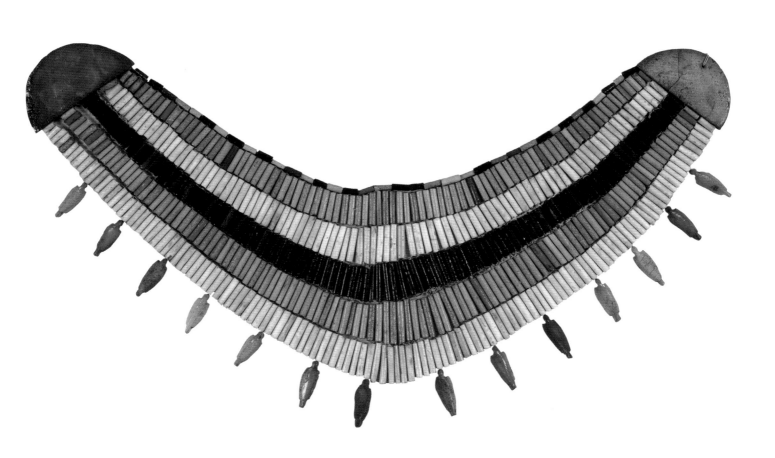

Model of a brewery

Later Eleventh Dynasty, *c.* 2050–2000 BC

From Deir el-Bahari, Tomb 3 in the temple of Nebhepetre Mentuhotep

Gift of the Egypt Exploration Fund in 1904

Wood

Length: 78 cm; width: 47 cm

EA 40915

WOODEN MODELS WERE PLACED in tombs from the late Old Kingdom until the late Middle Kingdom and could complement or substitute for tomb paintings. Such models provided a means of sustaining the deceased in the afterlife – in this case, it would ensure that the deceased had an eternal supply of bread and beer.

The flat wooden base of this model is pierced with holes for inserting the figures and implements to create a brewery scene. One side is occupied by thirteen women, each leaning over a quern with a grindstone. Opposite this row, another line of nine figures (originally thirteen) are crouching on the ground, sifting the flour ground by their companions opposite. A standing figure to their left oversees the work. Finally, a row of women faces outwards from the rest of the group: three women sieve mash into vats for beer production, while three (originally four) others crouch in front of ovens, presumably for heating the milled grain before fermentation, with one arm raised to shield themselves from the heat and the other originally holding an implement to fan the flames. The workers seem to be identified as women by their pale yellow skin colour (in contrast to the red skin of the male overseer), yet they wear simple kilts and have no hair; sexual differentiation in such models, in most of which the human figures are generally rendered rather schematically, is often done largely by skin colour.

The composition of the figures gives a lively impression of the movement and scale of a large grain-processing operation. Archaeological remains at Amarna show that large-scale production of bread and beer was achieved through endless duplication of small production units, rather than rationalizing the process into one large complex. The production of bread and beer were probably closely linked in ancient Egypt, although scientific studies have cast doubt on the theory that loaves were used to produce beer through fermentation. Models of breweries and bakeries often appear together, probably because they used the same raw materials, processed in different ways.

Tomb 3 was one of the subsidiary burials on the north side of the main platform of the mortuary temple/tomb of Nebhepetre Mentuhotep (see also the bead collar EA 41668 on pages 70–1, which comes from the adjacent Tomb 4). Burials on the west side of the platform were those of women who may have been royal concubines, but the occupants of the three tombs on the north side are unknown. This burial was located in a simple chamber at the bottom of a shaft, later reused for a simple burial in the Late Period. In addition to this model, parts of the owner's body were located, together with silver bangles, a bead necklace, a model granary, and a rather damaged boat, several of which are now in the British Museum. The occupant of the tomb was a young woman.

A fertility figurine

Late First Intermediate Period or early Middle Kingdom

Provenance unknown

Purchased at the sale of the d'Athanasi collection in 1837

Wood and mud

Length: 19.1 cm

EA 6459

A VARIETY OF FEMALE FIGURINES were included in burials from the Predynastic Period onwards, among them one of the earliest statuettes known from Egypt (the ivory figure of a woman, EA 59648, pages 24–5). Their general characteristics emphasize the sexual and reproductive aspects of the female figure, notably the breasts, hips, and pubic area.

This type of figurine is made of a flat piece of wood, and the shape employed has given rise to the modern nickname of 'paddle doll'. The body shape is very stylized, with a short stump of wood for the neck and the arms shown as rather short and lacking hands; the body terminates in an exaggerated depiction of the pubic region. The figure is painted with a collar in red and yellow round the neck, and the body is covered by a low–backed dress with shoulder straps, decorated in a geometric pattern of red, yellow, and black. It has been suggested that the patterns used on this object and others like it are inspired by Nubian dress. The head is made separately, from cloth wrapped around the wooden stump and then shaped and painted black, with two small objects, probably beads, representing the eyes. The impressive head of hair is composed of a number of small disc beads made of unfired mud, strung and attached to the head. Most objects of this type come from Upper Egypt, and are of early Middle Kingdom date; examples are particularly numerous at Thebes.

Early Egyptologists interpreted these figures as dolls, ignoring the emphasis placed on their sexual attributes. It has also been suggested that they are 'concubine figures', intended to provide sexual gratification in the afterlife. However, this fails to take account of the fact that the figures appear in the burials of women as well as men. The current preferred opinion is that these figures represent human fertility and birth and were placed in burials to guarantee eternal rebirth, symbolizing the sexual aspects of regeneration.

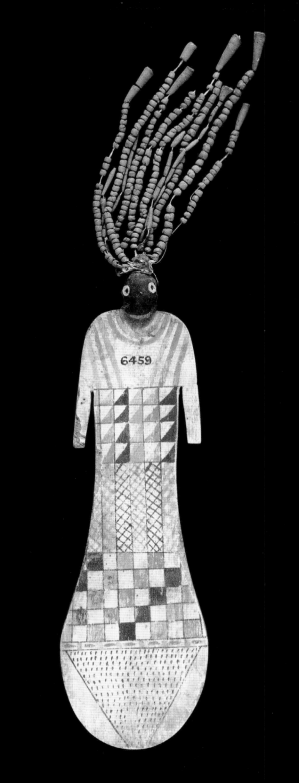

Stela of Senwosret I

Middle Kingdom, Twelfth Dynasty,
c. 1940 BC

From Elephantine

Acquired from Miss Selima Harris
in 1875

Pink granite

Height: 109 cm

EA 963

KING SENWOSRET I carried out a very active building programme all over Egypt during the early Middle Kingdom. This granite stela comes from the island of Elephantine, close to Egypt's southern border. The stela is roughly finished on the rear, indicating it was intended to be set into a wall or building. The scene at the top shows the god Khnum, called 'lord of the cataract region', on the right, with Khnum's consort Satis, 'mistress of Elephantine', standing at the left. Both deities are offering the gift of life to the king, represented by his Horus name, which is written as usual in a large *serekh* enclosure in the centre. Khnum presents an *ankh* (life) sign to the falcon on top of the *serekh,* while Satis' gift is expressed in the words 'may she give life'. Below are the remains of six damaged lines of hieroglyphs which begin with the king's names; the remainder consists of laudatory epithets, which also associate him with the goddess Satis and her daughter Anuket. Khnum, Satis, and Anuket were the local deities of Elephantine and the cataract region (where the river Nile became unnavigable). Triads of gods such as this were found in most major Egyptian religious centres, such as Memphis (see the Great Harris Papyrus, EA 9999, pages 226–7).

It seems very likely that this stela was set up in the area of the temple of Satis on Elephantine Island; it was probably placed near another stela of Senwosret I, now in Cairo (TR 19/4/2/1). The latter stela bears a longer text, which, in addition to praise of the king and gods, mentions 'repelling enemies' and 'destroying the bowmen', perhaps a reference to the king's campaigns in Nubia. Basing his opinion on the form of the writing of several hieroglyphs, Detlef Franke suggests that the stelae were not produced before about years 17/18 of the king's reign; he also argues that these stelae not only name specific gods but also refer indirectly to many more, including the king, who are both creators and the created. It is likely that this is the first depiction of the king as the creator. These stelae thus stressed both the importance of the king in the Elephantine area and his place in the cosmic order.

Reliefs from the tomb of Djehutyhotep

Middle Kingdom, middle of the Twelfth
Dynasty, *c.* 1878–1855 BC

From the tomb of Djehutyhotep
at Deir el-Bersha

Gift of the Egypt Exploration Fund
in 1894

Limestone with paint

EA 1147

Length: 169 cm

EA 1150

Height: 72 cm

DEIR EL-BERSHA, situated on the east bank of the Nile just north of Amarna, was the
necropolis of the First Intermediate Period and Middle Kingdom governors and officials
of the 15th Upper Egyptian province or 'nome'. There are a number of tombs, all now
rather damaged, arranged in several different levels of the side of a wadi. The site was first
systematically investigated in 1891–2 by the Egypt Exploration Fund (EEF). The most
impressive tomb is that of the nomarch (governor) Djehutyhotep, son of Kay, who seems
to have lived during the reigns of Amenemhat II, Senwosret II, and Senwosret III. His
tomb is particularly renowned for the scene (now badly damaged) of four teams of men
dragging a colossal statue.

The tomb had an impressive entrance portico with a pillar either side of the entrance,
with one main rectangular chamber, the walls of which bore most of the decoration. The
tomb had suffered destruction from earthquakes and robbers, but the EEF was able to use
records compiled earlier in that century to reconstruct much of the tomb decoration.
Many of the fragments of decoration had become detached, and were brought to the

Egyptian Museum, Cairo and the British Museum. In front of the tomb was a large courtyard, in which the burial of Gua was found in the mid 1890s (see pages 81–3). A mission from the Catholic University of Leuven is now re-examining the tomb, and has found over a thousand previously unrecorded fragments of decoration.

Both large pieces illustrated here came from the same wall, situated on the right as the tomb is entered. The female figure (EA 1150, shown on page 80) was the leader of a procession of women, evident from elsewhere as the nomarch's daughters, although no text survives with this fragment. She was faced by a smaller figure of an attendant holding a fly whisk, visible in this relief. The woman wears a tight sheath dress which accentuates the slim ideal form of a woman in Egyptian relief, and is a somewhat stiff and formal style of dress which broadly lasted for elite women until the middle of the Eighteenth Dynasty.

The other scene (EA 1147, below) was located in the register below the procession of women, just to the left of EA 1150. It shows a procession of attendants, probably members of Djehutyhotep's retinue. Two pairs of men carry what must be the tomb-owner's

carrying chair, below which is shown a dog, named Ankhu. The dog appears to be drawn at a somewhat larger scale than the men, suggesting that he must be of greater importance and thus perhaps Djehutyhotep's pet. He is shown as a rather short-legged dog, a far less common type than the more sporting sight-hound or saluki. Others among the procession carry weapons, including a man with a bow, a man with an axe, and one with an axe and shield. Perhaps they were Djehutyhotep's bodyguard. The dress of the men makes a distinction between their function and status; those with long kilts who only carry staffs are probably the senior officials, while those with short kilts are more likely the regular guards.

The quality of the carving of all fragments from this tomb is very high, and the colours of the painting are very well preserved. In EA 1147, many of the details are in fact applied only in paint. Analysis of the pigments on fragments from this tomb has shown that a number of unusual pigments were used in addition to the more regular ones; these include huntite for white, orpiment for yellow, and manganese oxide for black. Use of such exceptional pigments perhaps further stresses the wealth and importance of Djehutyhotep.

The burial assemblage of Gua

Middle Kingdom, Twelfth Dynasty,
reigns of Amenemhat II to Senwosret II
(*c.* 1911–1870 BC)

From Deir el-Bersha

Acquired in 1899

CANOPIC CHEST

Wood

Height: 53 cm

EA 30838

GUA WAS A PHYSICIAN during the Middle Kingdom. The British Museum has a number of objects which are believed to come from his tomb at Deir el-Bersha. The circumstances surrounding the discovery of these important objects are, to say the least, obscure. Interest in the Middle Kingdom tombs had been rising since the Egypt Exploration Fund's work in the painted chapels in the early 1890s (see pages 78–80), and from 1897 Daressy and Kamal worked on excavating burials for the Service des Antiquités. In late 1897, Daressy found several shafts in the courtyard of the local governor (nomarch) Djehuty-hotep, and excavated four of them, finding some fine coffins and other items. However, his map also shows the tomb of Gua, without further comment. It seems most likely that, after Daressy had finished excavating in 1897, illicit diggers, inspired by his finds, found more burials which were then sold to dealers; these were primarily the shafts of Gua and Seni, whose grave goods also belong to the Museum. Like Gua, Seni was a physician; their burials formed part of a small cemetery near the tomb of the nomarch Djehutyhotep,

whom they presumably served. Their coffins were doubtless fitted tightly into a rectangular burial chamber, like those excavated by Daressy.

The coffins and canopic box of Gua bear his name, and other objects acquired at or around the same time are also associated with the burial, including a headrest, some wooden models, a male figure, and a servant figure. The canopic container (shown on page 81) is a square box with a lid and four jars of Egyptian alabaster, with wooden covers in the shape of human heads, containing linen and traces of the internal organs.

The most spectacular objects are the wooden inner and outer coffins, which are quite similar in decoration. The photograph opposite shows the outer coffin. The coffin exteriors bear offering formulae for the deceased and the usual pair of painted eyes, which would allow the mummy to see magically outside the coffin. The interior decoration is much more elaborate. A 'false door' and an offering table are painted close to the deceased's head, enabling his spirit to pass freely in and out of the coffin and to receive nourishment. Below the texts at the top of the coffin is a 'frieze of objects', a narrow band filled with pictures of granaries, clothing, jewellery, tools, weapons, furniture, vessels, and many other commodities that the wealthy Egyptian desired for his afterlife and which would magically come into existence when needed. The objects include amulets and items of royal regalia, such as sceptres and kingly headdresses; whatever rank the deceased had held in life, these items would magically assimilate him with Osiris, ruler of the netherworld. To equip him with the necessary sacred knowledge of the afterlife, large areas of the coffin sides were inscribed in ink with writings now known as the Coffin Texts. These compositions derived ultimately from the Pyramid Texts of the Fifth and Sixth Dynasties. The spells offered magical assistance to the deceased on his journey into the next world. On the floor of the coffin is a composition called the *Book of Two Ways*, another guide to the hereafter (known only from coffins at Bersha), in which paths and watercourses are marked out for the deceased's guidance. The location of this text on the base reflects the idea that the images and inscriptions inside the coffin created a fully three-dimensional 'world', a sacred environment in which the rebirth of the occupant could take place and where he could live and travel. Thus, the internal space demarcated by the walls of a rectangular Middle Kingdom coffin was potentially more important than the exterior, since these surfaces were immediately accessible to the dead person. This explains why the interior decoration of these coffins is much more detailed and elaborate than that of the exterior. The male figure probably represented the deceased, serving as another place for Gua's spirit to dwell. The servant figure and wooden models provided service and sustenance.

A model funerary boat

Middle Kingdom, Twelfth Dynasty,
c. 1985–1773 BC

Probably from Thebes

Purchased at the sale of the third Salt
collection in 1835

Sycomore fig wood

Length: 66.7 cm

EA 9524

THIS PAINTED WOODEN MODEL represents a funerary boat bearing a mummy on a bier beneath a shrine-shaped canopy. Fore and aft of the mummy stand two bare-breasted women with short hair in attitudes of mourning; these women usually represent the goddesses Isis and Nephthys, the sisters of Osiris and archetypal mourners. The helmsman squats at the rear between a pair of steering oars, the supporting posts of which are topped with small falcon heads. A small offering table bearing two pots stands on the deck between the canopy and the prow.

The body of the boat is painted green, as if to indicate that it was made of a material like papyrus, although in reality any boat of this size could only have been made of wood. However, papyrus, and indeed the colour green, is symbolic of new life and rebirth and is appropriate for a tomb model; the yellow sickle-shaped prow and stern also imitate elements from papyrus boats. Lotus (lily) flowers are painted on the steering oars, giving further emphasis to the associations with rebirth. The *wedjat* eye of Horus, a symbol of healing and regeneration, is shown on the front of the body of the boat.

Models became a common feature of Egyptian tomb contents from the late Old Kingdom through to the Middle Kingdom; in some cases the models augmented the depictions which were painted or carved onto tomb walls, but in others they replaced what was shown in such scenes (see also the brewery model, EA 40915, pages 72–3). According to the sale catalogue of the 1835 Salt collection, this boat, another like it (EA 9525), and a model granary (EA 2463) were found in the same tomb, though regrettably the identity of the tomb is not specified. The granary was apparently seen by Robert Hay in the house of d'Athanasi, Salt's agent, at Luxor in about 1825.

Boats were particularly important models, to judge from the number that have survived. They were of course the main means of transport in Egypt, and the Egyptians saw the sky as a celestial river, on which the sun-god Re travelled every day in his own boat. Besides models of more conventional travelling boats, an important category is the funerary boat, as here. It is not clear whether this is a representation of the deceased's funeral, when the body travelled from the land of the living (the east) to that of the dead (the west), or whether it could represent a pilgrimage journey to Abydos so that the deceased could magically associate himself with Osiris. The latter scene became popular in the painted decoration of tombs of the New Kingdom.

Unfinished stela of Userwer

Middle Kingdom, Twelfth Dynasty, perhaps *c.* 1850 BC

Provenance unknown, perhaps Abydos

Acquired in 1834 from the collection of Joseph Sams

Limestone

Height: 52 cm

EA 579

THE TOP OF THIS ALMOST SQUARE STELA bears a prayer for offerings and a request to the living passer-by to say a formula to ensure offerings for the deceased. Two registers of depiction below the text show offering scenes and images of relatives. The upper scene shows (left) Userwer and his wife Satdepetnetjer seated before offerings; to the right of the offerings is a another wife, Satameni. On the right of this register are Userwer's father Senkhonsu and his wife Satnebniut, who are being presented with offerings by 'his son' Sneferuser. The scene of another wife in front of the deceased's offering table is rather unusual, and could perhaps suggest that Satameni was a wife who predeceased Userwer. The scene below shows a son, five daughters, 'his father Userwer', and a brother.

This stela illustrates how difficult it can be to follow the vagaries of Egyptian kinship terminology. In addition to the unusual scene of the second wife (where a son might normally be expected), the use of 'his' can be ambiguous. Whose are the relatives at the bottom? It has been argued that, since they face right, they might actually relate to Senkhonsu, and thus be siblings, an uncle, and a grandfather of Userwer.

The stela is also interesting for the evidence it provides of the techniques used in its manufacture. The lower scene still bears the grid for ensuring that the figures' proportions were correct, using the conventional Middle Kingdom grid of 18 squares from brow to feet which was employed for standing figures. Traces of grids also appear on the seated figures, who were drawn to a 14-square grid; a separate 18-square grid is used for the standing figures in the same scene. The figures in the lower scene show different levels of carving: as one moves to the left and upwards, less and less of the detail has been cut, with the two final figures still in fine black outline. It appears that the lower part of a figure was cut, then the upper part, and finally the facial and other details were added. Userwer bore the title of sculptor, but we have no way of knowing whether he worked on his own stela.

Where Userwer lived in Egypt is uncertain. The provenance of this stela is unknown but, like many others, it was probably set up at Abydos to be in the area of the cult centre of Osiris, the god of the dead. (See also the stela of Samontu, EA 828, pages 88–9 and the stela of Nebipusenwosret, EA 101, pages 94–5.) Because of the presence of cenotaphs as well as real tombs at Abydos in the Middle Kingdom, we cannot be certain that this stela was set up at the site where Userwer was buried.

579

Stela of Samontu

Middle Kingdom, Twelfth Dynasty,
reign of Amenemhat II, *c.* 1910 BC

Provenance uncertain, probably
from Abydos

Acquired at the sale of the Anastasi
collection in 1857

Limestone

Height: 136 cm

EA 828

THE MAGNIFICENT STELA of Samontu bears a mixture of texts and representations common on such Middle Kingdom objects. The small curved area at the top bears the date of year 3 of Amenemhat II, the third king of the Twelfth Dynasty. Below, in ten vertical columns, is a biographical text, followed by one horizontal line containing a simple offering formula.

The longer text begins with some of Samontu's titles of rank, and then tells us that he was born in the reign of Amenemhat I and was 'a youth who tied the headband' (an indication of achieving a certain age or rite of passage) in that of Senwosret I. It continues by mentioning some of the offices to which Samontu was appointed by the king (not specifically indicated, but probably Senwosret I, who reigned for 45 years). These included 'scribe of the hearer's enclosure', 'scribe of the cadastre (land registry)', 'accountant of northern barley in Upper and Lower Egypt', 'scribe of the great (labour) enclosure', 'royal document scribe' and 'overseer of works in the entire land'. These last two titles are quite high in Egypt's administrative hierarchy, but it is difficult to decide whether the other stages of his career were typical.

Two scenes appear below the texts. The upper one shows Samontu receiving choice offerings; he is seated and accompanied by a standing figure of his wife, Hedjeret. The lower scene depicts two sons and three daughters: the first son, Meriankh, is given titles which indicate that he was a legal official, while the other children are identified by their names: Satsatet, Senwosret, Samontu, and Neferu.

The stela is cut in sunk relief and the original paint is well preserved. The hieroglyphs were coloured blue, and the men and women the usual red-brown and yellow-brown, while the offerings are a mixture of all these colours. The style of the stela, with its slightly elongated figures, suggests that it was made in the same workshop as a number of similar pieces from the reign of Amenemhat II, a considerable number of which definitely came from Abydos.

Although the stela is dated to the reign of Amenemhat II, Samontu clearly lived most of his life in the reign of Amenemhat's father, Senwosret I. Historical discussion of the Middle Kingdom is often influenced by the question of whether the kings shared their thrones with their designated successor in a co-regency. A number of double-dated monuments exist which can be used to argue for such practices, and for many years, the Middle Kingdom was thought to be the one period during which this practice was common. However, recent research has reinterpreted much of the data, and current opinion regards co-regencies as less likely.

Statue of Senwosret III

Middle Kingdom, Twelfth Dynasty,
c. 1850 BC

From Deir el-Bahari, temple of
Nebhepetre Mentuhotep

Gift of the Egypt Exploration Fund
in 1905

Granodiorite

Height: 122 cm

EA 684

THIS STATUE IS A MASTERPIECE of Middle Kingdom sculpture, and belongs to a group of three in the British Museum (the others being EA 685 and 686). It depicts the king wearing the cloth *nemes* headdress, standing with both hands flat on the royal kilt, down the centre of which runs a beaded panel with two uraei (cobras) at the ends. Around his neck is an amulet, known primarily from Senwosret's statues and very occasionally on those of later kings of the Twelfth Dynasty. Its nature and meaning is far from certain; it has been likened to a double pouch, pierced by a thorn. On the belt of the kilt is a cartouche with one of his royal names, Khakaure; a full royal titulary is incised on the back pillar.

The quality and finishing of the stone are superb, as is the representation of the royal features. The latter are the 'serious' facial features particularly associated with Senwosret III, carefully and powerfully carved. There has been much discussion as to whether this is a true portrait of the king, or whether it is making a particular statement. Egyptian statues are rarely, if ever, 'portraits' in the modern sense of the term (although in this case we have no real clue as to Senwosret's appearance); rather, they usually exhibit a reasonably consistent range of features which, when tied in with inscriptional evidence, allow us to assign monuments to a king with some certainty. The characteristic features of Senwosret III may reflect the generally serious, or even pessimistic, tone of contemporary literary works; they might also represent concern and care for the world, a concept probably emphasized by the characteristic large ears of Middle Kingdom sculptures, perhaps symbolic of the ruler's readiness to listen. The degree of variability between the three British Museum statues, and indeed more generally, between different images of Senwosret III, is very interesting. Although the images are characterized by these serious features, no two are alike, even though it is reasonable to assume that the Deir el-Bahari statues were made by the same group of sculptors.

These statues and another now in Cairo, as well as two other examples, now headless, were erected around the platform base of the mortuary temple of Nebhepetre Mentuhotep (Mentuhotep II) at Deir el-Bahari. Senwosret seems to have been particularly dedicated to the Theban god Montu, the principal local deity until the rise of Amun; like Mentuhotep II (the name means 'Montu is satisfied'), he promoted the deity's cult. The statues are part of Senwosret's restoration and re-endowment of the temple of the earlier king, which is also recorded in a large granite stela, now in Cairo, that he erected in the temple.

Colossal head of Amenemhat III

Middle Kingdom, Twelfth Dynasty,
c. 1800 BC

From Bubastis

Gift of the Egypt Exploration Fund
in 1889

Granodiorite

Height: 79 cm

EA 1063

THIS HEAD COMES FROM ONE of a pair of seated statues of Amenemhat III which flanked the entrance to a temple at Bubastis in the Nile Delta. Fragments of the lower part of this statue are also in the Museum (EA 1064), while the head of the other statue is now in the Cairo Museum (CG 353). Few statues of this size have survived from before the New Kingdom, although there is plenty of evidence for colossal statuary as far back as the Old Kingdom. Temples were often flanked by pairs of colossal statues, the best-known examples being the so-called Colossi of Memnon at the entrance to the temple of Amenhotep III from the New Kingdom.

The massive and severe impression of this head is accentuated by the empty eye sockets, which would originally have been filled with inlaid eyes of black and white stone. These would have made the statue even more dramatic, while at the same time reducing its current air of severity. Close examination shows that the sockets were produced by drilling a series of holes and gradually removing the stone between them. Traces of a reddish ground on the stone indicate the presence of an original coat of paint.

The lower parts of these statues bore inscriptions: their original owner's name was replaced by those of others, the last being Osorkon I of the Twenty-second Dynasty. On grounds of style, however, they are likely to be from the later Middle Kingdom. The large ears are typical of much Twelfth Dynasty statuary, and are perhaps indicative of the rulers' desire to be shown as receptive to petitions and pleas from their subjects. Statues of the later Twelfth Dynasty, especially those of Senwosret III and his son, Amenemhat III, are particularly recognizable for their stern, almost careworn, features. There is more consistency in the portrayal of Senwosret III (see his statue, EA 684, pages 90–1) than in the statues of his son, which have been characterized as 'realistic', 'idealized', and 'stylized'; several statues of Amenemhat III even show the king with youthful features. The features of this statue's face are less detailed than in many of Amenemhat's other statues, perhaps less a result of craft or technical factors and more as the result of the simplification appropriate to objects designed to be viewed from a distance and from below.

The city of Bubastis was well known in Greek times, and a description of it by the historian Herodotos has survived. The temple of the goddess Bastet was excavated by Edouard Naville for the Egypt Exploration Fund in 1887–9, and revealed large-scale building work by Osorkon I and II of the Twenty-second Dynasty, who resided at Bubastis. Many reused blocks from older epochs came to light (for an example, see the lintel of Amenhotep II, EA 1103, pages 138–9). It is not certain whether this statue was originally set up at Bubastis or elsewhere.

Stela of Nebipusenwosret

Middle Kingdom, Twelfth Dynasty,
c. 1800 BC

From Abydos

Purchased at the sale of the third Salt
collection in 1835

Limestone

Height: 100.5 cm

EA 101

THE STELA TAKES THE FORM of a rectangular slab with a cornice at the top, with a round moulding (a 'torus', a representation of the original vegetation binding at the tops and sides of walls) at the upper, right, and left sides. The decoration is divided into three areas. The upper register displays the name of king Senwosret III in the centre, with a figure of the owner on either side, accompanied by a text referring to the gods Osiris (left) and Wepwawet (right). The central register shows Nebipusenwosret seated at an offering table, with a text to the right that lists some of his titles and gives some intriguing information about the stela's origin. The lower register consists of an address in seven lines to the priests of the Abydos temples and a prayer for offerings. The quality of the carving is uniformly good.

Nebipusenwosret served under both Senwosret III and his son Amenemhat III. The latter's *sed* or jubilee festival is mentioned in the central text, so it is possible that the stela was made after Amenemhat's thirtieth year, when the festival was probably first celebrated (though this might have been earlier: see EA 37996, pages 36–7). Perhaps the most interesting item in the stela is this text in the central register: 'This stela went south in the charge of the eldest lector-priest Ibi, when the priesthood of the temple came to see the king in his perfect festival of eternity.' Clearly the stela was not set up by its owner in person; Nebipusenwosret claims to have 'grown up at the feet of the king' and was probably an official in the royal residence at Lisht, just north of the Faiyum. He thus presumably took advantage of the convenient visit of a group of priests to have his stela set up at Abydos.

The sands of Abydos have produced more stelae, particularly of the Middle Kingdom, than any other site in Egypt. The reason is not hard to find: many people wanted to commemorate themselves in the presence of the god of the dead, Osiris, and the local necropolis deity, Wepwawet. Both are mentioned on Nebipusenwosret's stela. It is important to realize that most of these stelae belonged to people who were not buried there. People might have made a pilgrimage to the holy city and left a stela there, or, as in the present case, they might have someone else do it for them ('pilgrimage by proxy'). Many stelae were set up in small chapels, commemorating a whole family, and there could be several stelae per chapel. Only one other stela seems to mention Nebipusenwosret, if he is indeed identical to the Nebipu mentioned on Cairo CG 20235.

Gold openwork plaque showing Amenemhat IV

Middle Kingdom, Twelfth Dynasty,
c. 1795 BC

Provenance uncertain (initially
acquired in Beirut)

Gift of the Birmingham Jewellers' and
Silversmiths' Association in 1929

Gold

Width: 3 cm

EA 59194

THIS PLAQUE PROBABLY BELONGS to a pectoral. Three small pins on the back allow it to be set into another medium so that it could be worn more easily; presumably this also protected the delicate object. More elaborate examples of this type, first produced during the Middle Kingdom, took the form of golden openwork, with the cells in the gold filled with semi-precious stones (*cloisonné* technique; compare EA 54460, opposite). The design was cut out of sheet metal (*ajouré* technique), using a chisel to punch around the outline; the Egyptian craftsman did not possess shears or fine saws. The object is particularly carefully made, and all the smallest details of the figures are shown, from the facial features to the musculature of the legs. These details were chased onto the metal using a fine chisel and mallet.

The design consists of an almost square frame, with the top edge taking the form of the hieroglyph for 'sky'. Below is a figure of king Amenemhat IV (Maatkherure: see his sphinx, EA 58892, pages 98–9) presenting an oil jar to the god Atum, called 'Lord of Heliopolis' in the text above. Atum is standing, holding a sceptre in his left hand, and wearing the double crown of Upper and Lower Egypt. In his right hand he holds the hieroglyph for life, which he confers on the king in exchange for the offerings that the king presents to him. Below the jar presented by the king are hieroglyphs reading 'giving unguent'.

Scarab pendant

Middle Kingdom, Twelfth Dynasty,
reign of Senwosret II, *c.* 1877–1870 BC

Provenance unknown

Acquired in 1919

Electrum, lapis lazuli, green feldspar,
cornelian

Wingspan: 3.5 cm

EA 54460

THIS PENDANT IS SHAPED like a winged scarab. Two small tubes on the underside were used for suspension. The central ornament forms one of the names of king Senwosret II, Khakheperre, composed of the hieroglyphs of the sun-disc (*re*), the scarab (*kheper*), and the rising sun on the horizon (*kha*) beneath. Normally this name is written with the signs in the order *re-kha-kheper*, but the flexibility of the hieroglyphic writing system permits this change of order to achieve a symbolic image, in this case of a scarab appearing on the horizon pushing the sun-disc. On either side of the *kha* hieroglyph is a papyrus flower, a symbol of rebirth, like the scarab. The whole object thus expresses both an association with the king and a wish for rebirth after death. The use of the different coloured stones is partly guided by the association of the colours with the original object (red for the sun, green for the papyrus flowers), and partly decorative (as in the wings and the separately coloured head of the scarab). The stones for the wings are cemented into place, but all the other stones are set in cloisons – small 'cells' formed by soldering metal strips at right angles to the surface of a sheet metal base.

The first known examples of pectorals inlaid with semi-precious stones using the *cloisonné* technique come from the Twelfth Dynasty, although Old Kingdom tomb decoration sometimes shows jewellers making such objects. A similar object was found on a body excavated in a Middle Kingdom tomb at Riqqa in 1912–13. An extremely fine series of similar pendants, probably among the finest ever made in Egypt, is known from the tombs of the royal women of the reigns of Senwosret II and III at Illahun and Dahshur.

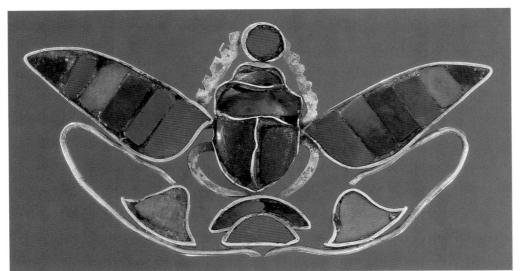

Sphinx of Amenemhat IV

Middle Kingdom, late Twelfth Dynasty, c. 1786–1777 BC

Discovered in the foundations of a building near Bab-Serail, Beirut

Acquired with the assistance of the National Art Collections Fund in 1928

Gneiss

Length: 58.5 cm

EA 58892

THIS SMALL SPHINX is one of the rare sculptures associated with Amenemhet IV, the last male ruler of the Twelfth Dynasty. The lion body sits on a large block base in the usual recumbent pose; its lower side has a hard protruding edge, known from other Middle Kingdom sphinxes. The breast is decorated with a pattern which recalls the mane of the famous sphinxes from Tanis attributed to Amenemhat III (Cairo, CG 393, 394), with their distinctive ruffs and leonine ears; however, the head is human here and wears a cloth *nemes* headdress. Another glance at the proportions of the head and the style reveals that something is not right: the head is too small for the body, the *nemes* is rather rounded, and the style and shape of the face is not in accord with Middle Kingdom styles. Examination of the *nemes* headdress shows traces of the same pattern as noted on the breast. The object has clearly been recut; in all probability it was originally a smaller version of the Tanis sphinxes, with the mane arranged into a tapering shape behind the head, not unlike the rough form of the *nemes* and thus making it relatively easy to convert. Most of the recutting would have taken place at the left and right sides of the face, where the ruff and mane had to be removed to allow for the creation of the ears. The recutting was doubtless carried out much later; the style of the face suggests this happened in the Late or, more probably, the Ptolemaic Period (664–30 BC).

The brief inscription on the breast between the forepaws reads 'Maatkherure, may he live forever, beloved of Atum, lord of Heliopolis'. A temple in Heliopolis thus seems a reasonable original location for this statue. Perhaps it was moved from there to some other site in the Delta, conceivably Alexandria if the recutting dates from the Ptolemaic or Roman Period; this hypothesis is supported by the fact that many other objects of Heliopolitan origin, including obelisks, have been found in Alexandria. From there it eventually found its way to the Lebanon. The head of a quartzite sphinx of Amenemhat IV has been found at Heliopolis; another comes from Thebes, while three larger sphinxes of his have been found at Abukir, near Alexandria, no doubt again as a result of their reuse.

Miniature sphinx holding a captive

Probably Middle Kingdom, perhaps
Twelfth Dynasty (*c.* 1985–1773 BC)

From Abydos, Tomb 477, probably west
of the Shunet ez-Zebib; excavations of
John Garstang in 1908

Gift of Mrs Russell Rea in 1920

Ivory

Length: 5.6 cm

EA 54678

THE FOREPART OF A SPHINX holds in its claws the head of a prostrate captive, probably a Nubian, a traditional foe of Egypt. The sphinx wears the traditional royal *nemes* headdress, with the uraeus (cobra) at the front and the snake's tail extending across the headdress. The captive's knees are drawn up and his arms extended beneath the sphinx's legs. He appears to be naked except for a belt at the waist and a short wig. His back is arched, and his expressionless face is angled up at the sphinx, whose gaze rises above and over him. The sphinx's face is characterized by rather large eyes and ears and prominent cheekbones. These somewhat exaggerated facial features were originally thought to represent a foreign king, perhaps one of the Syro-Palestinian Hyksos who ruled Egypt in the Fifteenth Dynasty, and the sphinx used to be dated to the later Second Intermediate Period. More recent research, based on both stylistic considerations and an examination of the material discovered with the sphinx, suggests that it is from the Twelfth Dynasty, and might even represent Senwosret I.

It seems likely that the object is substantially complete and was never intended as a free-standing three-dimensional piece; this is suggested by the two peg-holes underneath. It could have been a box handle or perhaps an ornament on a chair or some other item of furniture. It might have come from a royal context, since it displays the king's power over one of his traditional enemies. It might then have been given to a favoured official, who buried it in his own tomb as a mark of his status.

There are a number of casts of this object, including one in the British Museum (EA 48999) and another included in the sale of the MacGregor collection in 1922 (Lot 715). Presumably these were made because its excavator, John Garstang, wished the existence of the sphinx to be widely known, but had already given the original object to Russell Rea, MP, one of his sponsors.

The Ramesseum Papyri

Middle Kingdom, mid to late
Thirteenth Dynasty, c. 1850-1700 BC

From Luxor, the Ramesseum, Tomb 5

Gift of the British School of
Archaeology in Egypt and Sir Alan H.
Gardiner

Black and red ink on papyrus

EA 10610

EA 10752-72

EA 10610/5

Length: 44.2 cm; width: 30 cm

EA 10756/6

Length: 35.5 cm; width: 30.5 cm

IN 1895–6 W.M.F. PETRIE uncovered a shaft tomb in a late Middle Kingdom cemetery, in an area now covered by the brick storerooms of the 'Ramesseum', the much later funerary temple of Ramesses II. At the bottom of the 4-metre shaft he found a wooden box and a mass of funerary magical equipment, including a metal serpent wrapped in a mass of human hair, a statuette of an animal-headed girl wielding two serpent wands, and some ivory wands. This material had been discarded by ancient tomb-robbers when they plundered a burial from around 1700 BC. The box was two-thirds full of crumbling rolls of papyri, extremely fragile because of the occasional dampness of this level of the rock. The papyri were eventually unrolled and conserved in the early twentieth century by the German conservator Hugo Ibscher, who saved them by using various techniques, including mounting some fragments on sheets of gelatine. Some are now in the Manchester Museum and the Fitzwilliam Museum, Cambridge. Two rolls are in the Egyptian Museum, Berlin, and the rest are in the British Museum.

The box contained about seventeen papyri, a collection built up over several generations and one of the few personal manuscript collections found reasonably intact. This suggests the tomb-owner, possibly a lector-priest, was professionally interested in magical and liturgical texts. He was probably buried around 1700 BC. Some of the papyri have accounts and jottings on their backs which may relate to his household and lands, and he may have had close links with the local authorities. Some of the papyri are written in carefully-drawn linear hieroglyphs and seem to come from a temple context; these include spells for gaining respect (P. Ram VII = EA 10760), a funeral liturgy (P. Ram E = EA 10753), hymns to the royal crocodile god, Sobek (P. Ram VI = EA 10759), and a ritual for a royal festival with illustrations of the ceremony's scenes, the so-called 'Dramatic Papyrus' (P. Ram B = EA 10610). Most of the texts are written in hieratic and concern healing by medicine and magic. They include spells for mothers and young children and to aid pregnancy (P. Ram III–IV = EA 10756–7), rituals to protect a house from magic, ghosts, and serpents (P. Ram IX = EA 10762), 'a spell for the protection of the limbs against any male and female serpent' (P. Ram X = EA 10763), love-spells (P. Ram XI = EA 10764), invocations to demons against fever (P. Ram XII = EA 10765), and spells for protection on the dangerous epagomenal days at the turn of the year (P. Ram XVII = EA 10770). Many were written on reused papyri and in one case some of the earlier texts survive, preserving a sequence of late Twelfth Dynasty military despatches sent to the regional capital at Thebes from the chain of Nubian fortresses in the south (P. Ram C = P

EA 10610, sheet 5
Dramatic papyrus

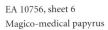

EA 10756, sheet 6
Magico-medical papyrus

BM EA 19752, 10771–2). This is a rare surviving example of the huge quantity of paperwork generated by the bureaucracy of ancient Egypt.

The collection also included literary texts, including two of the great masterpieces of Egyptian poetry, *The Tale of Sinuhe* and *The Tale of the Eloquent Peasant* (P. Berlin P 10499). A fine late Twelfth Dynasty roll (P. Ram I = EA 10754) contains the only known copy of the pessimistic *Discourse of the Scribe Sasobek*:

> This life of a span – what happens in it is unknowable;
> it starts suddenly,
> it ends in destruction.

Other texts include a word list (P. Berlin P 10495) and a collection of maxims (P. Ram II = EA 10755), such as:

> The grass dies even as it grows –
> but not the spoken word!

Although its social context remains obscure, this official's library provides a unique insight into contemporary spiritual and intellectual life. The tomb owner may have collected the manuscripts from various sources, since they were written at varying dates, or he may have inherited a library build up over several generations. The sheer number of manuscripts suggests that he was a person of some wealth and prestige, and not a travelling magician or village healer as was once thought.

R.B.P.

Jerboa

Middle Kingdom, Twelfth or
Thirteenth Dynasty, c. 1985–1650 BC

Probably from a tomb at el-Matariya

Gift of Richard Bethell in 1924

Faience

Height: 4.4 cm

EA 37097

THIS SMALL MODEL of a desert animal is made of blue-green and whitish faience with details of the eyes, ears, and markings painted in black. The reason for its presence in a tomb is uncertain, but it has been suggested that it may have helped to recreate the environment of the mythical beasts who would generate protective magic for the deceased.

The object probably came from one of the tomb-groups at el-Matariya (the site of ancient Heliopolis, north-east of Cairo) which were discovered by Bedouin in 1913. The tombs yielded other jerboas, now in the Metropolitan Museum, New York and the Fitzwilliam Museum, Cambridge, and a number of other faience creatures.

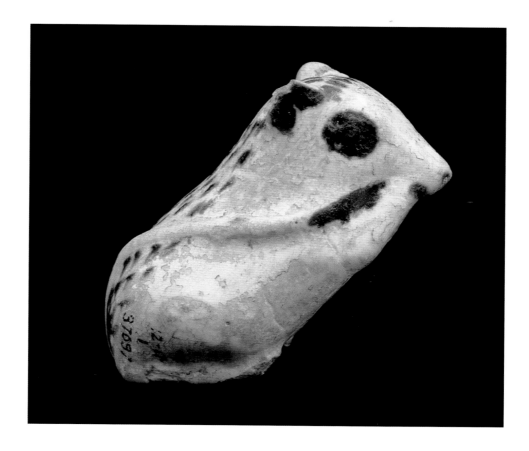

Statue of Rehuankh

Middle Kingdom, Twelfth Dynasty,
reign of Senwosret III or early years of
Amenemhat III, *c.* 1850–1830 BC

Provenance undocumented, but
undoubtedly from Abydos

Bequeathed by Lady Coote in 1944

Quartzite

Height: 71 cm

EA 1785

REHUANKH (called Ankhrehu in older publications) was mayor of an unnamed town, no doubt Abydos. The statue must have been the centrepiece of a tomb chapel in the town's Northern Necropolis, where two offering tables of the same man were also discovered. One, now in Cairo (CG 23045), was found by Auguste Mariette; the other, now in Kyoto, was excavated by W.M.F. Petrie. In addition to Rehuankh himself, both tables commemorate an extraordinary number of relatives and associates. His brother, mother and maternal relatives also appear on a stela whose relevance in this context has hitherto been overlooked (Cairo Museum, CG 20582); it too was found by Mariette in the Northern Necropolis and undoubtedly comes from the same family chapel.

As usual with late Middle Kingdom mayors, Rehuankh bears the additional title of 'overseer of god's servants', indicating managerial responsibility for his town's temple. His close involvement with its daily affairs is stressed by the inscriptions on the statue's robe and seat. Besides familiar titles such as 'senior lector', they contain effusive, title-like phrases emphasizing his care for a steady flow of offerings. We are left in no doubt as to where in Egypt this temple was sited. The cult recipient is identified as the 'Great God' and 'Lord of Eternity', in clear allusion to Osiris, and he is also called Rehuankh's 'lord'. There is also a reference to unnamed subsidiary gods 'who are in their shrines'. Rehuankh calls himself the 'god's sealer in the *neshmet*-boat', linking him to the sacred barque used in Abydos to carry Osiris' cult statue in festive processions. This is a unique variant of the regular title 'god's sealer', which on the Cairo offering table is borne both by Rehuankh and, in a secondary inscription, by his eldest son, who clearly inherited this office.

A full string of 'prefix titles' assigns supreme status to Rehuankh, on a par with Egypt's top officials. This is no surprise, since he administered a sacred and flourishing pilgrimage town. Rehuankh's importance is underlined by the high artistic quality of the statue and its relatively large size for a private subject at this time. It is also significant that the statue is of quartzite, a rare, hard stone from quarries as far away as Heliopolis, which had only begun to be used for some private statues in the late Middle Kingdom. The sculptor undoubtedly belonged to a royal workshop and the statue may have been carved in the north and then shipped to Abydos. Stylistic features date it to the reign of Senwosret III or the early years of Amenemhat III. This agrees with the date of the Kyoto offering table, which comes from a well-attested sculpture workshop based at Abydos itself and active during Amenemhat's reign. Rehuankh's long robe is not specific to his mayoral office but a common feature in male private sculpture from the mid-Twelfth Dynasty onwards. His shoulder-length wig likewise reflects the fashion of his day.

M.M.

Sphinx

Middle Kingdom, *c.* 1800 BC

From Serabit el-Khadim, Sinai, Egypt

Gift of the Egypt Exploration Fund in 1905

Sandstone

Length: 23.7 cm

EA 41748

THIS SPHINX WAS FOUND by W.M.F. Petrie in the temple of the mining settlement at Serabit el-Khadim, although further details of its provenance are not available. It is made from the local reddish sandstone, and, though initially dated by Petrie to the New Kingdom, is now thought more likely to be of the late Middle Kingdom, when the local mines were thriving and many other inscriptions at the site were made. Copper was mined here, starting in the Old Kingdom, but in the Middle Kingdom the site mainly produced turquoise. Hathor, 'mistress of turquoise', was the deity worshipped in Serabit el-Khadim.

The particular interest of this otherwise somewhat undistinguished statuette is in the inscriptions it bears. On the right shoulder is carved in hieroglyphs 'beloved of Hathor, mistress of turquoise'; between the paws Petrie saw a royal name, which is unfortunately now illegible. The most important inscription is that on the left shoulder and base, which is written in the Proto-Sinaitic script. This script is known from objects from Serabit el-Khadim and elsewhere, including the deserts to the west of Egypt. Attempts to decipher it have been based on the assumptions that the script was alphabetic, that the signs were derived from hieroglyphs, and that the language was West Semitic. The early work of Gardiner and Albright was the key to an attempted decipherment based on these ideas. Phonetic values have been derived for most of the signs, and a number of words can be recognized, including the name visible here, which is that of the Semitic goddess Baalat, perhaps identified with Hathor. This makes it likely that the inscriptions on the sphinx are bilingual. It seems more likely that the script originated in Palestine or Syria than in Egypt.

The Proto-Sinaitic inscriptions at Serabit el-Khadim were probably written by Asiatics working in Sinai alongside the Egyptians. Several hieroglyphic inscriptions from the site mention Asiatics or 'men of Retjenu', although they are usually quite small in numbers when compared with the Egyptian contingent (for example, 20 Asiatics and 200 [Egyptian] quarrymen in one text). It thus seems likely that they were not working as miners, but were either local guides or perhaps even traders, taking some of the materials to the Syro-Palestinian area.

Heart scarab of Sebekemzaf

Second Intermediate Period,
Seventeenth Dynasty, *c.* 1575–1560 BC

From Thebes

Purchased at the sale of the third
Salt collection in 1835

Gold and green jasper

Length: 3.8 cm; width: 2.5 cm

EA 7876

THIS JASPER SCARAB set in gold is the earliest known royal heart scarab. The first heart scarab hitherto found belonged to a private official about a century earlier than this example, but it seems unlikely that this type of object was first invented for a commoner. The scarab has a rudimentary human face and is set in a hollow sheet-gold plinth with a rounded back. Each of the insect's legs is made from a sheet-gold strip, with roughly incised marks representing hairs. The crudely-formed hieroglyphs incised around the plinth and in five horizontal lines across the underside give the king's name, followed by parts of Chapter 30B of the *Book of the Dead*. This text is the 'Spell for preventing the heart from opposing the deceased', and was thought to come into action when the owner's heart was symbolically weighed in the balance in the underworld in order to ascertain its owner's worthiness to enter the Egyptian equivalent of paradise (see EA 10470/3, pages 218–21).

To the Egyptians, the heart was the seat of intelligence, the origin of all feelings and actions, and the storehouse of memory. Thus, alone among the internal organs, the heart was left in place during the embalming process so that it could be weighed in the underworld. Should the heart be destroyed, an amulet could act as a substitute. This is why the spells usually found on a heart amulet are also intended to stop it being taken away from its owner, or, if such a dire event should occur, to return it to the deceased. In the inscriptions on this scarab, the legs of the bird-shaped hieroglyphs are missing, a feature usually termed 'mutilated hieroglyphs'. This was employed in texts in funerary and magical contexts from the later Old Kingdom to prevent the hieroglyphs magically coming to life and attacking the dead person. Like other aspects of reliefs and paintings, hieroglyphs were believed to be capable of being transformed into three-dimensional reality, and it was therefore necessary to render them harmless.

Two kings named Sebekemzaf are known from the Seventeenth Dynasty in the later Second Intermediate Period (see EA 871, pages 114–15). In particular, the tomb of king Sekhemreshedtawy Sebekemzaf is well known from papyri. It is mentioned in the Abbott Papyrus (see EA 10221, pages 232–3) as being the only royal tomb found robbed in year 19 of Ramesses IX. Coincidentally, the Leopold-Amherst Papyrus, now divided between Brussels and New York, bears an account of the robbery and the trial of the robbers. This scarab could have come from that tomb, but the burial of the other Sebekemzaf is also a possible source. The locations of the tombs of the two Sebekemzafs have not yet been ascertained, but recent work by the German Archaeological Institute has revealed the tomb of the Seventeenth Dynasty king Nubkheperre Inyotef (see his coffin, EA 6652, pages 112–13), which is believed to lie near that of Sekhemreshedtawy Sebekemzaf.

Coffin of king Nubkheperre Inyotef

Second Intermediate Period,
Seventeenth Dynasty, *c.* 1570 BC

From Thebes

Purchased at the sale of the third Salt
collection in 1835

Sycamore wood, gessoed and gilded

Length: 193.2 cm

EA 6652

THE BOTTOM OF THIS wooden anthropoid (human-shaped) coffin is painted blue, while the upper part is covered in gesso and gilded. The head and the hair or wig is gilded; the king wears a cloth *nemes* headdress. Traces remain of the places where the missing uraeus (protective cobra) and beard were attached. The eyes are inlaid with white and black stone. The body decoration takes the form of a feather pattern; in the centre is a vertical column of text. There are two gilded columns at the foot end, next to which kneel figures of the goddesses Isis and Nephthys with their hands raised in mourning. Inside the coffin are the blackened remains of some of the king's outer mummy wrappings, presumably part of the mummy shroud. Some fragments bearing cursive hieroglyphs were removed in the nineteenth century and are now registered as EA 10706, but it is not possible to ascertain the text to which they belonged.

The feathered pattern (Arabic: *rishi*) on such coffins gave rise to the modern use of this Arabic term to describe the type. The *rishi* coffin is a largely Theban development of the anthropoid type of coffin which first appeared in the Twelfth Dynasty. They are all made of local wood, and many of the non-royal examples are hollowed out of tree trunks. The feather pattern gives the impression that the deceased is enveloped by a pair of wings, presumably the protective wings of deities such as Isis and Nephthys. Most coffins employ the royal *nemes* headdress, which also appears in lists of objects required for the afterlife on Middle Kingdom private coffins such as that of Gua (EA 30839, pages 81–3). It doubtless expresses the wish for the assimilation of the deceased with Osiris, the archetypal king and god of the dead. Royal coffins like this example tend to exhibit more elaborate depictions of this headdress.

The precise position of Nubkheperre in the line of Seventeenth Dynasty kings, several of whom were called Inyotef, is difficult to determine, although he doubtless predates kings Seqenenre and Kamose, who fought against the Hyksos rulers in the later part of the dynasty. The Abbott Papyrus (see EA 10221, pages 232–3) refers to the inspection of this tomb in year 16 of Ramesses IX, when thieves were discovered tunnelling into it.

Nubkheperre's tomb was only plausibly identified in Dra Abu el-Naga at Thebes in 2001. This coffin was excavated by local diggers, perhaps in 1827, and came into the collections of Henry Salt via his agent d'Athanasi, but no record was made of the find-spot. The tomb was subsequently located by Mariette in excavations in 1860, but its location was lost again. Other unauthorized excavations between these dates brought to light funerary equipment belonging to other Seventeenth Dynasty kings, much of which is in the Louvre.

King Sekhemrewadjkhau Sebekemzaf

Second Intermediate Period,
Seventeenth Dynasty, *c.* 1560 BC

From Karnak

Purchased in 1907

Red granite

The height of the complete statue was
perhaps 180 cm

EA 871

ROYAL STATUES from the Second Intermediate Period are not common, and those of the Seventeenth Dynasty are particularly rare; this is the largest piece of royal sculpture known of this date. The king sits on a cube seat with a short back-pillar; he is shown wearing the traditional cloth headdress known as a *nemes* and the royal kilt or *shendyt*. His hands rest on his lap, with a bolt of cloth clasped in the right one. The empty eye sockets were once filled with inlays held in place by dowels passed through small holes drilled through the eyelids, a highly unusual feature.

A roughly-cut inscription survives on the front of the seat (on the statue's left), beginning 'The perfect god, lord of the two lands, Sekhemrewadjkhau', followed by a rather damaged text which can be restored as 'beloved of Amun-Re, lord of the thrones of the two lands' and 'may he live forever' or 'given life forever'. The damage to the text may be due to the persecution of the cult of Amun during the Amarna Period (*c.* 1352–1333 BC).

The three flat sides of the seat were originally decorated. On the statue's left are the remains of a winged sun-disc with uraei, flanked by the hieroglyphs for 'given life and dominion'. On the rear are two back-to-back figures of a standing hippopotamus deity, between which are the hieroglyphs for 'may protection and life be behind him'. The unnamed deity could be either the well-known goddess Taweret, perhaps somewhat out of place on a royal monument, or else the deity Ipi/Ipet, who protects the sun god and is known above all from the ivory magic or apotropaic (protective) wands of the Middle Kingdom.

The face is very carefully modelled in an almost naturalistic manner, but the eyes are a little close together, and the headdress is disproportionally large. The care given to the face contrasts strongly with what can only be described as a stylized carving of the very narrow torso, and the extremely sharp edges of the knees and shins. What might seem to be some awkwardness in carving the features is actually the official style of the period, the origins of which can be traced back to the late Twelfth and early Thirteenth Dynasties.

Little is known about Sekhemrewadjkhau Sebekemzaf, although he definitely undertook building work in the temple at Medamud. His position within the Seventeenth Dynasty (which controlled southern Upper Egypt only) is not certain, as there are two kings with the name Sebekemzaf; some authorities place him early in the dynasty, before the group of kings named Inyotef, while others (including the current author) place him after them. The location of his tomb is unknown; it was not among those inspected in the reign of Ramesses IX and recorded in the Abbott Papyrus (see EA 10221, pages 232–3).

The statue was discovered by Auguste Mariette in 1860, and then passed into the collection of the Luxor dealer and agent Maunier.

A Classic Kerma beaker

Classic Kerma Period (approximately
contemporary with the Second
Intermediate Period) *c.* 1750–1550 BC

From Kerma, Tumulus K IV

Excavated by G. A. Reisner; donated by
the government of the Sudan in 1922

Fired Nile silt

Height: 14 cm; diameter at rim: 11.5 cm

EA 55424

POTTERY IS ONE OF THE MOST IMPRESSIVE PRODUCTS of the Kerma culture, which flourished in Nubia (modern southern Egypt and northern Sudan) and formed the first kingdom of Kush (2500–1500 BC). Kerma pots are among the finest products of the potter's art to have been made in the Nile Valley at any period.

This beaker has a cavetto profile (shaped like an inverted bell), rounding into the small sagging base. The interior, rim, and upper part of the exterior are covered in a lustrous black slip, while the lower part of the exterior and the base are slipped in red. Overlying the red-slipped zone and the point of junction of the red and black is a very pale grey stripe, bounded by darker grey margins. The quality of execution is superb, and the vessel is extremely regular and fine, with walls only three millimetres thick. The beaker is a typical product of the Classic Kerma (*c.*1750–1550 BC) potters. The characteristic feature of this pottery is the grey band, the inspiration for which may have come from the accidentally-produced grey spots noted on some pots of the immediately preceding period. It is not certain how the potters were able to produce the band as a consistent feature. Although this beaker came from a funerary context, the type is frequently found on settlement sites throughout the kingdom, where they tend to be much less well preserved.

This vessel came from a subsidiary grave within one of the massive royal tumuli at Kerma (tumulus IV), where it formed part of a stack of five beakers and a bowl placed close to the head of the individual buried in the north-east corner of the grave. The massive royal tombs at Kerma date from a phase of the kingdom of Kush which was approximately contemporary with the Second Intermediate Period in Egypt. These tumuli are the largest burial structures in Nubia and contain many individual burials. Those near the royal burial appear to belong to people deliberately killed in order to accompany the dead king; other tombs are set into the tumulus above, and are slightly later in date than the main interment. These subsidiary burials, one of which yielded this beaker, are doubtless related to the main burial and were deliberately arranged to avoid interfering with it.

The Rhind Mathematical Papyrus

End of the Second Intermediate Period, *c.* 1550 BC

From Thebes

Acquired in 1865 from D. Bremner, who was given it by A.H. Rhind

Papyrus

EA 10057

Length: 295.5 cm

EA 10058

Length: 199.5 cm

The height of both sheets is about 32 cm

SEVERAL DOCUMENTS have survived that yield some insights into the ancient Egyptians' approach to mathematics. The best-known and longest is the Rhind Mathematical Papyrus, acquired by the Scottish lawyer A.H. Rhind in Thebes in about 1858. Budge's original introduction to the facsimile of the papyrus indicates that these fragments were found in a chamber of a ruined building near the Ramesseum. The two sections in the British Museum were linked by a now missing section about 18 cm long; the original may have been cut in half by modern robbers to increase its sale value. Fragments which partly fill this gap were identified in 1922, in the collection of the New York Historical Society, which had acquired them from Edwin Smith. Smith also acquired a surgical papyrus of about the same date as the Rhind Papyrus, suggesting that these two documents could have come from a cache of early New Kingdom manuscripts.

The papyrus is probably a mathematics textbook, used by scribes (the principal literate section of the populace) to learn to solve particular mathematical problems by writing down appropriate examples. The text includes eighty-four problems: tables of divisions, multiplications, and handling of fractions; geometry, including volumes and areas; and miscellaneous problems.

The sheet illustrated opposite, above shows problems 49–55, which deal with the calculation of the area of rectangles, circles, and triangles, and the division of areas of land into smaller fields. All the calculations are expressed in practical terms as areas of land. Take as an example the second problem in this column (problem 50): the area of a circle of diameter 9 *khet* measures is calculated by taking one unit off the diameter (= 8) and squaring that number (= 64). This is a practically-orientated approach; if we multiply π by the radius squared, the result is 63.61, giving an ancient error of only 0.6%. The description is followed by tables showing how the subtractions and divisions are worked out. This example is unusually straightforward, as many of the other problems are bedevilled by numerous scribal errors (as far as we can tell)!

The papyrus is extremely important as a historical document, since the scribe, Ahmose, dated it in year 33 of Apophis, the penultimate king of the Hyksos Fifteenth Dynasty (opposite, below). The other side of the papyrus mentions 'year 11' without a king's name, but with a reference to the capture of the city of Heliopolis. The late Second Intermediate Period context suggests this may refer to conflict between the Egyptians and the Hyksos before the beginning of the New Kingdom. Most scholars believe this refers to year 11 of the Theban ruler Ahmose, which would add to the evidence that Ahmose did not campaign against the Hyksos rulers until the middle or later parts of his reign.

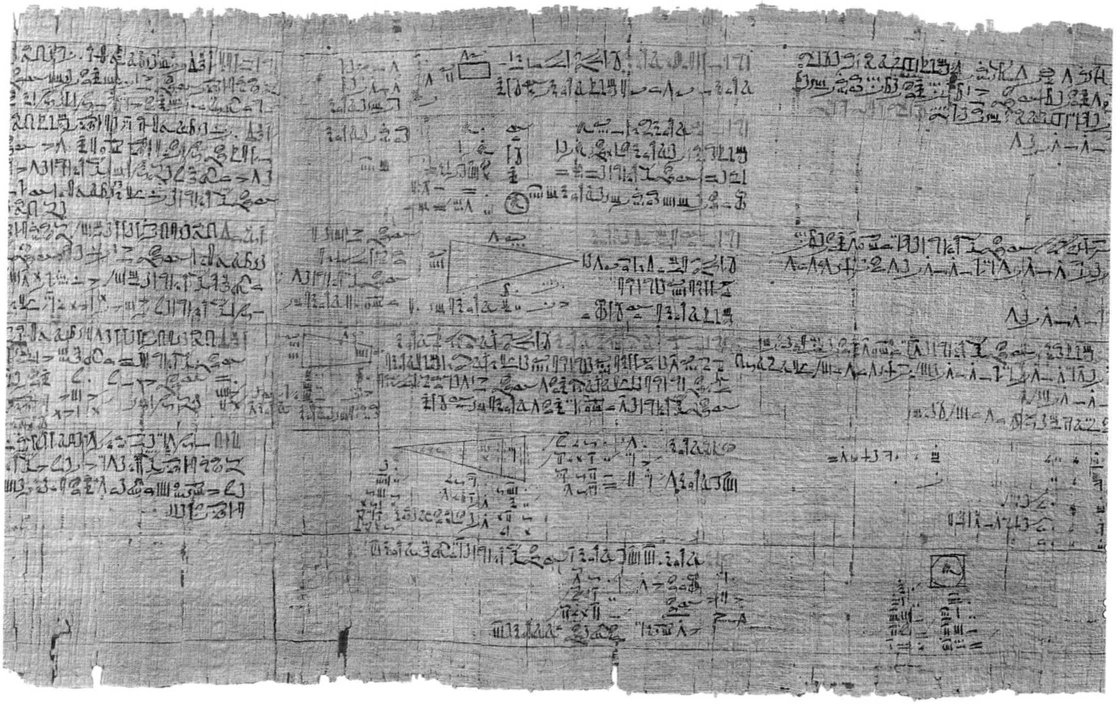

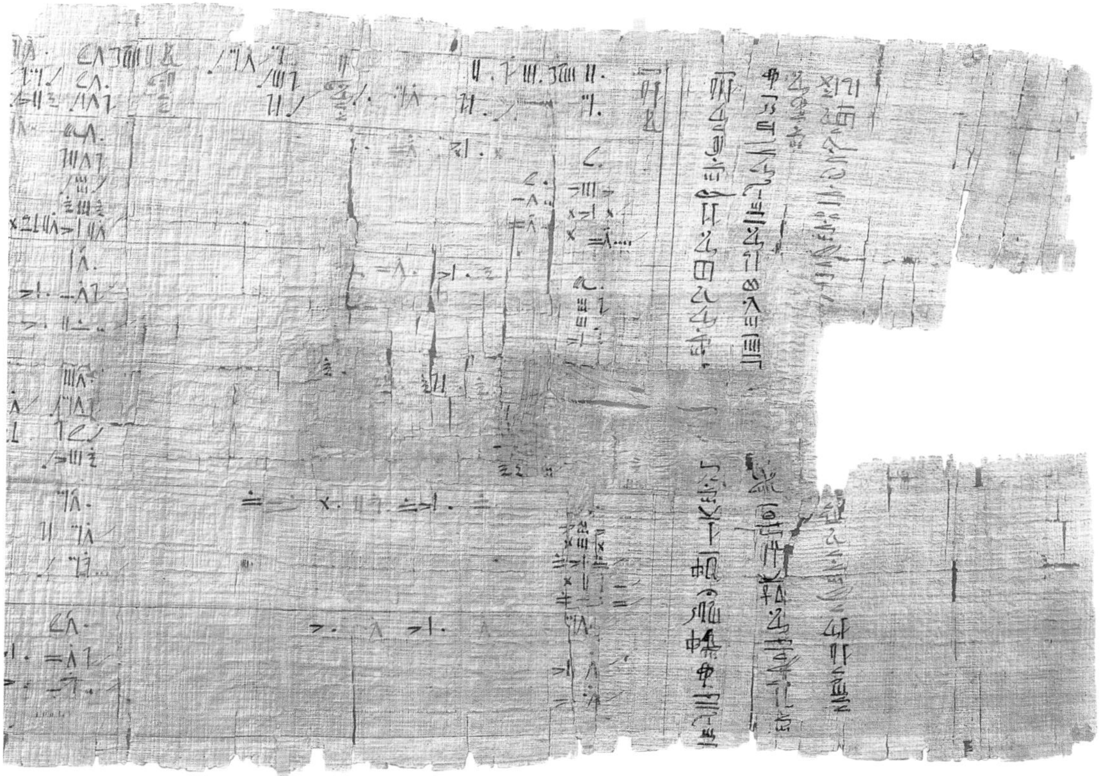

Shabti of king Ahmose

New Kingdom, Eighteenth Dynasty,
c. 1530 BC

Provenance unknown,
but probably Thebes

Acquired in 1899

Limestone

Height: 28.7 cm

EA 32191

SHABTIS, FUNERARY FIGURINES buried with the deceased, are among the most common objects in collections from Egypt. They appear first in the Middle Kingdom, and begin to multiply rapidly in private tombs from the Ramesside Period, although increasing numbers of royal shabtis are known from at least the reign of Amenhotep II (*c.* 1427–1400 BC).

The shabti of Ahmose is the earliest royal example known, and is one of only three inscribed three-dimensional images of this king to have survived (the others are a head, in a New York private collection, and a seated statue, found in Sai and now in Khartoum). Considerable stylistic similarities have been observed between these representations, notably in the depiction of the face, with its marked tapering shape, and the eyes. This suggests that this shabti is very much in the official representational style of the reign. It is thought that these and other products of the early New Kingdom were heavily influenced by major works of the Middle Kingdom which were still very much in evidence at the time, and formed a stylistic base from which Eighteenth Dynasty styles developed.

The figure wears the royal *nemes* headdress with a uraeus, sports a royal beard, and holds its arms crossed on the chest, without any royal regalia in the hands. Below the arms are seven lines of hieroglyphs, the first consisting of the king's names. The remainder of the text consists of the shabti spell. Like the shabti itself, this text developed in the Middle Kingdom, probably out of an original in the Coffin Texts, and became closely associated with the shabti's ability to carry out work for the deceased in the afterlife. Eventually it was included in the *Book of the Dead*. The shabti seems to have begun primarily as another image of the deceased which could function as a home for the spirits, but it also took over some of the servant functions of the wooden models known from First Intermediate Period and Middle Kingdom tombs. When Ahmose's shabti was produced, both functions were still important, but the servant aspect gradually became the main one.

Ahmose was the king responsible for the final ousting of the Hyksos rulers of the Fifteenth Dynasty and for reunifying the country and laying the foundations for Egypt's great imperial epoch, the New Kingdom. The location of Ahmose's tomb is unknown, but it was not in the Valley of the Kings, which did not come into use until the reign of Thutmose I. However, Ahmose's body was among the royal mummies discovered in the so-called 'royal cache' above Deir el-Bahari, and it seems reasonable to assume that he was buried somewhere in the Theban necropolis. His tomb is not mentioned among the tombs of the Seventeenth and early Eighteenth Dynasties listed in the Abbott Papyrus (see EA 10221, pages 232–3).

32191.

Mask of Satdjehuty

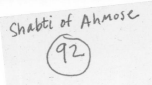

New Kingdom, Eighteenth Dynasty,
c. 1500 BC

From Thebes

Purchased in 1880

Cartonnage, painted and gilded

Height: 61 cm

EA 29770

BURIAL EQUIPMENT in any condition from the early Eighteenth Dynasty is seldom found, and such a superb piece as the mask of Satdjehuty is extremely rare. The wig is painted blue, in imitation of lapis lazuli; this and the gold leaf of which much of the decoration is composed symbolize the flesh of a divine being, expressing the wish for eternal life with the gods. Below the wig is a gilded collar, representing a mass of small gold beads with petal-shaped beads at the ends. The beginnings of two columns of texts with offering prayers are also visible. These would have continued on a protruding tab which has been broken off, but was perhaps originally similar in length to the tab at the back.

The feather effect of the winged headdress on this mask should perhaps be associated with the so-called *rishi*-type coffin popular in Thebes at the very end of the Second Intermediate Period and the early New Kingdom (see the coffin of king Nubkheperre Inyotef, EA 6652, pages 112–13). It has been suggested that the feathered headdress is also a mark of royalty or at least high status, but in the case of Satdjehuty, her status would have been amply indicated by the opulence of the mask.

There is little doubt that the mask's style dates it to the early Eighteenth Dynasty. The owner's name is not written on it, but from an inscription on a mass of linen which came to the British Museum with the mask, it is known that the linen was given to Satdjehuty 'in the favour of the god's wife, king's wife, and king's mother Ahmose-Nefertari'. Ahmose-Nefertari was the wife of Ahmose, the first king of the dynasty, and the mother of Amenhotep I, with whom she subsequently became associated as a local deity. That Satdjehuty should have received such an honour shows she was a woman of the highest rank. However, her name was quite popular in the early part of the dynasty, and it has not been possible to identify her further.

The burial was discovered about 1820, and probably consisted of at least a coffin, the mummy, papyri, a heart scarab, this mask, and a quantity of linen. Only the mask and linen are in the British Museum; the other items are presumed lost, but the mummy at least seems to have been purchased by 'an enterprising beerhouse keeper' in Uxbridge, Middlesex.

A bronze serpent

New Kingdom, early Eighteenth
Dynasty, *c.* 1550–1500 BC

Found in 1911 inside the coffin of
Mentuhotep in Chamber A of Tomb
37 in the Birabi, Thebes

Gift of the Fifth Earl of Carnarvon in
1913

Bronze

Overall length: 166.5 cm; height of
hood: 9 cm

EA 52831

THIS REARING COBRA, with extended hood and long body, is a very rare type of object, and was found under the shroud covering the mummy of a man named Mentuhotep. The only comparable object known is a much shorter example from a late Middle Kingdom tomb, found near the Ramesseum at Thebes and now in the Fitzwilliam Museum in Cambridge (E.63.1896), which was used as a wand in magical rituals. Other items found in the Ramesseum tomb indicate that the owner was a lector priest (see the Ramesseum Papyri, pages 102–4), although it seems unlikely that this was true of Mentuhotep. There are no texts in his burial that indicate this, and ritual implements such as this snake were often reused for mortuary purposes. In Egyptian religious iconography and mythology snakes are always symbols of great power, which can be negative or positive. For example, the serpent on the brow of the king (the uraeus) was believed to spit fire and represented the reptile's great power immanent in the king; on the other hand, the classic enemy of the sun-god during his travels through the underworld was the serpent Apophis.

Mentuhotep's coffin, discovered in 1911, was buried in a tomb in the 'Birabi' region, an area at the eastern end of the Assasif valley in front of the temples of Deir el-Bahari at Thebes, where Lord Carnarvon (later joined by Howard Carter) excavated in his early years in Egypt. The tomb was probably constructed in the Middle Kingdom or perhaps even the Seventeenth Dynasty. While it is not clear for whom it was originally cut, it was clearly used for several individual and family burials. Passages were used for burials and then blocked off; the blocking stones of Chamber A, where Mentuhotep was buried, seem to have borne one of the names of the early Eighteenth Dynasty king Thutmose I (*c.* 1504–1492 BC). From the manner in which the coffins were placed in the tomb, it would seem that there were at least three or four separate major groups and several minor ones. It is uncertain if any of the burials was that of the original tomb-builder; it seems very plausible that they are all examples of the reuse of an earlier tomb at the beginning of the New Kingdom.

Although several coffins were found with that of Mentuhotep in Chamber A, most of them did not bear names. The only one that did, that of a woman named Ahmose, carried no indication of her family connections. Her coffin and that of Mentuhotep are similar, and it is possible that they were husband and wife.

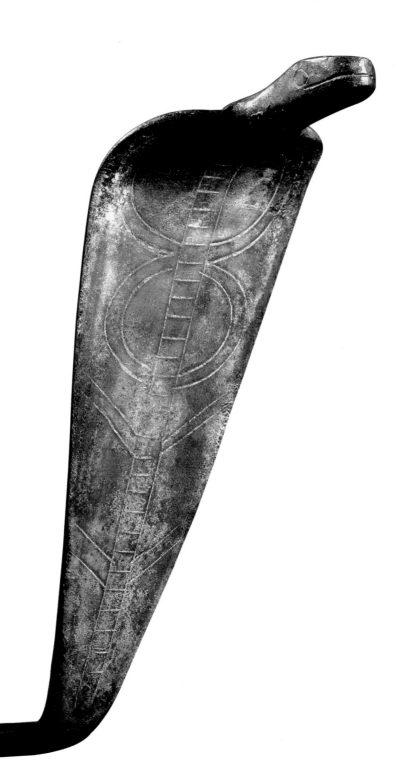

Statue of Amenhotep I

New Kingdom, early Eighteenth
Dynasty, c. 1510 BC

From Thebes, Deir el-Bahari

Gift of the Egypt Exploration Fund
in 1905

Limestone

Height: 269 cm

EA 683

AMENHOTEP I (c. 1525–1504 BC) is shown as Osiris, wrapped in a tight-fitting mummiform robe with his arms crossed on his chest. Holes in the clenched fists presumably held wooden royal insignia. On his head is the double crown of Upper and Lower Egypt; his chin bears a long, rather oversized, divine beard. The statue's back takes the form of a large flat slab, bearing a column of hieroglyphs. Colour remains in various places: white on the robe, red on the skin and the Lower Egyptian crown, and blue/black on the beard-strap and beard.

The osiride statue, as this type is termed, probably originated in the Eleventh Dynasty. The earliest examples come from the temple of Nebhepetre Mentuhotep (c. 2055–2004 BC) at Deir el-Bahari. More are known from the reign of Senwosret I (c. 1956–1911 BC), from Lisht, Abydos and Karnak, and the style became popular in the early New Kingdom. These early examples usually show the king with either the red or the white crown. Although Osiris himself is typically shown with the white crown (or variants like the *atef* crown), combining the two crowns in this statue type seems to be an innovation of Amenhotep I.

This is one of the very few statues which can be ascribed to Amenhotep I with any certainty and is one of the most important. Excavations at Deir el-Bahari have revealed fragments of other osiride statues of this king which show a strong consistency of style in the facial representation of Amenhotep I, and there is a head in the Bastis Collection which probably belongs to this group. The style of the Amenhotep statues seems to have been influenced by the representations of Mentuhotep II and Senwosret III (see Senwos-ret's statue, EA 684, pages 90–1) which were still standing in Mentuhotep's temple, although these Middle Kingdom pieces do not appear to have influenced subsequent New Kingdom royal sculpture.

The sacred associations of Deir el-Bahari, which go back at least to the Middle Kingdom, apparently encouraged Amenhotep I to build two small brick temples there. One was on the site of the later Hatshepsut temple, and these osiride statues may have graced it. Parts of this earlier temple were walled over to build the central ramp of Hatshepsut's temple; judging from this statue's findspot, the osiride figures were moved to Mentuhotep's temple, where they kept company with the statues of Senwosret III (EA 684). The history of this statue thus exemplifies the respect usually shown by one king to another when it was necessary to move a structure.

Amenhotep's temple was not a mortuary foundation but was probably dedicated to the particular form of the goddess Hathor revered at Deir el-Bahari, characteristically shown in later tombs as peering out of the Western Mountain (see EA 43071, pages 208–9).

Statue of a queen

New Kingdom, early to middle
Eighteenth Dynasty, *c.* 1500–1450 BC

From Karnak

Purchased as part of the first Salt
collection in 1823

Limestone

Height: 113 cm

EA 93

THIS LARGE BUST SHOWS a female figure wearing the so-called 'Hathor wig' with wide lappets either side of the face, curling at the ends, and a very broad lappet at the rear. This type of wig is named after the goddess Hathor because of its similarity to her hairstyle. On the figure's brow is an uraeus, with a broken head. Around her neck is a broad collar composed of five rows of beads. The statue's features have lost their sharpness as a result of the weathering of the stone.

The object has been dated to the Eighteenth or Nineteenth Dynasty. The stylistic evidence, notably the wig type, suggests strongly that it was carved during the reigns of Hatshepsut or Thutmose III (*c.* 1479–1425 BC). The statue was studied in the 1970s by Roland Tefnin, who came to the provisional conclusion that it might show queen Hatshepsut, but that it was necessary to seek the lower part of the statue for confirmation. The bust was discovered by Belzoni while working in Karnak in 1817, in the area now termed the eighth pylon, on the southern axis of the temple. He mentions that he found it 'divided at the waist', and that he removed the upper part and intended to return for the lower. Among the objects still on site is the lower part of the statue of a seated queen which closely fits Belzoni's description, and which has been shown to join with the London bust. It was found near a statue of Amenhotep I (*c.* 1525–1504 BC).

The (complete) statue shows a woman wearing a long conventional dress, with her hands laid flat on her knees. The inscriptions on the base are damaged but seem to name two queens. On the left is almost certainly the name of Ahmose-Merytamun, wife and sister of Amenhotep I, and on the right may be that of her sister Sitamun, also wife and sister of Amenhotep I. It would thus appear that the statue, placed next to one of the king himself, represented two of his principal spouses.

Tefnin has suggested that we reconcile the conflict between the statue's Thutmoside style and its attribution to an earlier queen by interpreting Belzoni's phrase 'was divided at the waist' as meaning that the statue was actually made of two halves. Since the adjacent statue of Amenhotep I was renewed by Thutmose III, perhaps the upper part of the damaged statue of the queens was also replaced by that king, using styles current at the beginning of his sole reign, in the 1450s BC.

Senenmut and Neferure

New Kingdom, Eighteenth Dynasty,
early reign of Hatshepsut, *c.* 1470 BC

From Thebes

Acquired in 1906

Granodiorite

Height: 72.5 cm

EA 174

SENENMUT BEGAN his career under either Thutmose I or II, and by the time that queen Hatshepsut became regent for the young Thutmose III, he was the tutor of the queen's daughter Neferure. He became perhaps the most important person in the kingdom once Hatshepsut ascended the throne in *c.* 1473 BC. He was the queen's 'steward' and also her 'overseer of works', and may have been responsible for the construction of many of the major monuments of her reign.

About twenty-five statues of him are known, more than of any other New Kingdom commoner. He commissioned at least seven statues of himself with Neferure, of which this is perhaps the finest example. Senenmut sits on a simple cubic seat with his robe wrapped protectively around the princess, who wears the sidelock associated with childhood; the bodies of the princess and the official merge together, thus emphasizing the closeness of the connection between them. The statue minimizes the shape of the human form, allowing fuller concentration on the two figures themselves, a trait also visible in the block statue that was so common in the New Kingdom (see the statue of Sennefer, EA 48, pages 134–5). This statue refers to Hatshepsut, who commissioned it as 'god's wife of Amun', indicating that it was made before she took on the attributes of kingship.

The statue is said to have been found in Karnak, but the circumstances of the 'find' have been disputed. It is said that this statue and another of Senenmut (now also in the British Museum, EA 1513) were found in a 'shrine' along with a now lost statue of Hatshepsut, but it now seems more than likely that this was a display set up by a local antiquities dealer (see the statue of Amenwahsu, EA 480, pages 166–7).

Senenmut possessed a large number of statues and a shrine at Gebel es-Silsila, and was mentioned on many of Hatshepsut's monuments. As befitting his status, he had a large and impressive tomb chapel (TT71) at Thebes, with a separate set of burial rooms far away from it (now known as TT353) in a quarry on the edge of his queen's mortuary monument at Deir el-Bahari. He does not seem to have been buried in the tomb, though what happened to him is unknown, nor is it clear whether he died before or after his patron. Deliberate damage to some of his monuments suggests that he was persecuted after his death, but whether this was linked to the attempted erasure of Hatshepsut from the stone record after about year 42 of Thutmose III is not at all clear. This particular statue escaped desecration, both in the Thutmoside era and during the attacks against the name of Amun in the Amarna Period, which suggests that it must have become concealed not long after it was set up.

Thutmose III with deities

New Kingdom, Eighteenth Dynasty, *c.* 1450 BC

From Karnak

Purchased as part of the first Salt collection in 1823

Red granite

Height: 178 cm

EA 12

THIS MOST UNUSUAL MONUMENT is made from a rectangular block of granite, with statues on each of the four sides. On both the longer sides stand king Thutmose III and the god Montu-Re, while on each of the shorter faces is a figure of the goddess Hathor, also standing. The royal figures are dressed in the short *shendyt* kilt, those of Montu-Re in regular short kilts, and those of Hathor wear the close-fitting ankle-length dress. One Hathor has her feet together, while the other has her left foot advanced; this is also the case for Montu-Re, while both royal figures are in the normal pose with left feet advanced. Each Hathor figure clasps one hand of Montu-Re and one of the king, and each Montu-Re figure clasps one hand of Hathor and one of the king. This arrangement expresses the king's association with both divinities. Hathor wears a tripartite wig surmounted by a winged sun disc. Montu-Re wears a composite crown of the sun-disc and the two-plumed head-dress normally associated with Amun, thus making a link between the older (Montu) and the younger (Amun) Theban deities; Montu-Re is himself a syncretistic divinity merging the Theban war god with the state solar deity.

The inscriptions are confined to labels identifying the figures; thus Hathor is called 'lady of heaven, mistress of all the gods' and '[she] who dwells in Thebes, lady of heaven, mistress of the gods'; Montu-Re is 'lord of heaven, who dwells in Thebes' and '[he] who dwells in Thebes, lord of heaven'. The name of Amun-Re in a royal epithet was damaged and restored, presumably in the Amarna Period, and the torsos of Montu-Re are flatter than the others, suggesting that they too were attacked and then recut in the post-Amarna style.

Although it was described as an altar in the nineteenth century, it seems more likely that this object was a pedestal, perhaps for an offering basin. There is an almost identical, although more damaged, example (possibly not *in situ*) in a corridor near the sixth pylon at Karnak, near Hatshepsut's buildings. The prototype may go back to the Middle Kingdom, to judge from a fragment of a similar object from the temples of Armant, which bears the name of Amenemhat I (*c.* 1985–1956 BC).

The object has a long modern history. It was first noted by the *savants* of Napoleon's expedition in the late eighteenth century, and was illustrated in the *Description de l'Egypte* (left). They thought it one of the most remarkable objects they had yet seen, and attempted unsuccessfully to remove it. Belzoni noticed it, probably near the temple of Mut at Karnak, during his first journey to Egypt in 1816. He collected it in 1817 as one of the items he assembled for Henry Salt, during his second journey. If the illustration in the *Description* is correct, one of the heads of Thutmose III was still intact when first noticed, and is shown wearing the white crown of Upper Egypt.

Block statue of Sennefer

New Kingdom, mid–late reign of Thutmose III, *c.* 1430 BC

From Western Thebes

Purchased as part of the first Salt collection in 1823

Granodiorite

Height: 89.8 cm

EA 48

THE BLOCK STATUE REPRESENTS a squatting man with his robe pulled tightly over his knees. The earliest block statues date from the Middle Kingdom, but they became particularly common in the Ramesside Period and later. They were usually set up in temples; the squatting pose, with arms crossed on top, was probably intended to express deference and devotion to god and king. The hands often hold symbols associated with regeneration and the afterlife, and being cloaked or wrapped was linked to death and rebirth in Egyptian thought. The placing of statues in temples would permit the owner's spirit to act as a passive participant in the rituals and partake of the offerings.

The statue of Sennefer is surely one of the finest examples of this type ever produced in Egypt. No personal details other than the face and hands were carved by the sculptor, concentrating attention on the superbly carved and polished face. The quality of the carving contrasts sharply with the rather roughly scratched hieroglyphs on the front and base. The large blank surfaces of this style of statue presented the Egyptians with the chance to cover them with texts. The texts here are in three parts: most of the front is taken up with an elaborate prayer for funerary offerings for Sennefer. The second part, beginning over his feet but extending onto the base, records Sennefer's request to be well provided for after his death, as he was on earth. The final elements are the names of his father Haydjehuty and his mother Satdjehuty, in columns flanking his feet. The short bottom line is intriguing; it seems to say 'the servant of the overseer of sealbearers, Minnakht'. Is this a reference to the person who organized the production of the statue?

Sennefer's principal title was that of 'overseer of the seal', a senior official concerned with financial matters, and thus an important person with access to considerable resources. He was able to obtain the services of the finest craftsmen to carve this beautiful statue (and two others, less well-preserved and now in the Cairo Museum), and to cut a large and originally impressive tomb in the Theban hills (TT99). He also possessed a shrine at Gebel es-Silsila, and is featured on monuments of Thutmose III in Sinai. A papyrus in the Louvre indicates that he was in office in year 32 of that king.

The statue's original location is far from certain, as Henry Salt's records indicate that it was found 'behind the statue of Memnon', in other words, to the west of Amenhotep III's mortuary temple at Thebes. This probably means that it came from the West Bank; as it is unlikely to have come from his tomb, one possible location might have been the mortuary temple of Thutmose III, the king whom Sennefer served. Salt clearly thought very highly of this statue, and it appears to have come to England before the rest of his collection as a sample of the quality of his objects.

Statue of Menkheperresoneb

New Kingdom, reigns of Thutmose III to Amenhotep II (*c.* 1450–1400 BC)

Said to be from Karnak

Acquired in 1909

Granodiorite

Height: 83 cm

EA 708

MENKHEPERRESONEB, SECOND PRIEST OF AMUN, is shown seated on a cube seat, wearing an enveloping robe or cloak, with his left hand flat on his chest and his right on his lap, holding a loop of cloth. Cloaked, seated statues are a sculptural type which is found most often in the Eighteenth Dynasty before the Amarna Period, in both tombs and temples. Most of the hard stone examples seem to have come from temples. The origins of this type of seated statue can be found in the later Middle Kingdom – there are some examples in the Egyptian Museum in Cairo – with variations in the arrangement of the hands, including one hand placed on the lap, holding a bolt of cloth, or grasping a lotus flower.

The texts on the sides consist of longer offering formulae plus Menkheperresoneb's names and titles, while those on the front and back are mainly his names and principal titles. The name of Amun has been chiselled out in all but one instance (that on the knees), along with the designation 'second priest'. The remainder of his titles and name are undisturbed – the damage is thus clearly the work of the agents of king Akhenaten who defaced the name of Amun throughout Egypt and Nubia. The original texts were later restored with great skill, so that the recut surface is only very slightly lower than the unaffected areas, although the degree of polish is noticeably less than on the original work. The damage and restoration strongly suggest that the statue was in a reasonably accessible location both before and after the Amarna Period, making a temple location for it likely.

The statue may have come from Karnak, placed there as a mark of Menkheperresoneb's favoured status with the king, and as a symbol of his devotion to the god whom he served, who would then return favours to him. However, as it was part of the so-called 'statue shrine' shown to Budge at the turn of the twentieth century (see EA 174 and EA 480, pages 130–1 and 166–7, for more detail), this suggestion cannot be proved.

For many years it was thought that this Menkheperresoneb was the owner of Theban Tombs 86 and 112, hewn in an earlier phase of his career before he became high priest of Amun. It has now been suggested that there were in fact as many as three men of the same name holding high office in the cult of Amun in and around the time of Thutmose III, and that the man represented by this statue was not the owner of these tombs.

Lintel of Amenhotep II

New Kingdom, Eighteenth Dynasty,
c. 1410 BC, restored in the Nineteenth
Dynasty, *c.* 1290 BC

From Bubastis

Gift of the Egypt Exploration Fund
in 1891

Red granite

Length: 200 cm

EA 1103

THE CENTRE OF THIS LARGE DOOR LINTEL shows two very similar scenes of Amenhotep II offering to the god Amun. The seated figures of Amun are almost back-to-back. The right-hand scene is the better preserved, showing the king with his arms raised, presenting a pot of incense or some other precious substance in each hand to the deity. In front of him are two offering stands bearing libation vessels. Above both figures of the king are his names and the usual epithets, while the speech of Amun on the right reads 'To you have I given all bravery and all health like Re forever' and on the left 'To you have I given all life, stability, and power and all joy'. The right-hand figure of the god is labelled 'Amun-Re, king of the gods, lord of heaven, who dwells (in) Perunefer', and on the left 'Amun-Re, foremost of Perunefer, the great god, lord of heaven'.

The history of this block is very interesting. The two vertical columns of hieroglyphs between the figures of Amun bear the names of king Sety I of the Nineteenth Dynasty and the texts 'for <lost> he renewed the monument' and 'who strengthened the house of his father like Re'. Such inscriptions from the beginning of the Ramesside era tend to refer to the restoration of monuments damaged during the Amarna Period, when, under king Akhenaten, the names of a number of deities, in particular Amun, were excised from inscriptions in tombs and temples, as part of Akhenaten's campaign to promote his god, the Aten, as paramount deity, and to reduce the power and influence of Amun. However, an examination of this block does not reveal any of the tell-tale recutting of names or figures of Amun, so perhaps the structure to which this belonged suffered damage from some other cause, and this lintel was the most convenient place to add the restoration inscription. Both the columns of the Sety inscription are unfinished.

Perunefer, a place-name not known beyond the Eighteenth Dynasty, has been interpreted as referring to a harbour in the city of Memphis, but recent excavations and research at Tell ed-Daba in the north-eastern Delta suggest that it should be located at this site, also known as Avaris. As this block was actually found at Bubastis, it seems that it was moved from its original location and re-employed in a building project of the kings of the Twenty-second Dynasty or later. Numerous blocks were found at Bubastis bearing the names of kings going back to the Fourth Dynasty (the Museum has blocks of Khufu and Khafre, EA 1097-8), and it seems quite likely that they did not all originate where they were found; they may also have come from the Memphite region, perhaps Giza. See also the head of Amenemhat III, EA 1063, pages 92–3.

Mummiform figures of Qenamun

New Kingdom, Eighteenth Dynasty,
probably reign of Amenhotep II,
c. 1427–1400 BC

Provenance unknown

Acquired in 1923

Wood

Height: 37.5 cm

EA 56929–30

THESE FIGURES HAVE OFTEN been called shabtis because of their similarity in shape to those well-known objects. The origins of shabtis lie in the Middle Kingdom, and generally they appear singly or in small numbers until the later New Kingdom. At that point they seem to have developed from being miniature figures of the deceased, and hence found in small numbers, to becoming workers for the dead in the afterlife, for which a greater number was evidently needed (compare the shabti of Ahmose, EA 32191, pages 120–1). Eighteenth Dynasty shabtis are usually of very high quality and resemble these figures, but closer examination of these two reveals tangs protruding from the bases, indicating that (unlike shabtis) they stood on separate plinths. Nor do they hold the agricultural tools characteristic of the shabti. The inscription on their fronts indicates that they were 'made as a favour of the king for ... Qenamun'; this man was a very high official of the reign of Amenhotep II (*c.* 1427–1400 BC) and owned a very elaborate painted tomb chapel in Thebes (TT93). Clearly Qenamun was a man of great means; he must have been extremely close to the king to receive such items from him.

Though not actually shabtis, the objects' mummiform shape suggests that they bear at least some association with them, and they have been categorized along with other so-called 'extra-sepulchral' shabtis – shabti figures discovered in locations other than tombs. This practice is known to have existed almost as long as the shabti itself, and several such figures from the Twelfth and Thirteenth Dynasties were found in holes near the Umm el-Gaab at Abydos. The Umm el-Gaab, originally the burial place of most kings of the first two dynasties, came to be regarded in the Middle Kingdom as the location of the tomb of Osiris himself. The cult was centred on the tomb of king Djer of the First Dynasty, which became a place of pilgrimage, so these shabtis would be commemorating persons in the presence of the god. Many other deposits of shabtis down to the Eighteenth and Nineteenth Dynasties are known at Abydos; similar objects belonging to Qenamun were found there during excavations in 1989. Another location was in the Memphite area, near the sacred site of Rosetjau, the entrance to the netherworld. A number of similar, royal figures (including Ramesses II and Merenptah) have been found in the Wadi Qubbanet el-Qirud on the West Bank at Thebes.

It is interesting to note that Qenamun features prominently among these other deposits, since many of his shabtis and mummiform figures, the latter bearing a text similar to that on the present examples, were found at Abydos and south of Giza. The Abydos examples were found in miniature coffins inside inscribed wooden boxes.

Kneeling figure of Thutmose IV

New Kingdom, Nineteenth Dynasty,
c. 1400–1390 BC

Provenance unknown

Acquired in 1946 from the Acworth
collection

Bronze with glass eyes and black
bronze inlays

Height: 14.7 cm

EA 64564

THUTMOSE IV (c. 1400–1390 BC) is depicted in an offering pose, kneeling and presenting two large round *nu*-pots at just above waist height. He wears the *nemes* headdress with a uraeus and the traditional royal *shendyt* kilt, with a wide belt which bears an elaborate diamond pattern. The belt's central rectangle bears the king's throne name, Menkheperure, rather crudely incised and lacking a cartouche. The facial features, with their high cheekbones and square jaw, are characteristic of representations of Thutmose IV.

The statuette is a hollow-cast bronze. The arms are attached to square tenons projecting from the shoulders; when the arms had been placed over the tenons, the protruding ends were hammered to smooth them down to the correct profile and to hold the arm in place. Four projecting tangs from the knees and feet allowed the figure to be set into a base of another material. The reddish colour of the bronze seems to be the result of excessive cleaning at some time in the past. The eyelids and the cosmetic eyeline extending from the outside corner of the statuette's eyes are inlays of an alloy known as *hesmen kem*, 'black bronze'. This was intended to react with the air and patinate into a black colour, imitating black eye paint. The surviving left eyeball and its brown iris are a glass inlay.

Far more royal bronzes survive from the Third Intermediate and Late Periods than earlier periods, though the Egyptians did apparently have the technology to make large copper statues as early as the Second Dynasty; a copper statue of Khasekhemwy, the last king of that dynasty, is mentioned in the annals on the Palermo Stone. Two large copper statues of (probably) kings Pepy I and Merenre of the Sixth Dynasty were found at Hierakonpolis, and are now in the Egyptian Museum in Cairo (JE 33034-5). There is a handful of Twelfth Dynasty royal bronzes, and one New Kingdom bronze earlier than the present example, showing Thutmose III, also in a kneeling pose (now in New York, MMA 1995.21). Since the Egyptians evidently had the requisite technology, perhaps the high value of metal, together with its reuseability, meant that statues were usually melted down when they no longer served their function.

The kneeling pose first appears frequently in Hatshepsut's reign (c. 1450 BC), although the oldest example seems to be a statue of Pepy I from the Sixth Dynasty (Brooklyn 39.121), and this is the most usual pose for these royal bronzes. It shows the king in his crucial role of offering to the gods in order to maintain the cosmic order, or *maat*: simply put, the king offers to the gods, and the gods protect Egypt and the king. These statuettes were probably originally placed in temples, and seem to have accompanied divine images. Perhaps they were placed on a divine barque to represent the king offering to the deity who owned the barque; small kneeling kings are sometimes seen in temple depictions of barques.

Masterpieces of Ancient Egypt

Barque bearing a figure of queen Mutemwia

New Kingdom, Eighteenth Dynasty,
c. 1370 BC

From Karnak

Excavated by the second Earl of
Belmore and Lady Belmore in 1817–18,
and in the Museum since at least 1834

Granodiorite

Length: 215 cm

EA 43

MUTEMWIA WAS THE PRINCIPAL WIFE of king Thutmose IV and the mother of Amenhotep III. She helped establish a temple to Mut to the south-east of the Amun temple at Karnak, where this sculpture may have originated. It was found reused in the floor of the main sanctuary at Karnak in the course of an excavation by the Earl of Belmore and Lady Belmore in 1817–18. It is likely that it was part of a small cache of temple statues, perhaps buried when the area was remodelled in the reign of Philip Arrhidaeus, son of Alexander the Great.

The barque bears a female figure seated in the centre; the figure's torso and head and the stern of the boat are lost. The woman's hands lie on her lap, the right grasping an *ankh* sign and the left lying flat. Behind her is the lower part of a bird, with its wings protectively overlapping part of the seat and (presumably) some of the figure. Its feathers are neatly carved.

At the boat's prow is a two-faced head of the goddess Hathor with a sistrum shape on her head; on the sides are the names of Amenhotep III, one of which has been deliberately damaged, presumably in the Amarna Period. The goddess' face is shown in the usual way with cow's ears, but the manner in which the sculptor has fitted the wig into the space is intriguing. The front-facing Hathor has tresses which extend roughly the conventional distance below the bottom of the face, but the tresses of the side facing the statue curve forward onto the body of the boat and are considerably longer than the head itself. Between these tresses and the statue's feet is an offering table and a cartouche with the name and titles of queen Mutemwia.

A lengthy cartouche on either side of the boat contains a series of laudatory epithets (slightly different on each side) and would probably have ended with the name of Mutemwia. The whole statue is an excellent example of a rebus, a visual play on words, otherwise known as an 'emblematic hieroglyph'. The Egyptian word for 'barque' is *wia*, the word for 'in' is *em*, and the statue shows a figure (presumably of Mutemwia as Mut) in a barque, which happens to spell out the name of queen Mutemwia.

This object is apparently unique. Perhaps the most intriguing aspect is the queen's figure protected by a bird. Images of kings protected by falcons are not unusual, because of the identification of the ruler with Horus, son of Osiris, but there are no parallels showing women. Perhaps the bird is the vulture of the goddess Mut, protecting the queen. It might also be Mutemwia's son Amenhotep III, named in the inscriptions, in the role of Horus protecting his mother.

Paintings from the tomb of Sebekhotep

New Kingdom, reign of Thutmose IV,
c. 1400 BC

From the tomb of Sebekhotep at
Thebes (TT63)

EA 37987 was purchased from J.W.
Wild in 1852. The rest were donated by
Henry Danby Seymour in 1869.

Paint on lime plaster on mud base

THESE FRAGMENTS ARE ALMOST AS WELL-KNOWN as the famous Nebamun tomb paintings (see pages 170–7). Sebekhotep's tomb is located on the West Bank at Luxor, at the north end of the hill of Sheikh Abdel Qurna, the site of the tombs of most of the high officials of the Theban region in the Eighteenth Dynasty before the reign of Amenhotep III. Unfortunately, the decorated chapel is quite badly damaged, and suffered the attentions of robbers in the twentieth century AD: photographic records of the tomb made by Harry Burton of the Metropolitan Museum of Art between about 1926 and 1940 show several substantial fragments which had disappeared when the tomb was studied and published in the early 1980s. Nonetheless, the paintings which survive *in situ* are brightly coloured and beautifully executed.

Sebekhotep was an important treasury official in the reign of Thutmose IV (*c.* 1400–1390 BC), bearing the title 'overseer of the seal', in effect the minister of finance. He was the son of Min, who had held the same title in Thutmose III's reign. It is likely that Sebekhotep was mayor of the Faiyum region before attaining his highest title in Thebes; as his father came from the Delta, it is possible that, like many other Theban officials, he came south at the king's request.

Six fragments of this tomb are in the British Museum. All but EA 37987 were donated in 1869 by Henry Danby Seymour, MP; EA 37987 was purchased from J.W. Wild in 1852. Wild was a draftsman with the Lepsius expedition to Egypt in 1842–5, and it seems plausible that he brought this fragment back with him. Another fragment originally in his possession was sold by his family to the Metropolitan Museum in New York in 1926. It is unclear how Seymour obtained his fragments, although his interest in biblical history may have taken him to Egypt; he said that his fragments were taken from the tomb in about 1844. This was around the time that Sebekhotep's tomb was first noted by Lepsius' expedition, and Lepsius himself commented that fragments had already been taken from tombs by travellers. The scenes were painted on a wall plaster consisting largely of mud, which unfortunately has made it easier to detach pieces from the walls.

ASIATIC WITH HORSES

Width: 60 cm

EA 37987

ASIATIC WITH HORSES

As a senior treasury official of the reign of Thutmose IV, one of Sebekhotep's responsibilities was evidently to deal with foreign gifts brought to the king. The wall from which this fragment (opposite, above) came almost certainly showed Sebekhotep receiving the produce of the Levant and Africa, which he then presented to the king. British Museum fragments EA 921, 922, and 37991 also come from this wall. A scene like this would have

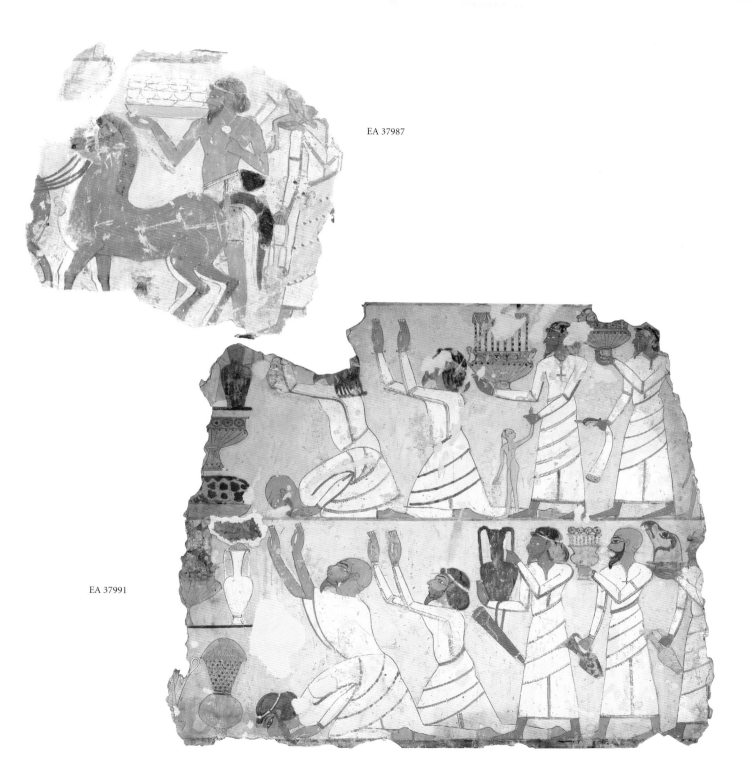

EA 37987

EA 37991

been placed in his tomb to illustrate his importance as an official and to represent his relationship with the king, so that it would be reflected in his life after death.

This fragment from the tribute scene (illustrated on page 147, above) was originally slightl y to the right of the lower register of EA 37991 (page 147, below). Chariot wheels are visible at the bottom left-hand corner, followed by two horses, with their reins extending into the chariot and perhaps tied to it. To the right, a man with an Asiatic beard and hairstyle carries a tray of white items with his left arm; over his left shoulder is a tall thin vessel painted blue, perhaps made of copper. The last figure on the right is a man in a long elaborate robe, bearing a child in his left hand and a blue vessel in his right.

ASIATIC TRIBUTE BEARERS

Width: 129 cm

EA 37991

ASIATIC TRIBUTE BEARERS

This (illustrated on page 147, below) is the largest fragment of the tribute scene. At the left of the sub-registers here are several vessels, similar to those shown elsewhere in the scene. Two pairs of men in Asiatic dress do obeisance to Sebekhotep and (by inference) to the king at the beginning of each sub-register, while behind each is a row of standing men carrying vessels. Several of these are most elaborate, and are made of gold inlaid with semi-precious stones; the others are probably also of metal. One man leads a small girl by the hand, while another bears a vessel probably made from an elephant tusk.

CRAFTSMEN AT WORK

Width: 79 cm

EA 920

CRAFTSMEN AT WORK

Another responsibility of treasury officials in Egypt was to oversee craftsmen producing luxury objects, as it appears that most of these workshops were attached to temples or palaces. Valuable items like jewellery fell into this category, and scenes of their manufacture on the walls of his tomb help indicate Sebekhotep's importance. These two registers (opposite, above) show some stages of jewellery production, primarily the broad collars so characteristic of festive depictions in tomb paintings. The men in the upper sub-register are probably stringing beads, while one man in the lower part is making them into the large collar shown on his lap. The man on the right in the lower register appears to be shaping an elaborate vessel; parts of other elaborate vessels can be seen in the register.

AFRICAN TRIBUTE-BEARERS

Height: 74 cm

EA 922

AFRICAN TRIBUTE-BEARERS

The upper register of the tribute scene described above shows the tribute of Nubia. Two fragments are in the British Museum. They were probably separated by one lost figure, whose arms are visible at the right of EA 921 (not illustrated). At the left of EA 921, three

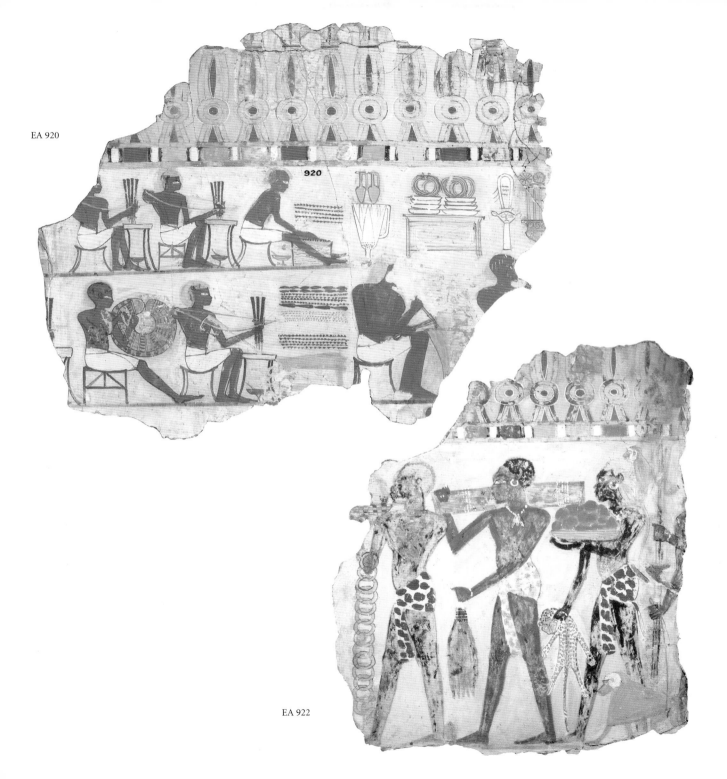

EA 920

920

EA 922

negroid men (probably Nubians) do obeisance to Sebekhotep and (by inference) to the king; they are followed by three men carrying plates of gold with interlinked rings of gold over their arms. The right-hand fragment (EA 922, page 149, below) shows four standing men. The first holds up a plate with blue items, with gold rings over his other arm. The second man holds pieces of ivory on his shoulder and unclear items in his left hand; the third man's right hand grasps a leopard skin and with the left he holds a tray of red fruit (?). On his shoulder is a monkey and by his legs a baboon, the latter on a leash held by the fourth (destroyed) man, who also grasps (possibly) a plant column.

Gold was one of the most important products of Nubia. Note the black and brown variation of the colour of the men's skin; this might represent different skin types, but could also be intended to make the individual figures stand out more, as it is not unusual for Egyptian painting to vary the skin colour of figures of the same sex for this purpose.

OFFERING-BEARERS

This fragment shows two offering-bearers located to the right of the false door painted on the southern wall of the front room of the tomb chapel. Two men dressed in white kilts and robes carry floral and food offerings for Sebekhotep. The false door (see EA 682, pages 54–5, EA 1324, pages 56–7 and EA 1848, pages 64–5) was the principal offering place in the tomb and the items carried by these painted figures could magically substitute for the real offerings, should they cease.

OFFERING-BEARERS

Width: 71 cm

EA 919

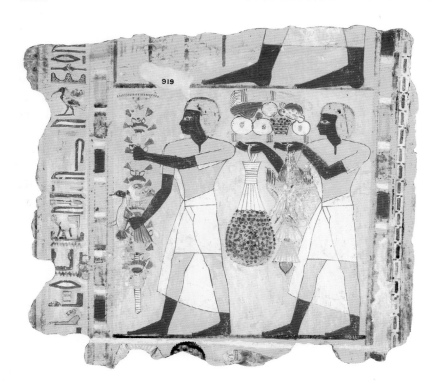

EA 5

Royal sculpture from the mortuary temple of Amenhotep III

AMENHOTEP III (*c.* 1390–1352 BC) probably constructed more buildings and erected more sculptures than any other king in Egyptian history (even Ramesses II) in the course of his 38-year reign. In particular, he was a great temple builder. Some locations, above all the city of Thebes, must have been one massive building site at this time. Hundreds, probably thousands, of statues of himself and deities in varying sizes, but particularly life-size and larger, were made for these temples; the largest statues are of himself.

Probably the greatest number of these statues stood in his mortuary temple at Kom el-Hitan on the West Bank. This structure was easily the largest on that side of the river, indeed almost certainly larger than the temple of Karnak, and contained over a thousand statues. Most of these were of gods (see the Sekhmets, pages 156–7), but a whole range of other divine beings was also present. The best-known of the colossal statues are the two figures which flanked the entrance, known today as the 'Colossi of Memnon'. They constitute the major surviving parts of the temple which, due to its location in the flood-plain, quickly seems to have fallen into disrepair. There were various other seated colossi, now almost vanished, and numerous standing figures, now shattered (EA 7). Other statue types included smaller seated and standing statues in granodiorite (EA 5), and pair statues of Amenhotep with his wife Tiye (EA 3).

The facial styles of statues of Amenhotep III tend to change according to the date in the reign at which they were produced, as his official manner of representation changed. Most interesting of all, the latest phase tends to show him in the most youthful style, perhaps indicating that in the last decade of his life, he had become a living youthful manifestation of all aspects of deity, probably after celebrating his jubilee *sed* festival in his thirtieth year on the throne.

This vast amount of colossal statuary in one temple was quite a new departure for Egypt. Large statues had been made before, but never in such quantity, and such a number of free-standing statues was also an innovation. The statues were perhaps used for 'ritual narration' in stone, whereby the king could join in his different aspects with the greater pantheon of gods. The location in the flood-plain might have been intentional, to symbolize the 'mound of creation' arising from the primaeval waters; unfortunately the real waters of the Nile flood were not conducive to the preservation of the temple. It was used as a quarry for stone and statues by many later kings, beginning with Merenptah of the Nineteenth Dynasty, some 140 years after Amenhotep's death.

These statues all came to the British Museum from the first collection of Henry Salt, purchased in 1823. They were excavated by Belzoni, who worked in Thebes and elsewhere as Salt's agent for several years. His workmen dug up a number of statues lying in the Amenhotep III temple in about 1816–18. In addition to the three statues here, there is another colossal quartzite head (EA 6) and a somewhat smaller seated statue (EA 4) in the collection.

SEATED STATUE OF AMENHOTEP III (EA 5)

This statue (illustrated on page 151) and a smaller example in the Museum, EA 4, both bear the intertwined symbols of the plants of Upper and Lower Egypt on the sides of the thrones. This symbolically represents the union of the two lands of Egypt, and illustrates the fact that it is the king who holds the land together. EA 5 also bears an inscription on its back pillar, which was defaced during the Amarna Period campaign against the names and representations of Amun, though these were later restored. This statue does not represent the king with the apparently rejuvenated features of EA 7, and was probably made earlier in the reign. Visitors to the British Museum will notice that Belzoni carved his name on the base of the statue.

COLOSSAL BUST OF AMENHOTEP III (EA 3)

This uninscribed bust of a king wearing the *nemes* headdress (opposite) has always been identified as Amenhotep III from its style and the fact that it was found in the area of his temple by Belzoni. Like EA 5, it is probably not one of the later products of the reign. The bust has been recently identified as one of the upper parts of a pair statue of Amenhotep III and queen Tiye, the lower part of which has now been re-erected in Merenptah's mortuary temple. Merenptah reused many blocks and statues from Amenhotep III's temple, which must have been in a state of decay a century and a half after the death of its founder.

HEAD FROM A STATUE OF
AMENHOTEP III

Purchased as part of the first Salt
collection in 1823

Quartzite

Height: 117 cm (max.)

EA 7

HEAD FROM A STATUE OF AMENHOTEP III (EA 7)

At the rear of Amenhotep III's temple were eight colossi about eight metres high, four of Aswan granite and four of brown quartzite from near Cairo, each with its arms (probably) crossed on the chest, identifying the king with Osiris. The granite examples wore the white crown of Upper Egypt and the quartzite ones the red crown of Lower Egypt, thus reflecting their geological origin. This head (opposite) is from one of the Lower Egyptian statues; a second head from one of the other statues is in the Museum (EA 6), and a third was discovered in excavations in the temple in the 1960s. Parts of the statues' bodies have come to light in recent excavations.

The head is a superb example of the Egyptian sculptor's art. The craftsman has taken advantage of the way that this particular quartzite can be polished to make certain features stand out: polishing more around the eyes and less around the mouth and leaving the line of the beard and eyebrows unpolished makes them stand out from the face. The eyes tilt down at an angle of 45 degrees, so as to look down on the viewer and thus accentuate the massiveness of the sculpture. It is thought that these statues were produced in the last decade of the king's reign to represent him as rejuvenated after his first *sed* festival.

The brown quartzite used in this sculpture comes from Gebel Ahmar near Cairo, and was particularly favoured in the reign of Amenhotep III. An inscription on a large stela erected within the mortuary temple describes the king as having filled it with monuments made from the 'mountain of wondrous stone (quartzite)'. A favoured official of Amenhotep III, Amenhotep son of Hapu, relates in a text on a statue how the king promoted him to be 'overseer of works in the mountain of wondrous stone'; he says that he brought many statues of the king from the area of Heliopolis to western Thebes.

Statues of Sekhmet

New Kingdom, Eighteenth Dynasty,
reign of Amenhotep III,
c. 1390–1352 BC

The four examples illustrated here are
from the temple of Mut at Karnak

The Museum's collection of these
statues came from several sources.
Some were given by King George III in
1802, though most were purchased
from the first collection of Henry Salt
in 1823

Granodiorite

Height:
EA 76: 236 cm
EA 57: 205 cm
EA 62: 218 cm
EA 80: 228 cm

This photograph shows (left to right)
EA 76, 57, 62, 80

SEATED AND STANDING STATUES of the lioness-headed goddess Sekhmet are a common sight in major museums. The largest single number of such statues outside Egypt is in the British Museum, where there are more than thirty complete or broken examples. Most were recovered from the temple of Mut at Karnak, where many are still visible. Their original provenance was without doubt the mortuary temple of Amenhotep III on the West Bank at Thebes, where the remains of others are still being discovered.

Amenhotep's temple fell into decay a century after his death, and was used as a convenient quarry by many later pharaohs (see EA 3/5/7, pages 151–5). Reliefs from the walls were reused in the nearby temple of Merenptah, and considerable numbers of the Sekhmet statues were moved to the Mut temple at Karnak. Some kings, in particular the Twenty-second Dynasty ruler Sheshonq I, added their names to the statues in their new locations (for example, on BM EA 517). The two goddesses Sekhmet and Mut were associated because both were shown in the form of a lioness, or a lioness-headed woman. In addition, most of the statues were erected near the temple's sacred lake, which has an unusual kidney shape; there are other places in Egypt where rituals honouring Sekhmet were performed near lakes of this type.

There is considerable variation among the statues. Some are particularly large, and the variability of the carving of the faces, for example, suggests that they were not produced by the same group of craftsmen – hardly surprising in view of their numbers. Some statues were carved with integral sun-discs on the head, but in many cases a separate sun-disc was added, fitting into a socket at the top of the head. Although many were left uninscribed, those with inscriptions mention a variety of epithets of the goddess. Most statues hold an *ankh* (life) sign and a *wadj* (lotus-headed) sceptre (or a plant with the same shape).

Texts in temples of the Ptolemaic and Roman Periods speak of a ritual to propitiate Sekhmet, a goddess who could be extremely dangerous, as when she took the form of the Eye of Re the sun-god. *Wadj* sceptres feature prominently in these texts and accompanying scenes, and many of the epithets found on the statues echo those in the texts. One text speaks of 730 Sekhmets following the king, and it is possible that, in the temple of Amenhotep III at Thebes, there were 365 standing and 365 seated figures of the goddess, forming a litany in stone to propitiate her permanently and prevent her from using her negative power against the king and, through him, Egypt. These litanies might only be associated with the new year, but there is also evidence that they could be celebrated in association with any momentous event. In the context of the mortuary temple, they may have been linked to the *sed* (jubilee) festival or Amenhotep's eternal cult.

Masterpieces of Egyptian Art.

A lion from Soleb

Originally New Kingdom, Eighteenth
Dynasty, *c.* 1370 BC

From Gebel Barkal in the Sudan

Gift of Lord Prudhoe in 1835

Pink granite

Length: 216 cm

EA 2

EVIDENCE FOR THE WIDE-RANGING BUILDING CAMPAIGN of Amenhotep III (*c.* 1390–1352 BC) is plentiful in the British Museum's collections. This lion and its mirror-image companion (EA 1), which greet the visitor at the southern entrance to the Egyptian Sculpture Gallery, show how his building projects extended into Nubia. They came from the temple of Soleb in Nubia, just north of the Third Cataract of the Nile, where they acted as guardian figures in front of a temple built by Amenhotep III in the second half of his reign (*c.* 1370 BC). The temple and associated town at Soleb show the extent to which the Egyptians were settling in Nubia, south of the Second Cataract, in the Eighteenth Dynasty, but the temple is also an elaborate monument to the cult of the king, as the deified 'lord of Nubia'. This deity was embodied by the lion.

An original text of Amenhotep III survives only on the statue EA 1, mentioning the temple of Soleb. Lion EA 2 bears on its breast an inscription in which the name of the king is unclear. Amenhotep III is a possibility, but it has also been suggested that it was Amenhotep's son Akhenaten, whose building activity is attested at Soleb. EA 2 bears a renewal inscription of Tutankhamun on behalf of Amenhotep III.

The two lions were not destined to remain at Soleb, as the Meroitic ruler Amanislo moved them south to his city of Gebel Barkal, beyond the Fourth Cataract, in the third century BC. He also added his names to the lions, on the breast of EA 1 and on the left forepaw of EA 2. It may have been he who removed the names of Tutankhamun, perhaps replacing them with his own in plaster which has now become detached. Moving such sculptures was not simply a way to obtain high-quality works cheaply to decorate new constructions; it was also very important in the link and parallel it established between the power of the third-century Kushite king and the powerful monarch of 1,000 years before. Moving this statue thus enhanced Amanislo's legitimacy.

The lions originally possessed inlaid eyes, and are often cited as examples of the skill with which the Egyptian artist could represent animals, even on a monumental scale. The mane of the animal is, however, highly stylized and looks more like a ruff.

They were given to the Museum in 1835 by Lord Prudhoe, who saw them in January 1829 during his travels in Egypt and Nubia. When he discovered them, they were apparently facing each other, flanking a gate. However, it is now thought that they were originally placed on a pinnacle of rock to the north of a palace now known as B1200. It is unclear how they were moved to Cairo, but they were certainly there in the care of the British Consul-General in 1830.

Colossal head

New Kingdom, originally Eighteenth
Dynasty, *c.* 1370 BC

From the temple of Mut at Karnak

Purchased as part of the sale of the first
Salt collection in 1823

Red granite

Height: 290 cm

EA 15

THIS STATUE, wearing the double crown of Upper and Lower Egypt, was found in front of the temple of Khonsupakhered in the temple enclosure of Mut at Karnak. It is uncertain whether it was originally erected there. An arm from the statue is also in the Museum (EA 55), while the body has been identified in the Mut enclosure. The broken statue was discovered by Belzoni and Beechey in the course of Belzoni's second journey in Egypt in 1817. They began work at a site where part of a statue protruded from the earth, and soon revealed the head. It took them eight days to move it one mile (1.6 km) to Luxor. The arm was presumably found with it, although Belzoni does not specifically say this.

For many years, the provenance of the statue was misunderstood and it was attributed to Thutmose III. It is now thought most likely that it was originally made for Amenhotep III, although the inscription on the torso from the Mut temple has been completely effaced. Various details of the face, such as the heavy cosmetic lines around the eyes, point to the style of Amenhotep III's reign, though it is also clear that it has been modified. The cosmetic lines have been largely abraded, and the lips have been adjusted by drilling in the corners to help create the illusion of a smaller mouth. The resultant features are thought to be those of Ramesses II, who is known to have ordered earlier statues to be modified to represent himself, in addition to inscribing them with his own name. In other cases (such as the statue Louvre A 20), Ramesses reduced the relatively plump stomachs of Amenhotep's images to make them conform to his model of the king's ideal physical shape.

Amenhotep III set up an enormous number of statues of himself in Thebes. This statue may have originated in Karnak, but it is also possible that it was removed from Amenhotep's massive mortuary temple on the West Bank at Kom el-Hitan (see also EA 3/5/7, pages 151–5, and the Sekhmet statues, pages 156–7).

A divine baboon

New Kingdom, Eighteenth Dynasty,
reign of Amenhotep III, *c.* 1370 BC

Provenance unknown

From the collection of John Barker,
purchased at Sotheby's in 1833

Quartzite

Height: 68.5 cm

EA 38

THIS ATTRACTIVE and beautifully carved statue of a squatting baboon is carved out of the brown quartzite of Lower Egypt so favoured by Amenhotep III. The ear has been restored and the muzzle repaired, but it is otherwise in excellent condition. The animal squats at rest, paws on its knees, and the artist has taken great pains to depict a highly detailed mane in very low relief, as well as representing the facial hairs with great care.

On the top of the base, between its rear legs, are texts which name Amenhotep III, describing him as 'beloved of he who cuts off the face of he who cuts off your face'. This is a very rare epithet, which cannot immediately be associated with a particular deity. The baboon was linked by the Egyptians with at least three main divinities. The first was the sun-god; as baboons screech at sunrise, they were thought to be particularly associated with this deity, and are often shown in religious papyri adoring the sunrise. The second deity is Thoth (also associated with the ibis); Amenhotep III set up four colossal baboon statues at Hermopolis, the centre of the cult of Thoth. The third divinity is Hapy, one of the four sons of Horus, who protected the embalmed internal organs of the deceased (he is usually associated with the lungs). The unusual epithet 'he who cuts off the face of he who cuts off your face' suggests that it might be Hapy who is represented here: spell 151 of the *Book of the Dead* contains a speech by Hapy in which he vows to smite the enemies of the deceased's face. However, no images of this deity in stone are known.

The statue's provenance is unknown. The possible association with Hapy, an over-whelmingly funerary deity, has led to the suggestion that it might have come from a tomb, presumably that of the king. However, stone statues do not appear in royal tombs, where statuary is invariably of wood (compare the wooden figures on pages 188–9). If the baboon represents Thoth, however, it probably came from a temple. A large number of statues of deities seem to have been made for Amenhotep III's mortuary temple at Kom el-Hitan on the West Bank at Thebes, and this object might have complemented the range of animal and human deities there.

The stone used is a most attractive type of veined quartzite from Gebel Ahmar, north-east of Cairo. The reign of Amenhotep III saw the most concentrated exploitation of this stone type, almost certainly because of its golden colour and proximity to Heliopolis, the centre of the sun cult, which became increasingly important during the reign.

John Barker was Henry Salt's successor as British Consul-General in Cairo.

Stela of Amenhotep III

New Kingdom, Eighteenth Dynasty, reign of Amenhotep III, *c.* 1360 BC

From Semna

Gift of Lord Prudhoe in 1835

Sandstone

Height: 82 cm; width: 90 cm

EA 657

IT BECAME CUSTOMARY for Egyptian kings to leave some physical record of their foreign expeditions and campaigns at strategic locations in the occupied lands. From the late Pre-dynastic Period to the early Old Kingdom, this simply took the form of a brief mention of the name of the king on a convenient rock (see EA 691, pages 46–7), but in the course of the next few dynasties the texts gradually increased in length, often including details about the expedition itself and its personnel. From the Middle Kingdom onwards the practice was to set up stelae, such as this one; compare the stela of Senwosret I, EA 963, pages 76–7, which was set up at the southern boundary of Egypt at Elephantine.

This stela was erected in the reign of Amenhotep III on the west bank of the Nile at Semna, south of the Second Cataract. The campaign recorded here was against the people of Ibhet, an area perhaps to the east of the Nile. The inscription relates how the army, under the command of the viceroy, was formed out of men from villages from Baky (probably Kubban) to Tery (location uncertain), a distance of 52 *iteru* measures, roughly 540 km, well beyond the Second Cataract. The text then claims that Amenhotep destroyed the enemies of Ibhet in an hour, and (probably, as it is damaged) took away their women-folk and cattle. The text gives a summary of the number of persons brought away from this victory: 740 men, women and children, plus another 312 hands, the latter indicating the slaughter which had occurred. It was standard practice to cut off the hands of dead enemies, and in some Nineteenth and Twentieth Dynasty temple reliefs, scribes are shown counting piles of these hands. The text concludes by recording a short hymn of praise to the king, uttered by the viceroy, Merymose. Parts of Merymose's sarcophagi are also in the Museum (see EA 1001, pages 168–9).

As always in this type of text, the king is shown as victorious. It must be remembered that, from the Egyptian point of view, stelae were not historical documents, as we might regard them, but rather statements of how things should be: the king always had to be shown as winning, often in superhuman ways, or else the concept of *maat*, the mainte-nance of the cosmic order, could not be realized. Nonetheless, it is likely that the stela also gives an account of an actual punitive expedition, presumably against a desert people who were threatening Egyptian occupation of the area. The stela does not bear a date, but the campaign is thought likely to have taken place in the later years of Amenhotep III's reign; this was not a very warlike period, and this campaign is only the second Nubian one recorded for the reign.

Statue of Amenwahsu

New Kingdom, probably middle of the Eighteenth Dynasty, c. 1450–1370 BC

Probably from Thebes

Acquired in 1907

Quartzite

Height: 56 cm

EA 480

THIS STATUE OF AMENWAHSU is of the stela-bearing ('stelaphorous') type, which shows the owner kneeling and presenting a stela, and came into common use in the New Kingdom. Amenwahsu wears a striated shoulder-length wig, and kneels with his hands held up in adoration of the deity and also supporting the top of the stela. The text on Amenwahsu's stela is a short hymn to Re-Horakhty at his (daily) rising in the east, plus the owner's name and title; at the stela's top is the figure of a ram-headed god, named as Amun-Re-Horakhty, merging the solar deity named in the hymn with the great god of Thebes, one of whose forms was a ram. On the back pillar, itself shaped something like a stela, are two pairs of columns of hieroglyphs, bearing prayers for offerings to Re-Horakhty-Atum and to Osiris, and Amenwahsu's names and titles.

Smaller versions of such statues, usually made of cheaper materials such as limestone and sandstone, were placed in small niches over the entrances to Theban tombs, orientated to the east to greet the rising sun. This example is perhaps too large to have been used in this way, and as there are many larger statues of this type, it is possible that it was placed in either a royal mortuary temple or a state temple.

The identity of Amenwahsu, who was overseer of priests of Montu lord of Thebes and of Montu lord of Tod (some 40 km south of Luxor), is not certain. The figure's face is in the style associated with the mid-Eighteenth Dynasty, perhaps from the reign of Thutmose III to the early reign of Amenhotep III, and the style of the stela is in accord with that date (the earliest stelaphorous statues are quite small, with a very small stela, but by the Ramesside Period the stela was often as tall as the owner himself). However, Labib Habachi has argued that it might belong to an individual of the same name known to have been involved in the Montu cults of (probably) the reign of Merenptah, who was buried in Theban Tomb 274. It is not easy to reconcile this suggestion with the style of this statue, unless a Ramesside Amenwahsu deliberately copied the style of a monument from two centuries earlier, so it is likely that we are dealing with two individuals.

The statue is said to have been found in Karnak, part of a cache of statues or statue shrine which was seen by Budge at the turn of the twentieth century, most of the contents of which were acquired by him for the British Museum over several years (see EA 174, pages 130–1). However, the circumstances of the 'find' are suspect, to say the least. T.G.H. James has argued that this 'shrine' was assembled by Mohamed Mohassib, a Luxor antiquities dealer, from illicitly excavated Theban statues.

Sarcophagus of Merymose

New Kingdom, Eighteenth Dynasty,
reign of Amenhotep III,
c. 1370–1350 BC

Presumably from Merymose's tomb
at Thebes

Inner sarcophagus fragments acquired
in 1875 from Miss Selima Harris;
middle fragments donated by Jean
Capart in 1938 and Earl Spencer
in 1965

Granodiorite

Length of restored sarcophagus: 197 cm

EA 1001

STONE SARCOPHAGI are rather rare for private individuals before the Nineteenth Dynasty; most anthropoid containers for mummies from the earlier New Kingdom are made of wood. Merymose had no fewer than three stone sarcophagi, nested one inside the other and all of the highest quality. The outer one was found in 1940 in a large anonymous tomb in the area of Qurnet Marai at Thebes, in the southern part of the necropolis, and there is little reason to doubt that this was the origin of all three sarcophagi and the tomb of Merymose himself. This tomb is now numbered TT 383.

Merymose was the viceroy of Kush (Upper Nubia) in the reign of Amenhotep III. Kush was an important source of wealth for the Egyptians, and in the New Kingdom produced much of the gold which the regime required. The quality of Merymose's sarcophagi indicates that he must have been very wealthy (see the stela of Amenhotep III, EA 657, pages 164–5, for evidence of Merymose's activities in Kush).

The inner sarcophagus (opposite) has been reconstructed at the Museum, and is a wonderful example of the stone-carver's art. The deceased is depicted with a long wig, short beard, and a broad collar; on his chest the sky-goddess Nut spreads her wings protectively over the body, while at the head and foot ends respectively, the goddesses Nephthys and Isis offer their protection, accompanied by texts. The coffin bears longitudinal bands of text which give Merymose's titles, while those at right angles to this name various deities whose images are to be found in front of the text bands, together with additional words spoken by them. On the left side of the sarcophagus are Hapy, Anubis, and Qebehsenuef, while on the more damaged right side would have been Imsety, Anubis, and Duamutef; in other words, Anubis plus the four sons of Horus, all of whom protect the deceased. At the head end on each side is a figure and text of Thoth. The sarcophagus' form and decoration are very similar to the contemporary common type of black wooden coffin.

The British Museum also has fragments of the middle sarcophagus, one of which joins a sarcophagus head now in Boston. The facial style of the latter piece is somewhat different from EA 1001, with the 'almond-shaped' eyes so characteristic of the middle period of Amenhotep III's reign; EA 1001 and the outer sarcophagus (the face of which is in Vassar College), are more typical of the earlier style, though of course the sarcophagi might have been produced by two different groups of craftsmen working in slightly different styles.

In addition to the elements mentioned above, the remainder of the outer sarcophagus is still in Luxor, and there are pieces of the others in Prague, Vienna, Oslo, Paris, and possibly Luxor. The number EA 1001 covers the fragments of both sarcophagi in the Museum.

Paintings from the tomb chapel of Nebamun

New Kingdom, Eighteenth Dynasty,
probably late reign of Amenhotep III,
or early Amenhotep IV, *c.* 1350 BC

From Thebes

Ten fragments purchased as part of the
first Salt collection in 1823; the eleventh
(EA 37981) was acquired by George
Waddington and Richard Hanbury in
1821 and donated to the museum by
Sir Henry Ellis in 1833

Paint on lime plaster on mud base

THE ELEVEN FRAGMENTS of the tomb of Nebamun in the British Museum are perhaps the finest surviving examples of the painters' art from ancient Egypt. The location of the tomb is very uncertain, as it has not yet proved possible to fit the fragments into any known chapel at Thebes. Besides the British Museum fragments, smaller pieces are in Avignon, Berlin, and Lyons, while three others were photographed in Cairo in the 1940s.

Ten of the Museum fragments were among the objects brought to Britain as part of Henry Salt's first collection. The paintings were discovered in 1820, but records give little information about the chapel's location. One of the Berlin fragments, showing men catching quails, was seen during the Marquis of Northampton's excavations in the area of Dra Abul Naga (northern end of the necropolis) in 1898–9. It is likely that the tomb was discovered there and some of the best paintings removed by Salt's agents. This probably caused considerable damage to the tomb chapel and the location was then lost, and the tomb may now have been covered by a more recent structure, somewhere at the northern end of the modern settlement of Dra Abul Naga.

Although the fragments are confidently termed paintings of Nebamun, the owner's name is nowhere clearly preserved. The least damaged example is at the end of the text on EA 37976, where, after the title 'scribe and counter of grain', 'Nebamun' is the most likely reconstruction. The name was damaged during the Amarna Period, when the name of the god Amun was systematically destroyed. The owner's title is not an especially elevated one, but there are several other small but beautifully decorated tombs of other holders of this and similar titles in the Theban necropolis, also of the middle to late Eighteenth Dynasty.

The tomb has been tentatively reconstructed as a small T-shaped chapel. The paintings are at present the subject of a comprehensive conservation and research project, and will be redisplayed in a refurbished gallery in the British Museum.

FOWLING IN THE MARSHES

FOWLING IN THE MARSHES

Width: 98 cm

EA 37977

The best-known of the paintings shows Nebamun taking part in the common scene known as 'fowling in the marshes'. He stands in a small papyrus boat, with his wife bedecked in her best clothing behind him and a child seated between his legs. He is about to throw a stick at a range of species of birds in and above a papyrus thicket, and grasps three birds in his other hand. Within the thicket, a cat has a duck in its mouth and two other birds in its claws. The colouration and attention to detail in the painting are astonishing. One remarkable feature noticed in the 1990s is the use of gold leaf on the cat's eye.

BANQUET SCENE

Above left:

Width: 99.5 cm

EA 37984

Above right:

Width: 50 cm

NOT THIS SIDE.

6 . 2 . 11

A scene such as this is usually balanced by a matching one showing the tomb owner spearing fish, and the spear can be seen in the bottom left corner of the fowling scene. Two of the Cairo fragments show the head of the tomb owner and the child between his legs. The composition is, however, not a representation of the pleasures of the hunt, but is an integral part of the decorative programme of the tomb; the most plausible interpretation is that the scene is formed of a complex series of symbols which allude to reproduction and rebirth, in this case in the afterlife, which would be ensured by such depictions in the tomb chapel.

BANQUET SCENE

Three fragments have survived, which, when arranged as here, represent four registers of a banquet scene. Three of the registers show guests at this event, some as couples, some in groups of the same sex. Both men and women are dressed in fine white robes with thin overgarments which give a yellow colour to the main fabric. All the women have thick long wigs and the men mostly wear shoulder-length hairstyles, although some are shaven – the difference seems only to occur in groups of men, where the styles alternate. The third register shows two groups of female musicians, with a pair of naked dancers in the left-hand group. Serving men and women minister to all the couples; all the guests and the musicians have festive cones of fat on their heads. The musicians are one of the rare examples in Egyptian art in which the subjects are shown from the front rather than in profile. Such departures from the normal conventions are only ever found in subsidiary figures in scenes such as this.

Although the banquet scenes are thought to be connected with the celebration of the Theban Festival of the Valley, when the statue of Amun came from Karnak temple to visit the shrines on the West Bank, it is not simply a reflection of a celebration. Drink rather than food is being consumed, and the figures hold lotus (lily) flowers or mandrake fruit to their noses. Intoxication seems an important element, and the lotus and mandrake may have narcotic or hallucinogenic properties which help the banqueters to approach closer to the deity. These and other symbols suggest that these scenes once again express the wish for rebirth after death, which was one of the purposes of the tomb chapel.

NEBAMUN SEATED

Height: 67.5 cm, EA 37979

GEESE

Width: 115.5 cm, EA 37978

CATTLE

Width: 97 cm, EA 37976

NEBAMUN INSPECTING CATTLE AND GEESE

In addition to the more esoteric scenes, Eighteenth Dynasty tombs contain many scenes apparently depicting daily life. These three fragments come from the same wall, which showed the tomb-owner twice, seated on a stool inspecting two scenes, one of geese and one of cattle.

One of the seated representations of Nebamun has survived (left), showing him sitting on a folding seat with a back. In his left hand he holds a staff, and in his right a sceptre of authority and a small floral bundle. The black and white shape immediately beneath him is a representation of the soft leather of the chair seat.

In the upper fragment (opposite, above), the gooseherds are shown with their charges in two sub-registers; to the left a scribe, differentiated by his more elaborate dress and the palette under his arm, presents a piece of papyrus with accounts, presumably of the geese, to Nebamun. In the lower scene (opposite, below), herdsmen drive their cattle, which are being counted and recorded by scribes at the left. The scenes are accompanied by idealized captions of what some of the men in them might have said; the longer text in the cattle scene is also full of praise for Nebamun. As with all these paintings, the level of detail is remarkable; every creature is clearly differentiated, usually by careful use of different pigments so that no animals of similar colour are adjacent. Such scenes as these have a deeper meaning too; they project Nebamun's personality and wealth into the afterlife and help create a world in which his spirits can reside after death.

FROM: BM MASTERPIECES OF ANC. EGYPT

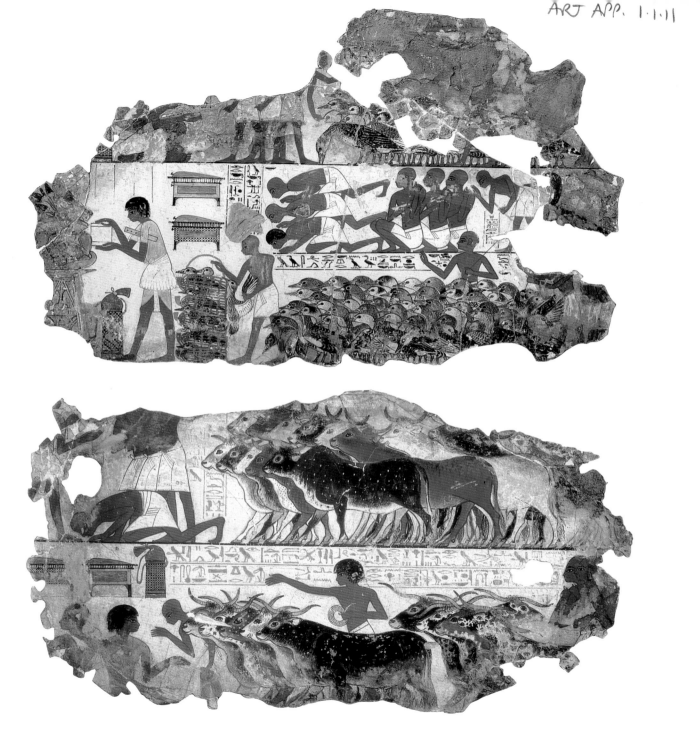

A POOL IN A GARDEN

This depiction of a pool surrounded by trees (left) may have come from the same wall as the fowling scene. The pool is filled with fishes, plants, and birds, while the trees around it include date-palms, dom-palms, sycomore figs, and mandrakes. At the top right, a female figure forming part of a dom-palm – a tree-goddess – holds out a tray of offerings, mostly fruit of the adjacent trees. Parallel scenes indicate there would have been a figure of the owner to the right, receiving the offerings. The remains of text at the top left are a speech of another tree deity, the sycomore. Once again the scene drips with symbolism – the plants, birds, and fish allude to rebirth, and the fruit of the dom, which contains water, is a potent sustenance for the next life. As in the banquet, the mandrake may have narcotic significance.

A POOL IN A GARDEN

Width: 73 cm.

EA 37983

A FIELD SCENE

Width: 83 cm

EA 37982

A FIELD SCENE

This scene (opposite) was part of a larger one of agricultural activities. At the left, in front of a standing grain crop, an elderly man holding a staff bends before a small boundary marker or stela, and swears an oath, recorded in the text above, that the stela is in the correct place. To his left are the remains of a procession of figures who accompanied him; above the corn are the remains of a flying quail. The right-hand part of the scene has two sub-registers: the upper shows a pair of horses with a chariot, and the lower a pair of a different type of equid, also with a chariot. The latter animals are probably browsing in the tree to the right. The most interesting feature of this scene is the unusual lower animals, since they do not seem to be the normal Egyptian horse. They may have been some other breed of equid, but precisely which is open to debate.

The scene is another of those which help recreate Nebamun's world for the tomb spirits. Very few other examples of similar scenes exist. There are two others which show the same unusual type of horse, and three the checking of the boundary stela. All these other tombs date from the middle to late Eighteenth Dynasty, all are at Thebes, and all belong to men of similar professions – clearly it was a decorative motif which was in vogue among a particular social group for only a short time.

Statue of queen Nefertiti

New Kingdom, Eighteenth Dynasty, later reign of Akhenaten (the Amarna Period), *c.* 1340 BC

From Amarna, House L.50.12

Gift of the Egypt Exploration Society in 1925

Sandstone with traces of colour

Height: 71 cm

EA 935

NEFERTITI was the principal wife of the pharaoh Akhenaten. This headless and footless statue of Nefertiti depicts her standing, wearing a full-length pleated gown, originally white. The flesh was painted red, and traces of red and blue colour indicate that the figure wore a collar. Nefertiti stands with both hands extended forward and carrying something, now lost along with her forearms and hands. It has been suggested that what she held was an altar or a flat table, but other Amarna sculptures which hold such items show the hands supporting them from below, whereas Nefertiti grasps the object by its sides.

The head, back of the neck, and the top of the back pillar are made from a separate piece of sandstone. This bears remains of plaster: one area at the top of the back pillar has the beginning of the text cut into it, and there is a roughly 2 cm square area of plaster on the front, sloping side. While the statue might originally have been composite in nature, perhaps because the stone broke during carving, it is also possible that it was later damaged and repaired – the presence of the plaster might even suggest that it was repaired twice.

The text on the back pillar gives the full name of Akhenaten's preferred deity, the sun-disc or Aten, in cartouches (the so-called 'dogmatic' or 'didactic' name), and the name and titles of Nefertiti. The dogmatic name of the Aten changes in the course of Akhenaten's reign, and this form is found from year 9 onwards. The earlier form of the name had included the gods Shu and Horus as well as the Aten, but the later name includes only the sun-god Re and the Aten, suggesting that this was part of a move towards a purely solar concept of the god. The name also conveniently dates the statue to the later part of the reign. This date accords well with the stylistic features, which illustrate the move from the more exaggerated appearance typical of the earlier Amarna Period towards a more naturalistic one.

The figure of Nefertiti was found with a statue of Akhenaten in a similar pose (now Ashmolean Museum 1924.162). The pair probably stood together in a shrine in Amarna house L.50.9, next to the house where the statues were found. Presumably these statues were a more elaborate form of the depictions of the king and queen on stelae found in shrines in other houses (see the shrine stela of Amenhotep III, EA 57399, pages 180–1), and formed the focus of the domestic piety of the house owner.

Shrine stela of Amenhotep III and queen Tiye

New Kingdom Eighteenth Dynasty,
c. 1340 BC (the Amarna Period)

From Amarna, house R.44.2
(of Panehsy)

Gift of the Egypt Exploration Society
in 1924

Limestone

Height 32.5 cm

EA 57399

THIS STELA was discovered in several pieces in the house of Panehsy, first servant of the solar disc (Aten). It shows Amenhotep III and his wife Tiye, seated in front of a large pile of offerings on the left. Above them is the Aten, with its arm-like rays extending down to those below. This scene is set inside a frame consisting of floral bouquets to the left and right, and at the top a row of bunches of grapes with a cavetto cornice above, surmounted by a frieze of cobras. Some traces of paint remain, principally on the king's body. The couple are shown in the rather relaxed, almost slumped, style in which seated figures were normally depicted at Amarna; Amenhotep (referred to only by his throne name Neb-maatre, as it would have been inappropriate to mention the god Amun at Amarna) is shown as rather fat, and possibly elderly, if the images are to be taken at face value.

A number of other houses found at Amarna have revealed small shrines containing a stela depicting Akhenaten and Nefertiti in the presence of or worshipping the Aten. These reflect the official religious practice of Amarna, whereby all contact with the Aten had to go via his intermediary the king, although amulets of Bes and the like show that popular domestic deities from the years before the Amarna episode were not ignored. What is interesting about this particular stela is that it depicts Akhenaten's father, and it is also unique in being in raised rather than sunk relief. The form of the Aten's name (compare the statue of Nefertiti, EA 935, pages 178–9) indicates that it must have been made after year 9 of Akhenaten's reign, and the stela has been used as the basis for a variety of view-points on the history and religion of the period. For example, obese depictions of Amenhotep III have been interpreted as images of him as a creator god; the presence of his images at Amarna might indicate that he had a long co-regency with his son; his portrayal in this style means that he had concurred with the artistic and religious changes of his son; or that he was simply elderly and somewhat fat. One must be careful about taking any Egyptian art at face value, as it is almost always intended to promote a particular view of its subject.

In addition to the house in which this stela was found, Panehsy also possessed what has been termed an 'official residence', from which came an elaborate gateway bearing scenes of Akhenaten and Nefertiti worshipping the Aten. This was adjacent to the great temple of the Aten in the centre of the city of Amarna.

57389

Fish-shaped bottle

New Kingdom, Eighteenth Dynasty, reign of Amenhotep III or Akhenaten, *c.* 1360–1340 BC

From Amarna, east of house N.49.33

Gift of the Egypt Exploration Society in 1921

Glass

Length: 14.5 cm

EA 55193

NEW KINGDOM GLASS VESSELS are highly colourful and distinctive objects, and the British Museum fish is perhaps the best-known example of this genre. The vessel resembles a *tilapia* fish. It was produced by first making a core in the rough shape of the desired item (in this case perhaps an irregular oval); molten glass was then trailed over it to give the basic body, and more coloured trails of glass were added to produce the decorative effect. A tool was used to drag the coloured trails to produce the festooned pattern, and the body was then smoothed. Extra pieces of glass were added to create the eyes and the fins; the tail was probably pinched into shape.

Glass workshops did exist at Amarna and the fish could have been made there. An alternative suggestion, based on examination of the colours and manufacture, is that it might have come from the same workshop as a pear-shaped vessel in the tomb of Kha at Thebes and a glass fish-tail found in the Theban palace of Amenhotep III at Malqata. If this is the case, it might have been made in Thebes in the reign of Amenhotep III and then taken to Amarna.

Glass vessels were mainly used as containers for cosmetics or precious oils, and this object was found in a domestic context, a house at Amarna. It may have been buried by its owner, as it was found under a double layer of plaster. Glass vessels seem to have been primarily functional rather than ritual objects, but the choice of the relatively uncommon fish shape (at least three other examples are known, all of about the same date) might hint at some further meaning, other than its novelty value. The Nile *tilapia* fish is what is known as a 'mouth brooder': the female keeps the eggs she has laid in her mouth until they hatch, and thereafter will take her brood back into her mouth at any sign of danger, releasing them when it passes. This apparent production of new life through the mouth was seen by the Egyptians as a symbol of rebirth, and the appearance of *tilapia* in wall paintings in tombs (and elsewhere) contributes to the regenerative aspect of such scenes. (*Tilapia* can be seen in Nebamun's fowling and garden scenes, pages 171 and 176). This complements other forms of regenerative symbolism at Amarna, such as the paintings of papyrus and lotus/lily seen in the palaces. Such symbolism seems to have been quite compatible with the religious changes instituted in the reign of Akhenaten.

King Tutankhamun presenting offerings

New Kingdom, Late Eighteenth
Dynasty, *c.* 1330 BC

Probably from Karnak

Believed to be part of the first Salt
collection, purchased in 1823

Granodiorite

Height: 167.7 cm

EA 75

THIS STATUE SHOWS a bearded king wearing the *nemes* headdress, with a broad collar round his neck, holding a tray (now destroyed) of offerings, from which hangs a mass of additional offerings. These consist mainly of lotus flowers, fowl, and sheaves of grain and would almost certainly have extended to the ground. Part of the missing lower section of this statue has been identified in the Cairo Museum, bearing a number of papyrus plants.

Using both fragments, the inscription on the rear pillar reads 'May the perfect god live, he who does what is beneficial for his father Amun-Re, the king of Upper and Lower Egypt Djeserkheperure-Setepenre, the son of Re, Horemheb' (last king of the Eighteenth Dynasty). However, the facial features are of particular interest, since the elongated face and slightly protruding chin do not resemble the accepted style of Horemheb's reign, but rather that of Tutankhamun, many of whose statues Horemheb is known to have usurped. In this case there is no sign that the inscription has in any way been recut, but few would query the stylistic attribution to Tutankhamun. Presumably this statue of the young king was not completed at his premature death, and was usurped by Horemheb when the latter came to the throne.

This particular type of representation is not common during the New Kingdom, perhaps even being inspired by statues from the reign of Amenemhat III in the Twelfth Dynasty; two or three other such statues are known, all from the Eighteenth Dynasty before the Amarna Period. In addition, a similar statue (and perhaps even that of Thutmose III now in Cairo, CG 42056) is shown in a painting in the tomb of Rekhmire at Thebes, among gifts for the temple of Amun (without doubt, that at Karnak) and other sanctuaries. All these statues have been interpreted as depicting the king in the guise of the Nile god Hapy, the personification of fecundity. This assumption has been questioned, however, since conventional 'fecundity figures' are shown with pot-bellies and breasts, and are most definitely not royal representations (compare the statue of Hapy, EA 8, pages 248–9). There can be little doubt that the simpler interpretation of the king presenting offerings is to be preferred.

The history of this object in the British Museum is far from clear. It has been here at least since the opening of the new Egyptian Saloon in 1834, appearing in the annual *Synopsis* for 1835 as object no. 75 in the display. No more definite evidence has yet been found about its acquisition, although there is a strong suspicion that it is one of the otherwise unassigned objects described in the lists of the collections of Henry Salt from 1818 and 1821, mentioned as being found in Karnak.

Stela of Horemheb

New Kingdom, late Eighteenth Dynasty,
c. 1330 BC

Saqqara, tomb of Horemheb

Acquired as part of the Anastasi
collection in 1839

Limestone

Height: 194.5 cm

EA 551

HOREMHEB HELD THE RANK of military general in the reign of Tutankhamun, and began building a tomb in the New Kingdom cemetery at Saqqara. He was not buried in this tomb; when he became king, after the deaths of Tutankhamun and Ay, he had a new tomb cut in the Valley of the Kings (KV 57). However, several reliefs in his Saqqara tomb (including pilasters EA 550 and 552) were altered to show a small uraeus (royal cobra) on Horemheb's brow. Perhaps the scene at the top of the stela was too high for the workmen to make the alteration.

This stela was originally set up against the west wall of the Saqqara tomb's first colonnaded court. It shows Horemheb worshipping Re-Horakhty, Thoth, and Maat, and is cut in high-quality sunk relief, typical of the immediate post-Amarna period. Beneath is a hymn of praise to these three deities, the longest preserved inscription from the tomb. Several parts of this text have parallels, in particular the opening lines, which are reflected in the opening of the *Book of the Dead* of Nakht (Papyrus BM EA 10471). The royal aspect of the sun-god is the central theme of this hymn. The text also expresses the wish for the active support of these deities for Horemheb in the next world, so that he may attain new life in the appropriate way.

The New Kingdom tombs at Saqqara were first located early in the nineteenth century, during the frenetic and unsupervised search for antiquities. A number of statues, stelae, and fragments from these tombs came into the collection of Giovanni Anastasi; some, including three statues from the tomb of Maya, went to the Leiden Museum the 1820s, while his next collection was sold to the British Museum in 1839, and a subsequent one to the Louvre; the last Anastasi collection was auctioned in Paris in 1857, and the objects dispersed, with some coming to the British Museum. Parts of the tomb of Horemheb were still accessible in the 1860s, when the text of a companion stela was copied by Emmanuel de Rougé. The location of the tombs was then lost until they were rediscovered by a joint British-Dutch expedition which began work in Saqqara in 1975. This huge cemetery lies south of the pyramids of Netjerikhet (Djoser) and Unas.

Horemheb's Saqqara tomb, with its pylon gateways and colonnaded courts, is termed a 'temple tomb'. The tomb's focus has moved away from the complex mixture of scenes seen since the Old Kingdom to a concentration on the character of the deceased, the provisioning of his spirits, and the display of his piety towards deities who would assure his survival in the next world. This stela functions in the latter category.

Protective figures from the Valley of the Kings

New Kingdom, late Eighteenth Dynasty
to the Ramesside Period

Wood, resin

EA 50702, 50699 AND 50703

Originally said to be from the tomb of
Thutmose III, but now thought to be
from that of Horemheb, *c.* 1300 BC

Acquired in 1912

Heights: 57 cm; 32.5 cm; 40.5 cm

EA 61283

Thebes, Valley of the Kings, found in
the tomb of Ramesses IX, *c.* 1110 BC

Purchased as part of the first Salt
collection in 1823

Height: 42.5 cm

THE BRITISH MUSEUM holds a number of most unusual wooden figures from royal tombs of the New Kingdom. Illustrated here are a seated figure with a human body and a ram's head (EA 50702), a human figure with a gazelle's head (?) seated on the ground (EA 50703), and two figures which appear to be seated robed hieroglyphs, one with a hippopotamus' head (EA 50699) and the other (illustrated on this page, below left) holding a human mask over its face (EA 61283). The bodies are carved out of blocks of wood, but, as usual with Egyptian wooden figures, the arms of the first two are made separately and pegged onto the body. All the figures were originally covered with a layer of linen and gesso and painted with black resin. The unusual twisting of the body of EA 50703 must have presented particular challenges to the craftsman; another example has the head of a turtle (not illustrated, EA 50704) and there the awkward join between the human body and the turtle head was conveniently obscured by the figure's wig.

The base of EA 61283 is considerably later than the object itself, probably dating from the Late Period, and could be the base of a Ptah-Sokar-Osiris statue. Several other figures from the Valley of the Kings which came to the Museum through Henry Salt are mounted on miscellaneous ancient pieces of wood. This mounting may have happened after their discovery in Egypt or even on arrival at the Museum.

Several similar figures were found in the tomb of Horemheb in the Valley of the Kings, and some of the Museum's examples may have come from this tomb. Belzoni acquired others from the tombs of Ramesses I and IX. They are believed to represent various protective deities, whose images were placed in the royal tomb to protect the dead king in the afterlife. Royal tombs of the late Nineteenth and early Twentieth Dynasties often show such figures on their walls, in similar poses, carrying knives and serpents to show their power; perhaps the ram-headed wooden figure originally clasped such items. The wall figures may have played a protective role in the enactment of embalming rituals, repelling evil, and also in the rituals by which the murdered Osiris was 'reassembled' and revivified by Isis and Nephthys. These scenes were played out daily in the Egyptian concept of the royal afterlife, and were depicted in tombs. These wooden statuettes may testify to similar practices before these rituals were shown in the wall decoration. No comparable examples were found in the almost complete burial equipment of Tutankhamun, so it seems likely that the figures are a funerary development of the end of the Eighteenth Dynasty. Such figures were painted on Twenty-second Dynasty coffins of private individuals, and were represented in stone in the tomb of Montuemhat at Thebes (Twenty-fifth Dynasty).

Figure of Bes

New Kingdom, probably late
Eighteenth Dynasty, *c.* 1300 BC

Said to be from Akhmim

Acquired in 1888

Wood, gesso, paint

Height: 28 cm

EA 20865

THE DEITY BES IS first known in the Middle Kingdom, and first appears in wall scenes in the New Kingdom. By this time he had acquired the form by which he is best known, that of a rather grotesque bandy-legged dwarf with a lion's mane and protruding tongue.

This example is one of the most elaborate statuettes of the god known. Bes dances with one leg on a lotus flower support, and the other leg raised behind him, with arms spread apart and a small round tambourine in his left hand. On his head is what is probably an ostrich-feather crown. His body is black, with cream spots, and he wears an elaborate painted necklace. The original function of this figure is uncertain, but it could perhaps have been a decorative element on a large harp.

Bes had many functions. He did not have a national cult centre, but he often appears in the same contexts as Hathor, so images of him can be found in major temples such as those at Dendera and Philae. He was above all a god of popular religion, worshipped at home; one of his main responsibilities was ensuring fertility, and protecting mother and child during childbirth. This statue may be associated with this function, or perhaps with Hathoric or solar rites. Music – and the tambourine in particular – was associated with childbirth in the New Kingdom: there is a painting of Bes figures playing tambourines in the sleeping room of a house in the workmen's village at Deir el-Medina. In temples of the Ptolemaic and Roman Periods, Bes, playing a tambourine or dancing, is sometimes associated with a ritual to welcome back and appease the goddess Hathor, but he can also be found dancing and playing for the sunrise, perhaps evoking the traditional image of baboons welcoming the sun's return.

As with so many symbols in Egypt, this image of Bes may have multiple layers of meaning. One which links them all together is the concept of new life and (re)birth, an essential part of the Egyptian concept of the cycle of life. An elaborate image like this might have been placed, perhaps attached to an instrument, in an elite New Kingdom burial to help ensure the continued existence and rebirth of the deceased in the next world.

Limestone statue of an unidentified couple

New Kingdom, late Eighteenth or early
Nineteenth Dynasty, *c.* 1300–1250 BC

Provenance unknown, but perhaps
Saqqara

Acquired at the sale of the Anastasi
collection in 1839

Limestone

Height: 130 cm

EA 36

THIS ANONYMOUS STATUE of a couple is a striking element of the Egyptian sculpture display in the British Museum. The husband and wife are seated on high-backed chairs with lions' legs; the man wears a long curled lappet-wig, a pleated kilt, and sandals. A pair of long baggy sleeves are visible on his upper arms, perhaps from a tunic, or possibly from a wrap-round cloak or shawl. Other traces of this garment only appear round the lower back, so it must either have been a cloak or sufficiently diaphanous to have been depicted by means of paint, now worn off. The woman wears a long enveloping wig, of the type which came into fashion in the second half of the Eighteenth Dynasty, and a long wrap-round garment, also fashionable for roughly the same length of time, which is tied together under the right breast. The noses have been restored and there is some damage to the hands and breasts, but otherwise the statue is in excellent condition.

These dress styles are characteristic of the late Eighteenth and early Nineteenth Dynasties. The earliest examples are known from the reign of Amenhotep III, around 1370 BC, and the style formed the basis for non-royal dress of the Amarna Period.

The statue's provenance is unknown, but might be either Thebes or Saqqara. Of these, Saqqara seems the more likely, especially as the object was collected by Anastasi, who was probably more active in the Memphite than the Theban area. In addition, several similar statues come from Saqqara, all free-standing, whereas statue groups of this size at Thebes would normally be cut from the rock. The best-known group from Saqqara is that of Maya and his wife, now in Leiden. The tombs in which these statues were placed only began to be systematically excavated in the late twentieth century. The largest examples include the tombs of Horemheb (see his stela, EA 551, pages 186–7) and Maya, which, with their impressive gateways, colonnaded courts, and complex chapels, are often termed 'temple-tombs'.

The statue was particularly admired by the sculptor Henry Moore (1898-1986), and was the inspiration for his *King and Queen* (1952-3), now in the Tate Gallery, London. In 1998, as part of a tribute marking the centenary of his birth, the Tate Gallery lent the *King and Queen* to the British Museum. The two couples were placed together in the Egyptian Sculpture Gallery as if in conversation.

Wig

New Kingdom, probably Eighteenth
Dynasty

Said to be from Thebes

Purchased at the sale of the third Salt
collection in 1835

Human hair, beeswax and resin

Height: 49.5 cm

EA 2560

THIS WIG is made of human hair, and is said to have come from a tomb at Thebes. It was found in its original box, made of reeds (now EA 2561). An examination by a modern wigmaker concluded that the standard of craftsmanship was as high as in a good modern wig. Indeed the foundation was not unlike that of 'fashion' wigs of the 1970s. It is thought to be a man's wig.

The wig consists of two elements, a mass of naturally curly hair on top with several hundred thin plaits hanging from ear to ear around the neck of the main wig. The foundation is composed of a net of human hair, finely plaited, with rhomboidal apertures approximately 1.27 cm long at the sides. The curls are formed from naturally curly hairs, heavily impregnated with a mixture of beeswax and resin. The thin plaits are each made of three strands of hair originally 30–38 cm long, though most of the ends are now broken off.

Overall there are some 300 strands of hair in the wig, each strand containing about 400 hairs. The hairs seem to have been attached to the foundation as follows: all the hair was coated with beeswax and resin, and about 2.5 cm of each strand was looped around the foundation and pressed back into the wax on the strand. A thin sub-strand was wound around this to ensure good attachment. As beeswax melts between 62 and 65° C, this method of fixing should have been more than adequate in Egypt.

A number of wigs have been found in Egypt. This example is perhaps the most famous, but false braids are known from the Predynastic Period, and several wigs and boxes have been found in Twelfth Dynasty tombs at Lisht. Other New Kingdom wigs include that of Merit (wife of Kha, Eighteenth Dynasty) from Deir el-Medina (now in Turin), which is longer and structurally less complex. It would appear that women's wigs were less complex than those worn by men – could this mean that men wore wigs on only very special occasions?

Egyptologists normally interpret most hairstyles shown in painting and sculpture as showing wigs. If this was indeed the case, and wigs were regularly worn for special occasions, then there must have been a considerable number in use. However, it would perhaps be naïve to take representations of festive formal garb shown in tomb paintings (such as those of Nebamun, pages 170–3) as accurate representations of actual festivals. Wigs may also have a symbolic purpose: there are a number of literary allusions in which hair and wigs are evoked in a sexual context – one of the best known is in the seduction scene in the literary text known as the *Tale of the Two Brothers* (Papyrus BM EA 10183). In Egyptian thought sexual activity and rebirth after death were closely linked, and the presence of a wig in a burial might thus be an allusion to hopes for rebirth, as well as representing the inclusion of precious possessions in the tomb.

Wooden stool

New Kingdom, perhaps mid-late
Eighteenth Dynasty, *c.* 1400-1300 BC

Provenance unknown, but perhaps
from Thebes

Details of acquisition unknown

Ebony and ivory

Height: 37.5 cm

EA 2472

THE ELABORATE NATURE of this stool, perhaps one of the finest surviving examples from ancient Egypt, suggests it was made for an elite official. It once had a deeply concave seat made of leather glued onto the frame, perhaps used together with a cushion. Similar though simpler stools appear in paintings from the tomb of Nebamun in the British Museum (see EA 37984, pages 172–3). The cylindrical legs are incised and inlaid with small pieces of ivory in lotus petal and drop shapes. The braces between the legs end in ivory ferrules, to cover the joins of the wood. The upper parts of the legs bear an inlaid pattern in ivory of lotus petals and drop shapes. The lower legs look as though they were turned on a lathe: they taper and then flare out again and have a ring decoration. It has been suggested that some other stool legs of the New Kingdom in the British Museum may have been produced with simple turning equipment, but this has also been queried; the first pictorial evidence for the practice comes from much later, in the early Ptolemaic Period (the tomb of Petosiris at Tuna el-Gebel).

The ferrule at the end of each stretcher, concealing the joint with the leg, is in the shape of a papyrus head. The contrast between the dark wood and the light-coloured inlays is particularly effective. The stretchers and braces are also made of ivory.

A similar example, although not quite so elaborate, was found in the tomb of Kha, the foreman of the workmen at Deir el-Medina in the reign of Amenhotep III (now in the Museo Egizio di Torino). Turin also has an unprovenanced stool with similar decoration to this one, but painted rather than inlaid.

The Egyptians acquired ebony from Nubia in the south, but stools exactly like this are sometimes depicted among goods brought as tribute to the king by Nubians. Although the use of stools was widespread in Egypt during the Eighteenth Dynasty, the workmanship evident in this example and the expensive materials used suggest that it belonged to an important individual. The poor preservation of domestic remains in Egypt, in contrast to the excellent potential for survival in funerary contexts, makes it certain that this stool was found in a tomb. It is not clear whether such objects were domestic items of the owner's, subsequently placed in his tomb, or were specially made for the burial. Whatever the case, the soul of the deceased was thought to need furnishings in the afterlife.

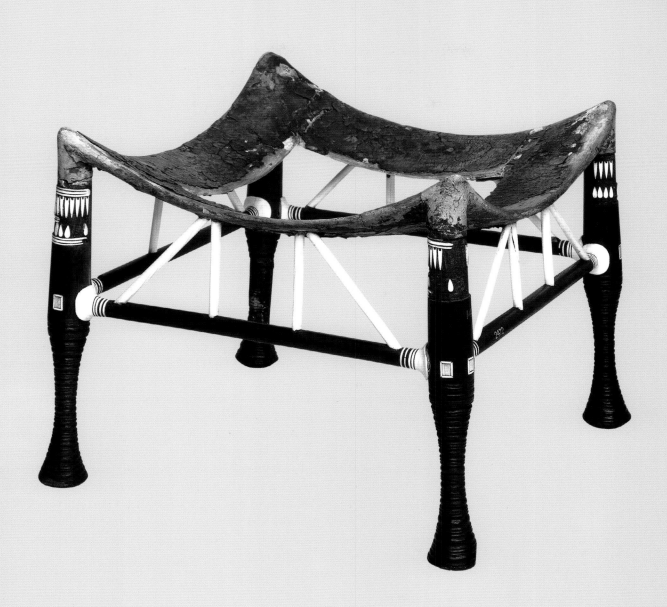

The London Medical Papyrus

New Kingdom, perhaps later
Eighteenth Dynasty, *c*.1300 BC

Provenance unknown

Details of acquisition unknown

Ink on papyrus

The complete papyrus was 210 cm
long, 17 cm average height (now in
two frames)

EA 10059

EGYPTIAN TEXTS concerned with healing are of two main types: those which deal with illnesses and injuries in a way which can be related to a modern medical perspective, and those which handle them using religious and magical means. Few fall exclusively into the first category, and the best-known example is the Edwin Smith Papyrus, now in New York, which deals primarily with fractures and similar injuries. The London Medical Papyrus falls into the second group.

Medical papyri of this type are among the hardest Egyptian texts to understand, because of their difficult medical and magical terminology. They usually consist of a series of magical spells or prescriptions against particular ailments, which can rarely be identified with any certainty. The contents of the London Papyrus can be grouped into spells against skin complaints (two groups), eye complaints (two groups), bleeding (especially miscarriage), burns, and a final hymn concerning the image of the sun-god Re.

Here is an example of a spell to deal with a burn: 'Another spell for a burn on the first day. Your son Horus has burnt himself in the desert within a place where there is no water. Water is in my mouth. Nile flood is between my thighs. Herewith I come to extinguish the fire. Flow out, burn! This incantation is to be spoken over the milk of a woman who has given birth to a boy; resin cat's hair. To be placed on the burn' (col. X, 14–XI, 2).

Thus the ailment is described and a similar injury to a deity is mentioned. The text asserts the speaker's ability to cure the problem, and a remedy to work in conjunction with the spell is proposed. Some of this is clearly superstitious folk medicine, but some natural ingredients prescribed might have had beneficial side effects (such as the antiseptic effect of urine, which is often mentioned).

A particularly interesting selection of spells relating to skin complaints includes words to be spoken in foreign languages. One specifically mentions 'the language of Crete' and refers to the treatment of 'the Asiatic disease', which has been tentatively identified as leprosy (col. VII, 4). It is not yet possible to translate the Cretan text, but we can obtain some idea of the consonants used from the Egyptian practice of writing foreign words in a syllabic form. Some of the other spells contain texts in a Northwest Semitic language, perhaps a mixture of Phoenician and Aramaic. These spells are among the earliest attested examples of these languages, and illustrate the greater contact between Egypt and the rest of the Mediterranean world in the New Kingdom.

Column X

Column VII

Cult image of Amun

Perhaps New Kingdom, early
Nineteenth Dynasty, or Third
Intermediate Period, *c.* 1295–750 BC

From Karnak

Purchased at the sale of the third Salt
collection in 1835

Silver and gold

Height: 21.3 cm

EA 60006

THIS STATUETTE DEPICTS AMUN, paramount god of Thebes and supreme state god of the New Kingdom and later. He is shown in human form, wearing a cap similar to the base of the red crown of Lower Egypt, topped by two feathers with a sun-disc at the bottom. This is his most common manner of depiction, although he is also represented as a ram (compare the emblem held by the king on the statue of Sety II, EA 26, pages 224–5). His divine status is also marked by the beard with a curled tip, worn only by deities and the transfigured dead. The statue is made of silver, with the kilt, collar, and feathers enhanced by an overlay of gold leaf.

Very few other statues of silver and gold have survived, no doubt largely due to their value, which led to their reuse or recycling. The figure's opulence suggests that this is either a very lavish votive offering or perhaps a cult image, placed in a shrine in the temple of Karnak, and tended by priests during the daily rituals of feeding, cleaning, and clothing the god. Few similar cult images are known: there is a gold Amun, perhaps from the Twenty-second Dynasty, in New York (MMA 26.7.1412), and a silver falcon-headed figure in Kyoto. Study of the latter suggests it might be from the Ramesside Period, and the similarity of the statues, particularly in the rendering of the torso, is the reason that the silver Amun is sometimes given a Nineteenth Dynasty date. The alternative, later date is suggested by the solar disc on the crown, which is almost unknown before the Third Intermediate Period. Although the actual size of the principal cult image of Amun is unknown, it is reasonable to think that it would have been larger than this figure, which might have resided in a subsidiary shrine. For comparison, the Kyoto figure is 41.9 cm high and weighs no less than 16.5 kg.

The discovery of this statuette in the Karnak complex is described by Giovanni d'Athanasi, Henry Salt's agent: 'a rich store of valuables [was opened] to our view – amongst which were several statues of bronze and stone of various shapes and dimensions, and one of silver, nine inches in height, representing the God of Thebes'. Clearly d'Athanasi came across a small cache, a concealed group of disused statues which, rather than being melted down or reused, were buried in the sacred ground of the complex in which they had stood. Better-known examples include the massive cache discovered in the early twentieth century in front of the seventh pylon at Karnak, or the small cache of statues found in the Luxor temple in 1989.

Bust of Ramesses II, the 'Younger Memnon'

New Kingdom, Nineteenth Dynasty,
c. 1250 BC

From Thebes, the Ramesseum

Gift of Johann Ludwig Burckhardt and
Henry Salt in 1817

Granodiorite

Height: 267 cm

EA 19

ONE OF THE LARGEST PIECES of Egyptian sculpture in the Museum, this fragment was retrieved from the mortuary temple of Ramesses II at Thebes, the so-called Ramesseum. The king's names appear on the back pillar. It was originally part of the southern statue of a pair which flanked the entrance into the temple's hypostyle (pillared) hall. The lower part of the statue was identified and restored to its place in the Ramesseum in the late 1990s.

The sculptor(s) of this colossal statue varied the usual convention, angling the eyes down slightly so that the statue appears to gaze at those looking at it, as opposed to the straight-ahead pose normal in Egyptian sculpture. The craftsmen also used the lighter vein of stone here for the head of the statue, thus deliberately emphasizing it.

The statue has been known for many years; it was first mentioned by Diodorus Siculus in the first century BC, and was later noticed by Frederik Norden, a early traveller to Egypt from Denmark, in the eighteenth century AD. Norden's description records that the statue had fallen but was still intact, but by 1799, when Napoleon's expedition visited the temple, the bust had become detached from the base. When the great rush to obtain antiquities from Egypt started some fifteen years later, the Swiss explorer Burckhardt claimed it and arranged for it to be acquired by the British Consul-General, Henry Salt, who later presented it to the British Museum. Salt engaged the Italian former circus strong man, Giovanni Belzoni, to retrieve the bust. It took Belzoni the best part of six months in 1816 to transport the statue to Cairo, thanks to problems with the local administration and with others who would have liked to acquire it. Belzoni's account of his difficulties, both political and technical, is fascinating. The bust finally arrived in London in 1817 and was put on display in the Egyptian Room in the relatively new Townley Gallery.

For many people, this was the first example of large-scale Egyptian sculpture they had seen, and it produced many favourable reactions, especially when it is remembered that at that time Egyptian culture was considered far inferior to that of Greece and Rome. The nickname 'Younger Memnon' was apparently given to the piece by early travellers; Memnon was a mythical Ethiopian king who came to the aid of Troy, was slain by Achilles, and was rendered immortal by Zeus. In classical times, the two statues at the entrance of the mortuary temple of Amenhotep III were associated with this hero, and the Ramesseum seems to have been known as the 'Memnonium'; the association was transferred to this statue.

The Abydos king-list

New Kingdom, Nineteenth Dynasty,
c. 1250 BC

From Abydos, temple of Ramesses II

Acquired from Jean François Mimaut
in 1837

Limestone

Length: 370 cm

EA 117

THE TWO MAIN TEMPLES that survive at Abydos, the cult centre of Osiris, are memorial temples to two of the most prominent kings of the Nineteenth Dynasty, Sety I and his son Ramesses II. The decoration of both temples included a list of kings of Egypt. That of Sety I is complete and is still in the temple, while the five remaining fragments of the list of Ramesses II were excavated by Bankes in 1818, and in 1837 taken to France by the French Consul-General in Egypt, J.F. Mimaut; his collection was acquired for the British Museum in the same year.

As far as can be discerned, the two lists were very similar, although the list of Ramesses may have been physically shorter, with more rows to accommodate the same number of royal names. A figure of Ramesses II would have stood at the right side of the scene, perhaps with a son. The royal figures were probably depicted making offerings to their predecessors and to Osiris, partly preserved at the left. The list's surviving part contains sections of three rows of cartouches. The upper two are those of earlier kings, while the bottom row gives the two alternating names of Ramesses II.

The upper row names several kings who belong between the known rulers of the Sixth Dynasty and those of the later Eleventh Dynasty, as is clear from Sety's list, and are usually assumed to be the relatively short-lived kings of the Seventh and Eighth Dynasties. The Sety list omits the kings of the Ninth, Tenth and early Eleventh Dynasties. The middle row names kings from Senwosret II (Twelfth Dynasty) to Ramesses II, but omits Sebekneferu, the last ruler of the Twelfth Dynasty (a woman), all the kings of the Second Intermediate Period, the female pharaoh Hatshepsut, and the Eighteenth Dynasty monarchs between Amenhotep III and Horemheb (the Amarna Period).

The importance of both Abydos lists is twofold. Most of the Seventh and Eighth Dynasty kings are not recorded elsewhere, but of perhaps even greater importance is the light these lists shed on who were regarded as legitimate kings. That it should omit the kings of the Intermediate Periods is hardly surprising, but all female rulers are missing too, and the list confirms the view that the Ramessides regarded the Amarna kings as best expunged from history.

Such king-lists were not compiled to present an objective history to subsequent generations. Rather, their context is a temple which glorified the king and the deities. By showing themselves worshipping their predecessors, Sety and Ramesses were stressing how well they fitted into the age-old kingship of Egypt, thus enhancing their legitimacy. The list tells us as much about Egyptian ideas of history as it does about their sequence of kings.

Ostrakon bearing an attendance record of workmen

New Kingdom, Nineteenth Dynasty,
year 40 of Ramesses II, *c.* 1239 BC

Said to be from the Valley of the Kings

Purchased as part of the first Salt
collection in 1823

Limestone

Height: 38.5 cm

EA 5634

THIS LARGE OSTRAKON (flake of stone used for writing) bears writing on both sides. At the top of the first side is the date 'year 40'; as the handwriting can only be from the Ramesside Period, this must refer to the fortieth year of Ramesses II's reign. In addition, many of the persons mentioned here are known from other documents of this period. The hieratic texts are in red and black ink. Each line begins with the name of one of forty individuals, followed by a number of dates, and above each date is entered an observation in red. These men belonged to the gang who worked on the construction and decoration of the royal tomb in the Valley of the Kings, and who lived in the village of Deir el-Medina.

It is clear from the contents that the list is a summary of workmen's absences from duty, with the red comments giving explanations for a particular date. Many of the entries consist of the word 'sick', on two occasions qualified by the phrase 'of the eyes', and there is another example of a man absent after being stung by a scorpion. One man was often 'with' another workman, and presumably served as a doctor. Three workmen were away for two to three days dealing with the death of a female relative, while another was absent bandaging (less likely mummifying) his colleague Hormose. Some five absences can be associated with purification rituals surrounding childbirth. Far more are linked with men doing work for the foreman or the scribe elsewhere; the work is not described here, but other sources indicate that this could have been making objects for or working on that person's tomb, an activity which may have been illegal. Others were away doing work for themselves. The excuse 'drinking with Khonsu' may refer to a celebration associated with a festival, as is 'libating'.

Rather than being compiled on a day-by-day basis on one ostrakon, it is thought that the scribes of the tomb would compile daily notes on smaller flakes of stone and then write more formal accounts for the administration records. This ostrakon probably covered a period of 280 days, of which only 70 days seem to have been working days. The Egyptian 'week' consisted of ten days, with a normal 'weekend' of two days, so it seems that the workmen were probably working less than half the time. Other sources indicate that working for only half a period of time was not unusual, and, after forty years of work on the royal tomb, it is very likely that it was all but finished. Ramesses II of course went on to reign for a further twenty-seven years; there is plenty of evidence that work on his tomb was cut back, and that workers were moved, for example, to the tombs of queens in the Valley of the Queens.

Votive tunic

New Kingdom, possibly Nineteenth
Dynasty, *c.* 1275 BC

From Thebes, perhaps Deir el-Bahari

Acquired in 1906

Coarse linen with painted design

Length: 34.3 cm

EA 43071

THIS TUNIC, with one long sleeve attached, bears a painted image of the goddess Hathor, shown as a cow emerging from the mountain of the West. Hieroglyphs above the cow describe her as 'Hathor foremost of Thebes, lady of heaven, mistress of the gods'. Around the animal's neck is a necklace with a sistrum (an emblem of Hathor) attached; between the horns are two feathers and a solar disc. The first line of the inscription below gives the title 'mistress of the house' and the name (unfortunately unclear but ending in '-imentet') of the woman who dedicated the tunic; the second line repeats the name and epithets of Hathor.

It has been described as a child's tunic, but it is more likely that it was specially produced as a votive offering to the goddess. Many types of votive objects were deposited in temples all over Egypt as gifts expressing devotion to deities, who, it was hoped, would in turn favour the donor. This and similar textiles may have been donated by women to the cult, perhaps accompanying specific prayers for children or successful childbirth. However, none of the inscriptions make reference to this. Another suggestion is that the tunics may have been used to clothe divine images; there is some evidence from the titles of the persons named on them that only those connected with the Hathor cult presented such garments. They presumably had to be stored carefully in the temples to maintain and protect the decoration and efficacy of the object.

Hathor was a popular deity with associations ranging from joy to music and dance, and was also one of the few state gods to whom ordinary people could appeal. Her cult was very prominent on the West Bank at Thebes, near the temples of Deir el-Bahari. The motif of the cow emerging from the western mountain, associated with burial and rebirth, is extremely common at Thebes. The rock-cut Hathor shrine containing a statue of the goddess as a cow, which was discovered in 1906 between the Middle and New Kingdom temples, embodies this idea in three dimensions (Cairo, JE 38574-5).

The tunic is said to come from Thebes. Around the time that it was acquired by the Museum, the Egypt Exploration Fund's excavations in the area of the temple of Nebhepetre Mentuhotep II at Deir el-Bahari were revealing a number of cloths and other votive textiles (as well as many other votive objects) related to the later cult of Hathor, practised there from at least the New Kingdom onwards. The Museum acquired several objects from these excavations. It thus seems possible that this tunic might have been discovered in a contemporary illicit excavation carried out at the same site.

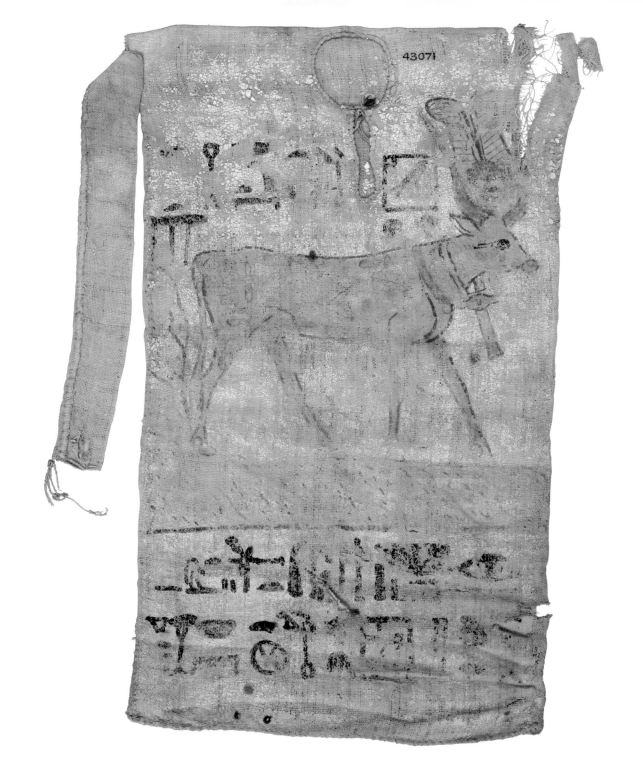

Statue of Khaemwaset

New Kingdom, Nineteenth Dynasty,
reign of Ramesses II, *c.* 1250 BC

From Asyut, but almost certainly
originally from Abydos

Gift of Samuel Sharpe in 1866;
previously in the possession of E.A.
Diamandidi and C. Cuny

Conglomerate

Height: 138 cm

EA 947

IN THE COURSE of his long reign Ramesses II had many sons, the best-known of whom is his fourth son, Khaemwaset. This statue shows Khaemwaset wearing a kilt and a short wig with vertical striations. He carries a standard in each hand. That in his left hand is in the shape of the symbol ('fetish') of the town of Abydos; that in his right is damaged at the top but originally bore three figures. As the central one appears to have been mummiform it probably represents Osiris, with the other two depicting his spouse Isis and son Horus, the triad of Abydos.

The text around the base is a prayer to the god Atum, while that on the top of the base refers to Khaemwaset's setting up of the statue in the Thinite nome (the province in which Abydos is located). The two inscriptions on the back pillar, which begin on its flat back and extend onto its sides, relate to Osiris, and include prayers and offering formulae. Many of the expressions in the text are unclear and enigmatic. The names of Ramesses II appear on the two standards; in one case he is called 'beloved of the Thinite Nome' and in the other 'beloved of Osiris foremost of the Westerners'.

It is thus clear that the statue was set up in a temple in the precinct of Osiris (at Abydos), but it is unknown whether it was found at Asyut or just spotted there for the first time in the collection of Dr Cuny. A photograph of the statue in his house taken by Teynard in 1851–2 must be one of the earliest photographs of an object now in the Museum. Cuny was a French physician who was then the chief medical officer in Middle Egypt; the writer Gustave Flaubert is also said to have seen this statue.

The object is an example of the so-called 'standard bearer' statues, a type of representation which appears in the course of the Eighteenth Dynasty and is most commonly found in the Nineteenth. These statues are thought to be related to the cult of the royal *ka* spirit. The execution of the statue in a stone with a very difficult vein of pebbly conglomerate shows the skill with which sculptors could work even the most problematic material.

Early in his life Khaemwaset was attached to the cult service of Ptah, the god of Memphis, and spent most of his time in the area. He is renowned as being perhaps the 'first Egyptologist', as he visited the pyramids of Giza and Saqqara, clearing and renewing parts of a number of them and leaving large inscriptions to this effect. He was also responsible for work on the burial places of the Apis bulls at the Serapeum, and may even have been buried there himself. In later times he was recalled as a magician, as attested in the Demotic Setne-Khaemwaset stories (one of which is in the British Museum, Papyrus EA 10822).

The door of a tomb

New Kingdom, perhaps early
Nineteenth Dynasty, *c.* 1285 BC

From Thebes, perhaps the area of
Dra Abul Naga

Purchased as part of the first Salt
collection in 1823

Sycomore fig wood

Height: 204 cm

EA 705

THIS DOOR BELONGED TO THE TOMB of a high priest of Amun named Khonsuhotep, and is made of six planks of wood fixed together with nails and supports on the back. A large protrusion survives at the bottom for insertion into the lower door socket. In the centre is an incised depiction of the owner adoring and offering to Osiris and Hathor of the West, with the outline filled with white paint. This scene makes it evident that it came from a tomb rather than a house. Nothing more is known about Khonsuhotep.

Very few Egyptian doors have survived, because of the poor survival of organic material in domestic contexts, the reuse of the tombs, and the high value of wood, which was not a common commodity. Doors in Egypt usually were made of a single leaf, with protrusions at the top and the bottom which fitted into sockets in the doorway on which the door pivoted; very similar doors are still in use in modern Egyptian villages. More often than not the principal traces of their existence are stone sockets in temples. Tomb doors are particularly rare, and few traces of sockets have been noted. Most doorways were probably closed with single-leaved doors, although larger doorways (as in temples) were probably made of two leaves and secured with bolts.

The best surviving tomb door is from the tomb of Sennedjem at Deir el-Medina (Cairo, JE 27303). This closed the doorway between the shaft and the burial chamber, and is thus smaller than Khonsuhotep's door (117 cm), which without doubt sealed the entrance to his tomb chapel, which would have been much grander. Sennedjem's door was also decorated, but in colour, with scenes of him and his family worshipping Osiris and the West, and an additional scene of the worship of Ptah-Sokar-Osiris and Isis. Perhaps bright colours were used because this was an internal door, to complement the bright painting of the burial chamber.

EA 705 was collected for the Earl of Belmore in his travels in Egypt in 1817–18 by Giovanni d'Athanasi. Belmore presented it to Salt, and it came to the British Museum as part of the latter's first collection:

'Next morning, the 14th of January [1818], we proceeded, in company with Mr. Salt, to view the antiquities …; one of the most curious and interesting articles which he had discovered, was an ancient door made of what appears to be common deal. … This ancient relic was found near one of the tombs that have been cut in the southern aspect of the mountain above the village of Gornou, a little to the west of the road that leads into the valley of the tombs of the kings … The noble Earl made a present of it to Mr Salt, and it is now in the British Museum.' (Dr Richardson, physician to the Earl of Belmore, who travelled to Egypt with him.)

The burial assemblage of Henutmehyt

New Kingdom, early to middle
Nineteenth Dynasty, *c.* 1250 BC

From Thebes

Acquired between 1905 and 1913

Wood: the coffins are a mixture of
cedar of Lebanon and sycomore.

OUTER COFFIN

Height: 206 cm

INNER COFFIN

Height: 187 cm

MUMMY-COVER

Height: 173 cm

All three EA 48001

CANOPIC CHEST AND JARS

Chest height: 48.2 cm

Jar height: 40.6 cm

EA 51813

HENUTMEHYT WAS BURIED in Thebes during the Nineteenth Dynasty, about 1250 BC. She held the title of 'singer of Amun in Karnak', which is extremely common in New Kingdom Thebes. Judging from the richness of her burial, she was an important woman, and it is possible that someone in her family could have had connections at the highest level. Little else is known about her. Henutmehyt was quite a common name in the Nineteenth Dynasty, but the style of the burial equipment makes the long reign of Ramesses II perhaps the most likely date. Henutmehyt's tomb seems to have been found by clandestine diggers in about 1904, and the objects came to London over the next few years.

The assemblage consists of two wooden coffins, a mummy-cover (opposite, all EA 48001), four magic bricks (EA 41544-7), a canopic chest and jars (below left, EA 51813), four shabti boxes with shabtis (EA 41548-51), and a box containing mummified food (EA 51812). The Museum of Reading owns a funerary papyrus, on loan to the British Museum.

The outer coffin (opposite, left) is painted and gilded, and provides a splendid image of Henutmehyt, wearing a huge wig, with gilded bands and a lotus (lily) flower on top of her head. The lotus symbolizes the idea of rebirth and new life. Henutmehyt's face and upper body are gilded to emphasize that she is now a divine being; the remainder of the coffin is painted yellow in imitation of gold. The sky-goddess Nut spreads her wings protectively across the front of the coffin. Vertical and horizontal bands divide the remainder of the lid into compartments which are occupied by figures of the Sons of Horus (Imsety, Hapy, Duamutef, and Qebehsenuef) and the goddesses Isis and Nephthys, all of whom protect Henutmehyt. On either side of the coffin is a row of gods with Thoth at the start and end; two of the sons of Horus are shown on each side, along with Anubis.

The lid and sides of the inner coffin (opposite, centre) are completely gilded. The decorative programme is very similar to that of the outer coffin. The underside of this coffin is covered with a thick layer of resin, which must have been poured in after the burial was assembled, causing the two coffins to adhere to one another. Embedded in this resin, itself an important symbol of rebirth, are a number of grains of barley and wheat. It is most unusual to find these, but their presence should perhaps be associated with the Osiris beds and corn Osirises found in this period and later, in which grains germinating in the tomb evoke the symbolism of the new life granted by Osiris. Remains of the mummy are embedded in more resin poured into

the inner coffin. The rest of the mummy has not survived, and it might have been destroyed when the coffins were opened.

The mummy was covered by a two-piece gilded wooden mummy-cover (page 215, right). The iconography of the upper part is very similar to the upper parts of the coffins. The openwork lower part consists of a series of images of Henutmehyt worshipping deities, including Anubis and the four Sons of Horus. The reddish colouring of the gilding is probably due to tarnishing of the metal.

The canopic jars (illustrated on page 214) have animal and human heads. They were painted black and placed in a two-lidded box.

The shabti boxes (one is illustrated opposite) contain forty brightly painted figures. The magic bricks (below), made of unbaked mud, were almost certainly placed in niches in the burial chamber to protect the mummy. Each is decorated with the appropriate magical spells to protect the deceased, with an amuletic figure inset into it: a mummiform statuette, a *djed* pillar, a reed for a torch, and a figure of Anubis. X-rays of the food in the wooden box have identified it as consisting of four linen-wrapped ducks and some joints of meat, probably goat. The papyrus seems to have been placed in the tomb as a sheet and not rolled up, although there is some evidence that there may have been more sheets: Budge claims that the mummy was wrapped in the papyrus, which cannot be confirmed. The text on the sheet is that of Spell 100 from the *Book of the Dead*.

The papyrus of Any

New Kingdom, Nineteenth Dynasty,
c. 1275 BC

From Thebes

Gift of E.A. Wallis Budge in 1888

Papyrus

Average height of a sheet: c. 42 cm.

EA 10470

MANUSCRIPTS of the *Book of the Dead* come no finer than the papyrus of Any. It was acquired in Thebes in 1887–8 by Budge, who describes how he was taken at the dead of night to its place of storage. He claims that it was found in a niche in a burial chamber, although, as is often the case with Budge's later accounts of his purchases, this should not be taken too literally, as he acquired objects from dealers for whom truth was not necessarily essential. No tomb of Any has ever been located. On its accession by the British Museum, the papyrus was unrolled and found to be about 23.5 m long.

The *Book of the Dead* was intended as a text to be buried with the deceased. It would, through its presence and its spells, provide the dead with special knowledge and magical powers to ensure a safe passage into the afterlife. The origins of the text, which comprises almost 200 spells, not all of which appear in each manuscript, are in the Coffin Texts (see the coffin of Gua, EA 30839, pages 81–3). The *Book of the Dead*, called in Egyptian the *Book of Going Forth by Day*, took its basic form during the Seventeenth Dynasty, and remained broadly the same down to the Roman Period in basic content. By the early Nineteenth Dynasty, when Any's papyrus was made, illustrations (termed 'vignettes') accompanied the texts. Any's vignettes are probably the finest known, although he was not a particularly elevated individual, judging from his main title of 'royal scribe', and this papyrus would have been very expensive. His name is written in a different hand, and so it is likely that this was a ready-made product to which the name of the purchaser was added.

THE JUDGEMENT OF THE DEAD (SHEET 3)

The judgement of the dead (opposite, above) was crucial to the New Kingdom concept of the hereafter. On the left, Any and his wife enter the judgement area. In the centre are the scales used for weighing the heart, attended by Anubis; the process is also observed by Any's *ba* soul (the human-headed bird), two birth-goddesses, and a male figure representing his destiny. On the left pan of the scales is Any's heart, being weighed against a feather, the symbol of *maat,* the established order of things – in this context meaning what is right. The Egyptians believed that the heart was the seat of reasoning, and where knowledge of good and bad deeds was stored. If the heart and feather did not balance, then the deceased was condemned to non-existence, and was consumed by the ferocious 'devourer', the strange beast shown at the right of this scene. Once the judgement was completed successfully (as ensured by the papyrus), the deceased was declared 'true of voice' or 'justified', a standard epithet applied to dead individuals. The process is recorded by the ibis-headed deity Thoth. Above are twelve deities who supervise the judgement.

Sheet 3

Sheet 35

LIFE IN THE AFTERWORLD (SHEET 35)

The scenes in the left part of this frame (page 219, below) accompany Spell 110 and illustrate the world which Any entered after the successful judgement. In the next world, the deceased was expected to undertake agricultural work in the Field of Offering and Field of Rushes. The scene schematically renders areas of land surrounded by water. Any is shown offering to three deities of the ennead (group of nine gods) at the top, and then paddling his boat across the Lake of Offerings. He is also shown worshipping the Western Falcon and the Heron of Plenty. He is depicted reaping, winnowing, and ploughing below. Moored at the edge of the water at the bottom, and shown with a snake's head, is the boat of Wennefer (a name for the god Osiris).

The right-hand section gives part of Spell 148, which makes provision for a spirit in the realm of the dead. Any is shown adoring the sun-god Re, shown as a falcon-headed mummy wearing a sun-disc. In fuller versions of the accompanying text, the deceased makes his claim for provisions based on his knowledge of the names of the seven celestial cows and their bull, shown at right, and of four steering oars of the sky (in the next frame).

HYMN TO OSIRIS (SHEET 2)

Sheet 1 of the papyrus is not as well preserved as sheet 2 (opposite, above) but shows Any and his wife Tutu adoring the sun-god Re. The image at the left of sheet 2 logically belongs with this previous text but also provides a link to the contents of this sheet. It shows the sun-disc (Re) being lifted up to the heavens by an *ankh* sign, and adored by two groups of baboons symbolic of the sunrise. The *ankh* is supported on the *djed* symbol of the god Osiris, and is a symbolic depiction of the rebirth of the sun from its overnight passage through the realms of the dead. The process is watched and protected by two figures representing Isis and Nephthys. The text to the right is a hymn to Osiris.

THE END OF THE PAPYRUS (SHEET 37)

The shrine at the left of this frame (opposite, below) contains the falcon-headed mummiform deity Sokar-Osiris, which actually belongs with the text of Spell 185 on the previous sheet. The remainder of the image shows an offering made to the hippopotamus deity Opet, who holds the symbols of life and flame for the deceased. She rests against the *sa*-amulet of protection. To the right Hathor emerges from the mountain of the West into the marshes of the valley, beside a small picture of Any's tomb. These images symbolize returning from the West (death) into life, the aim of the papyrus and the tomb itself.

Sheet 2

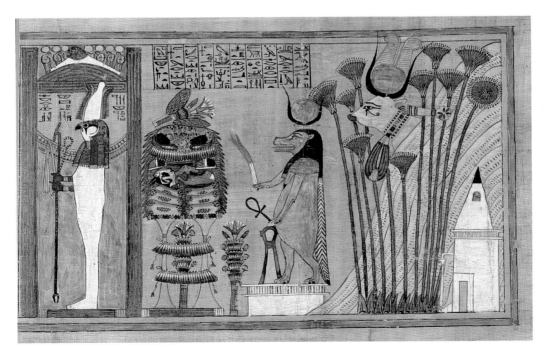

Sheet 37

Statue of Roy

New Kingdom, Nineteenth Dynasty,
c. 1220 BC

From Karnak, temple of Mut

Gift of King George III in 1802

Granodiorite

Height of the original fragment: 88 cm;
as restored, the height is 113 cm

EA 81

ROY IS SHOWN SQUATTING, wearing a long pleated robe with his arms folded on top of his knees. His head is represented in typical Ramesside fashion, with a somewhat oval face and an elaborate shoulder-length double wig. Below his arms is a large sistrum, a musical instrument sacred to the goddess Hathor. Doubtless he is presenting this to the goddess Mut, who, along with Amun-Re, is named in the inscription on the statue's back pillar. Two columns of inscription express similar wishes that these deities permit Roy's statues and name to remain forever in the temple. The object is of the type known as a block statue, which originated as a much simpler form (see EA 48, pages 134–5) but was then elaborated in the later Eighteenth and early Nineteenth Dynasties to indicate more of the features and clothing of the deceased. One result of these elaborations is that the large area for text seen on EA 48 was no longer available, and inscriptions had to be added elsewhere (as on the back pillar here, a feature not evident in earlier examples).

Roy, or Roma-Roy to give the longer version of his name (not on this statue), was the high priest of Amun in the later reign of Ramesses II, and may have survived into the time of his successor, Merenptah. He probably succeeded his brother Bakenkhonsu as high priest, for he is shown in the latter's tomb as the second priest of Amun. He clearly came from a priestly family, since his father, Roma, was also high priest. He was able to commission several statues of himself, four of which were found in Karnak (including this one) and one near his tomb on the West Bank at Thebes. He also usurped two statues of the vizier Mentuhotep from the early Twelfth Dynasty, and is known from other fragments and inscriptions. Roy was buried on the West Bank at Thebes in the area known as Dra Abul Naga, where there is a large and prominent group of tombs of Ramesside high priests; his tomb has the number TT 283.

The Theban high priest of Amun commanded great power in the city, since the cult of his deity was one of the main reasons for the importance of Thebes. He oversaw a large bureaucracy and was in charge of a considerable amount of wealth. At the end of the New Kingdom the high priests effectively ran Upper Egypt, and some of them even used the title of king.

The lower part of the statue is restored, and the upper fragment was discovered by Napoleon's expedition to Egypt during work in the temple of Mut at Karnak; it came to the British Museum after the Treaty of Alexandria in 1801.

Seated statue of Sety II

New Kingdom, Nineteenth Dynasty,
c. 1200-1194 BC

From Karnak, temple of Mut

Purchased as part of the first Salt
collection in 1823

Sandstone

Height: 164.7 cm

EA 26

THIS IS PERHAPS the most perfectly preserved royal statue in the Museum's collection, as only the muzzle of the ram's head held by the king and the head of the uraeus have been damaged. The statue was discovered by Belzoni in 1816, apparently in a cache with six Sekhmet statues in the temple of Mut, and passed into the collection of Henry Salt, for whom Belzoni was collecting antiquities. The statue was clearly one of Salt's favourite objects, and he sent it to England in the autumn of 1819, well in advance of the rest of the collection, no doubt to persuade the British Museum's Trustees to purchase his other objects.

The king is seated on a cubic throne with a small cushion at the rear. He wears a wig of a type favoured in the Nineteenth Dynasty, with long lappets framing the face, and a uraeus (cobra) on his brow; his kilt is pleated with a decorated waistband or belt, and there are sandals on his feet. On his knees he holds a ram's head, a symbol of the god Amun. Royal figures holding emblems such as this tend to stand, kneel, or prostrate themselves, as they are usually presenting the emblem to the deity, so a seated statue of this type is quite unusual.

The cartouche on the king's left shoulder gives the personal name 'Sety, beloved of Ptah', and that on the right his throne name, 'Usermaatre-meryamun'. Framing the sides of the throne is a 'block border' pattern, and at the bottom rear corners appears the *sematawy* emblem of the intertwined heraldic plants of Upper and Lower Egypt, symbolizing the unity of the two lands. The king's names and epithets are also inscribed on the back pillar and around the base. It is intriguing that the quality of the carving of the inscriptions and decoration does not match that of the remainder of the object: note the relative roughness of the block pattern on the throne and the awkwardness of the hieroglyphs.

Sety II was the short-lived successor of his father Merenptah, and was buried in Tomb 15 in the Valley of the Kings. There may have been civil conflict during his reign, since there seems to have been a rival ruler, Amenmesse, in the southern part of Egypt, who also owned a tomb in the Valley of the Kings (KV 10). To the tourist, Sety's best known building work is the triple barque shrine in the first court of the temple of Karnak, but he also constructed the first pylon of the Mut temple; it seems likely from the provenance of this statue that it was part of the same building project.

The Great Harris Papyrus

New Kingdom, reign of Ramesses IV,
c. 1200 BC

From Thebes, probably Deir el-Medina

Acquired from Miss Selima Harris
in 1872

Papyrus

Average height of sheets: *c.* 45.8 cm

EA 9999

IN 1855 A.C. HARRIS, a British merchant and commissariat official in Alexandria, purchased this papyrus. He is said to have acquired it in Thebes from local inhabitants who were digging for antiquities. Descriptions of the discovery of this and a number of other papyri 'behind the temple of Medinet Habu' suggest a location on the eastern side of the valley of Deir el-Medina; it is possible that several documents from the temple, the centre of the administration of the West Bank, were buried together at the end of the New Kingdom.

At 42 metres in length, the Great Harris Papyrus, or Papyrus Harris I, is one of the longest papyri surviving from ancient Egypt. The text relates to the reign of Ramesses III (*c.* 1184–1153 BC). Written mostly in hieratic, it is divided into five sections. The first three record the king's donations to the major gods and temples of Thebes, Heliopolis, and Memphis. Each is preceded by an illustration of the king with the gods of that area. Thus the first section shows the triad of Thebes (Amun, Mut, and Khonsu), the second Re-Horakhty, Atum, Iusaas, and Hathor (Heliopolis), and the third (sheet 43, opposite) Ptah, Sekhmet, and Nefertum (Memphis). In each section, the king recites what he has done for the deity in a particular temple, including offerings and temple-building. Some items can be reasonably assumed to be actual things the king did, but others are more ideological in nature, such as bringing the god the 'nine bows', the traditional enemies of Egypt. The detailed lists which follow the recitations show that the amounts were colossal, for example 309,950 sacks of grain and large quantities of metals and semi-precious stones from one list relating to Thebes alone.

The fourth section deals with several minor temples, and another royal recital plus more detailed lists. The last section is often called the 'historical section' or 'discourse to mankind'. This recounts events of the reign, beginning with the start of the Twentieth Dynasty, a time of of chaos that was ended by the accession of Ramesses' father Sethnakht. Other passages cover Ramesses' campaigns against the Sea Peoples, desert dwellers, and Libyans, and several peacetime expeditions. It ends with a description of the golden age that the king has brought to Egypt, and then describes the passing of the king and the accession of Ramesses IV. The entire section is written in a very propagandistic tone; it is essential not to take it at face value, since its purpose was to glorify the king rather than present a modern historical narrative. Only positive events are mentioned, so the possible harem conspiracy which may have ended his life does not appear. Nonetheless, the text contains many important pointers to the history of the reign.

Sheet 78 (illustrated this page, left) shows accounts of expeditions to Timna and Serabit el-Khadim, and the beginning of the 'golden age' text.

Face from the sarcophagus of Ramesses VI

New Kingdom, Twentieth Dynasty,
c. 1140 BC

From Tomb KV 6 in the Valley of
the Kings

Purchased as part of the first Salt
collection in 1823

Conglomerate

Height: 83.8 cm

EA 140

NEW KINGDOM KINGS were buried in magnificent stone sarcophagi – in some cases more than one, as with Merenptah, who had four sarcophagi. Several Eighteenth Dynasty examples have survived intact, but many of the later ones are broken. Substantial parts of the lower sections of Ramesses VI's sarcophagus still lie in his burial chamber. This fragment gives one of the few known three-dimensional representations of the successors of Ramesses III, and is extremely well carved, showing the king with the conventional divine beard of a deceased person. Ramesses V (*c.* 1147–1143 BC) was actually responsible for the commencement of the cutting of this tomb, which was finished by Ramesses VI (*c.* 1143–1136 BC); it is unknown whether Ramesses VI removed the body of Ramesses V, or if the two kings shared the tomb. Some rivalry is possible between the two, as Ramesses V was a grandson of Ramesses III, and Ramesses VI was the former's uncle.

The tomb of Ramesses VI seems to have been robbed shortly after his burial. Reports which date at the latest from Ramesses IX's reign report the interrogation of five robbers who took four days to break into the tomb. Whether these robbers broke the sarcophagus is unclear – it would have taken a considerable degree of force to do so, and it would not have been strictly necessary in order to to rob the burial. However, it has been noted that streaks of oil on the sarcophagus might indicate that the damage happened before these oils had time to set, perhaps not long after the burial.

This royal tomb has lain open since antiquity, as indicated by the various graffiti in Greek and Latin, and the sarcophagus was still lying there in pieces when this fragment was collected in the late 1810s. In 2001–2004 an American-led conservation project reassembled as many parts of the sarcophagus as were available. The base, though severely damaged, could be reconstructed to the level of where the lid rested. More than half the lid is missing, but a replica of the head sent from the British Museum has been incorporated into the reconstruction.

Ramesses IX with a prince and a vizier

New Kingdom, Twentieth Dynasty, *c.* 1120 BC

Said to be from the Valley of the Kings

Purchased as part of the first Salt collection in 1823

Limestone

Length: 76 cm

EA 5620

MOST OSTRAKA are relatively small, as perhaps to be expected from flakes of stone from quarrying work, but there are some notably large exceptions, of which this is an example. It bears a drawing showing Ramesses IX (*c.* 1126–1108) on the left, receiving two men. The one wearing a sidelock is the crown prince and the other is the vizier, to judge from his high-waisted robe. The drawing is accompanied by columns of hieroglyphs.

Much can be learned about this ostrakon from comparison with the temple scenes from which it apparently was derived. Two parallel texts have been identified, a very fragmentary one in the small temple of Ramesses III at Karnak and a much more complete version in the same king's mortuary temple at Medinet Habu. In the latter, Ramesses III is shown reviewing prisoners and the spoils of war from his Libyan campaign, and the text consists of a royal address to the crown prince and two viziers, and a response by the crown prince in the form of a paean of praise of the king. The rest of the scene is an enumeration of the spoils.

The text of the British Museum ostrakon is in two main parts. The first twelve columns are a speech by the crown prince, more or less repeating the equivalent text from Medinet Habu. It compares the king to the sun-god Re and stresses how mankind cannot live without the king, the son of Amun, the god who has placed the king on the throne. The next three columns of text are a series of laudatory epithets of the king; these were not found on the parallel wall scenes, but, like the previous text, are of a type which might be expected in a temple context.

This ostrakon was either a preparatory sketch for a similar inscription of Ramesses IX, or just a copy of a very prominent text made by a trainee artist who wished to practise. The latter hypothesis seems more likely, since the temple of Medinet Habu was the main functioning structure on the West Bank at Thebes in the late Twentieth Dynasty, and is assumed to have been the centre of the scribal administration; in addition, Ramesses IX had no such wars to proclaim (although this would not necessarily stop a king from making such a claim). The king's figure would also be expected to be proportionally larger if it were a preparatory sketch for a temple scene, although there is at least one example of an unusual scene in Karnak in which Ramesses IX is shown the same size as his high priest Amenhotep.

The tomb robbery papyri

FROM THEBES COMES a fascinating group of papyri concerning events at the end of the New Kingdom, in particular trials relating to the robbery of various tombs and the interrogation of suspects. It is likely that most of these papyri, most of which are in the British Museum, with others in Liverpool, Brussels, Turin, New York, and Vienna, originally came from an archive kept somewhere on the West Bank. This might have been in the administrative centre at the temple of Medinet Habu; they may subsequently have been stored in a tomb. Their hiding place seems to have been discovered in the middle of the nineteenth century, when they appeared on the antiquities market.

THE ABBOTT PAPYRUS

The Abbott Papyrus takes us into the world of tomb robbers and quarrelling politicians in ancient Egypt. The events it describes are dated to four days in year 16 of the reign of Ramesses IX (c. 1110 BC). Sheet 2 is shown opposite.

It begins with a report of a commission of inspection to examine several tombs on the Theban West Bank. Several royal tombs were inspected in the northern part of the necropolis, including those of Nebehepetre Mentuhotep of the Eleventh Dynasty, Amenhotep I of the Eighteenth Dynasty, and almost all the tombs of the kings of the Seventeenth Dynasty. Of these, only one was found to have been robbed: that of Sekhemreshedtawy Sebekemzaf. Note that the Valley of the Kings was not included in the visit! The commission stated that all the private tombs they examined had been robbed, however; then they moved on the next day to the Valley of the Queens. An accused robber was brought along to see if he would confess, but even under duress he denied having been in any of the tombs there. The burials were decreed to be intact.

This part of the papyrus is an important source of information about the tombs of the Seventeenth and early Eighteenth Dynasties, as the location of Amenhotep I's tomb is still unclear, and the Seventeenth Dynasty royal tombs were found in the mid-nineteenth century and subsequently lost. On the basis of the Abbott Papyrus it is thought that they lay in the area of Dra Abul Naga, and one of them, that of Nubkheperre Inyotef (see EA 6652, pages 112–13), was rediscovered by a German expedition in 2002. The Leopold-Amherst Papyrus, now in New York and Brussels, contains a graphic account of the robbery of Sebekemzaf's tomb and associated events. It is just possible that the scarab of Sebekemzaf (EA 7876, pages 110–11) came from this tomb.

The rest of the papyrus deals with disputes between the authorities of Thebes and the commissioners about the inquiry's results. The commission seems to have been set up

THE ABBOTT PAPYRUS

New Kingdom, late Twentieth Dynasty, reign of Ramesses IX, c. 1110 BC

From Thebes

Acquired from Dr Henry William Charles Abbott in 1857; previously in the possession of A.C. Harris

Papyrus

Originally one long sheet, 218 x 42.5 cm, now divided into three frames

EA 10221

The Abbott Papyrus, EA 10021

originally because Paser, the mayor of the eastern part of Thebes, had been receiving complaints about robberies in the West Bank necropolis, particularly in the royal tombs. The discussions in the papyrus would appear to vindicate the position of Paweraa, the mayor of the west of Thebes, that no robberies had really taken place, with the one indisputable exception. However, commentators on the text have noted that the way the discussions are reported seem to be intended to pour scorn on Paser; his charges are ridiculed when they appear to be true, and loudly denigrated when they are found to be false. Paser seems to have suffered some humiliation as a result, and there can be little doubt that the Abbott Papyrus was probably written largely from Paweraa's point of view. It would appear that the whole matter can be put down to a personal feud between these two important men; we have no idea of how it started, though Paser might have suspected that Paweraa had a hand in some of the criminal acts.

PAPYRUS BM EA 10054

Papyrus 10054 (the recto is illustrated on page 234) contains several unconnected texts, the first of which relates to year 16 of Ramesses IX (c. 1110 BC), when the outbreaks of tomb robbery seem to have come to the attention of officials (see the Abbott Papyrus above). Several of the robbers named in this papyrus appear in others of this group, and were clearly prominent criminal figures. Another text in this papyrus relates to year 18, and another to

PAPYRUS BM EA 10054

New Kingdom, late Twentieth Dynasty,
c. 1110–1093 BC

From Thebes

Acquired from Miss Selima Harris in 1872

Papyrus

Whole sheet 116 x 41 cm

EA 10054

a year 6, either of Ramesses XI or perhaps of that era in the later part of his reign termed the 'repeating of births' or 'renaissance' era.

The texts from year 16 record confessions extracted by force from various robbers by the vizier Khaemwaset and the mayor of Thebes. Several describe breaking into and robbing tombs. Thus the robbery of the tomb of Tjanefer, Theban Tomb 158, is described thus: 'We opened it, and we brought out his inner coffins, and we took his mummy, and left it there in a corner in his tomb. We took his inner coffins to this boat, along with the rest, to the Island (?) of Amenopet. We set fire to them in the night. And we made away with the gold which we found on them.' (A detail of this text is shown below left.) Setting fire to the coffins was a way of removing their gilding, which could then be sold or melted down. The robbers also described the division of their spoils.

The year 18 text describes the theft of gold from a statue of the god Nefertum and the theft of other silver objects, which were replaced by wooden copies. The texts make it clear that what the robbers sought above all else was metal, the value of which could be easily realized and traded. No intrinsic value was seen in the objects themselves. The remaining text on the papyrus concerns grain distribution. The writing of three separate texts on the same piece of papyrus is perfectly normal, and suggests that the material was quite valuable and had to be used economically.

PAPYRUS BM EA 10068

This papyrus consists of three groups of lists. The first, on the recto, dated to what is almost certainly year 17 of Ramesses IX (*c.* 1109 BC), consists of five lists of plunder recovered from thieves which was handed over to various temples in Thebes, including

PAPYRUS BM EA 10068

New Kingdom, late Twentieth Dynasty,
c. 1109–1087 BC

From Thebes

Acquired from Luigi Vassalli in 1856

Papyrus

Originally one sheet 156 x 44 cm; now
cut into two frames

EA 10068

the temple of Maat and the Ramesseum. The handing over of such items by the vizier and the high priest of Amun almost on the same date is attested in the so-called Necropolis Diary Papyrus, now in Turin. The quantity of material recovered is remarkable, exemplified by the totals at the end of the first list: just over 236 *deben* of gold and silver. As a *deben* of gold weighed probably 13.1 g, the amount of precious metals was at least 3 kg – this gives a fascinating insight into the quantities of valuable metals in circulation, and of course does not even include copper.

Two lists appear on the document's verso. One is a list of levies, not fully understood, but the second (below) is a fascinating list, dated to year 12 of (probably) Ramesses XI (*c.* 1087 BC). It lists the houses on the West Bank, from the temple of Sety I at the north end of the site to a settlement named Maiunehes, probably adjacent to the temple of Ramesses III at Medinet Habu. One hundred and eighty two houses are listed, ten between the temples of Sety I and of Ramesses II (the Ramesseum), fourteen from there to Medinet Habu, and the remainder in the area of Maiunehes. The professions of the owners are given – a mixture of officials, priests, and tradesmen. Doubtless there were other settlements on the West Bank at this time (no workmen of the royal tomb are mentioned), but it does present us with a remarkable picture of contemporary demographics.

EA 10068

Osiris figure and papyrus of Anhai

Late New Kingdom, Twentieth Dynasty,
c. 1100 BC

Probably from Thebes

Acquired in 1888

PAPYRUS

Ink on papyrus

Length: 69.9 cm; height: 46 cm

EA 10472/7

OSIRIS FIGURE

Wood, painted

Height: 63.5 cm

EA 20868

WHEN THIS UNINSCRIBED Osiris figure (left) was examined, the funerary papyrus of Anhai was found in a recess in the base. Figurines of this type are the forerunner of the more common and later Ptah-Sokar-Osiris figures, and take the form of a mummiform figure of the god of the dead; the presence of this deity in the tomb would help ensure resurrection and new life after death. This example is particularly elaborate and wears the feathered *atef* crown, a floral collar, and an elaborately decorated red covering on the upper body, with a decorated white covering from the waist down. This bright colouring can also be seen in depictions of Osiris in tomb paintings from the Eighteenth and Nineteenth Dynasties. As in many other depictions, Osiris' face is green – the colour of vegetation, another symbol of new life associated with this deity. Some other figurines of this type are painted black, symbolizing the fertility of the earth with which Osiris was associated. He carries the crook and flail of kingship.

The end of the papyrus of Anhai is illustrated opposite. Anhai was a 'mistress of the house' (a married woman) and 'singer of Amun of the great musical group', perhaps of the god. It is thus probable that she came from Thebes, but she also held titles associated with cults at Esna. Funerary papyri of women are by no means unknown, though less common than those of men. The practice of placing papyri inside figures may date back to the Eighteenth Dynasty; one of the earliest osiride figures, of king Amenhotep II, contained a similar recess. Doubtless Osiris guarded the papyrus, as well as assisting the deceased, a function also performed by texts on papyri.

Anhai's papyrus contains several spells from the *Book of the Dead*. This sheet (opposite) is particularly interesting: the scene at the left is the final illustration from the *Book of Gates*, more usually associated with the decoration of royal tombs of the New Kingdom (only one other example of this scene is known in a funerary papyrus). It shows the god Nun, personification of the primaeval waters, raising the boat of the sun-god, a representation of the sun's daily birth at its rising. The sun-god is represented as a large scarab beetle pushing a solar disc, and is accompanied in the boat by several other, unnamed, deities, known to include Geb, Shu, Heka, Hu, and Sia from fuller depictions. The sun is propelled towards the sky goddess Nut, shown upside-down receiving the disc. A brief text mentions 'Osiris who surrounds the netherworld', and the whole composition can be seen as a complex representation of the daily passage of the sun, from its rising to its setting in the underworld. Anhai stands at the right in an attitude of adoration. The intervening scene probably shows two ram-headed creator gods with her mummy in symbolic apotheosis, having ascended to heaven to join the stars.

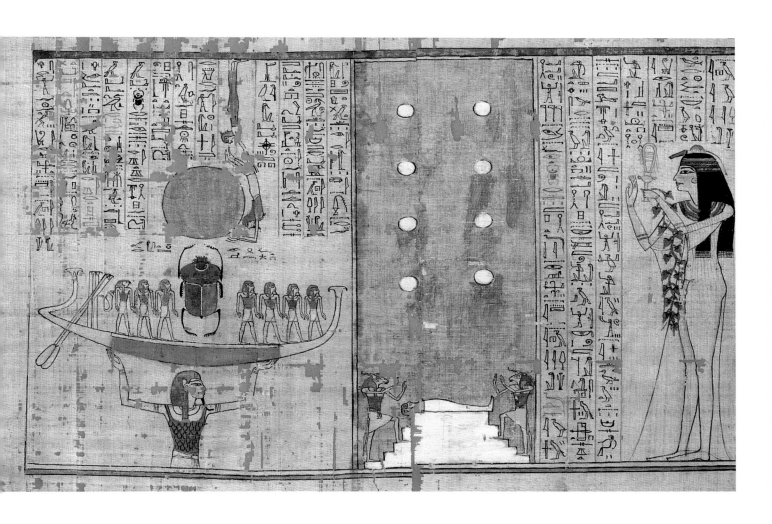

A letter to Paiankh

New Kingdom, late Twentieth Dynasty,
c. 1080–1070 BC

From Thebes

Purchased from the collections of
Henry Salt, date uncertain

Papyrus

Height: 44 cm

EA 10375

A LARGE NUMBER OF PAPYRI, known as the 'Late Ramesside letters', was found in Western Thebes in the early nineteenth century. The circumstances of the find or finds are not recorded, but several of them appeared in European collections in the 1820s; some now in Turin were collected by Bernadino Drovetti, who acquired many objects in the area of the workmen's village of Deir el-Medina. A possible place of origin might have been the temple of Medinet Habu, the administrative headquarters of the West Bank at the end of the New Kingdom; the workmen of the royal tomb moved there early in the reign of Ramesses XI since their desert village was becoming too dangerous and isolated.

These letters come primarily from the family archive of the scribe Djehutymose and his son Butehamun, whose house survives at Medinet Habu. Most are from the very end of the New Kingdom, the last years of the reign of Ramesses XI known as *wehem mesut*, often translated 'renaissance'. Real power in Thebes lay with the general Paiankh, but for much of this time he was in Nubia, fighting Panehsy, the former viceroy of Nubia, who had turned against the monarchy about 1090 BC. It is unlikely that Paiankh succeeded in controlling Panehsy, since Nubia was soon lost to Egypt, although he probably managed to prevent Panehsy from harassing Thebes. Djehutymose was often in Nubia with Paiankh, and many of the letters are between him and his son.

A typical Egyptian letter such as this begins with a long passage of effusive greetings to the recipient before turning to business. This letter is a response from Butehamun and senior officials in western Thebes, including the foremen of the workmen of the royal tomb. It relates to several tasks that Paiankh has asked Butehamun to do and the Theban response. As with so many letters and documents from ancient Egypt, or indeed personal correspondence of any period, it is rather cryptic, as we do not have the previous correspondence from Paiankh, though of course both the sender and recipient knew exactly what was meant. Some of the damage coincides with where the papyrus would have been folded for delivery; it would also have been sealed.

The most interesting of all is the request from an earlier letter from Paiankh, 'Uncover a tomb among the ancient tombs and preserve its seal until I return', which elicited the response 'We shall enable you to find it fixed up and ready'. The text refers to placing markers on it. This rather cryptic reference might perhaps indicate that Paiankh had begun an 'official' programme of opening up tombs, especially those of earlier kings, with the aim of stripping them of their wealth to finance his campaigns. Apart from the occasional opportunistic robbery, this would be the first stage in the journey of the royal mummies which eventually led to the caches in Deir el-Bahari and the Valley of the Kings.

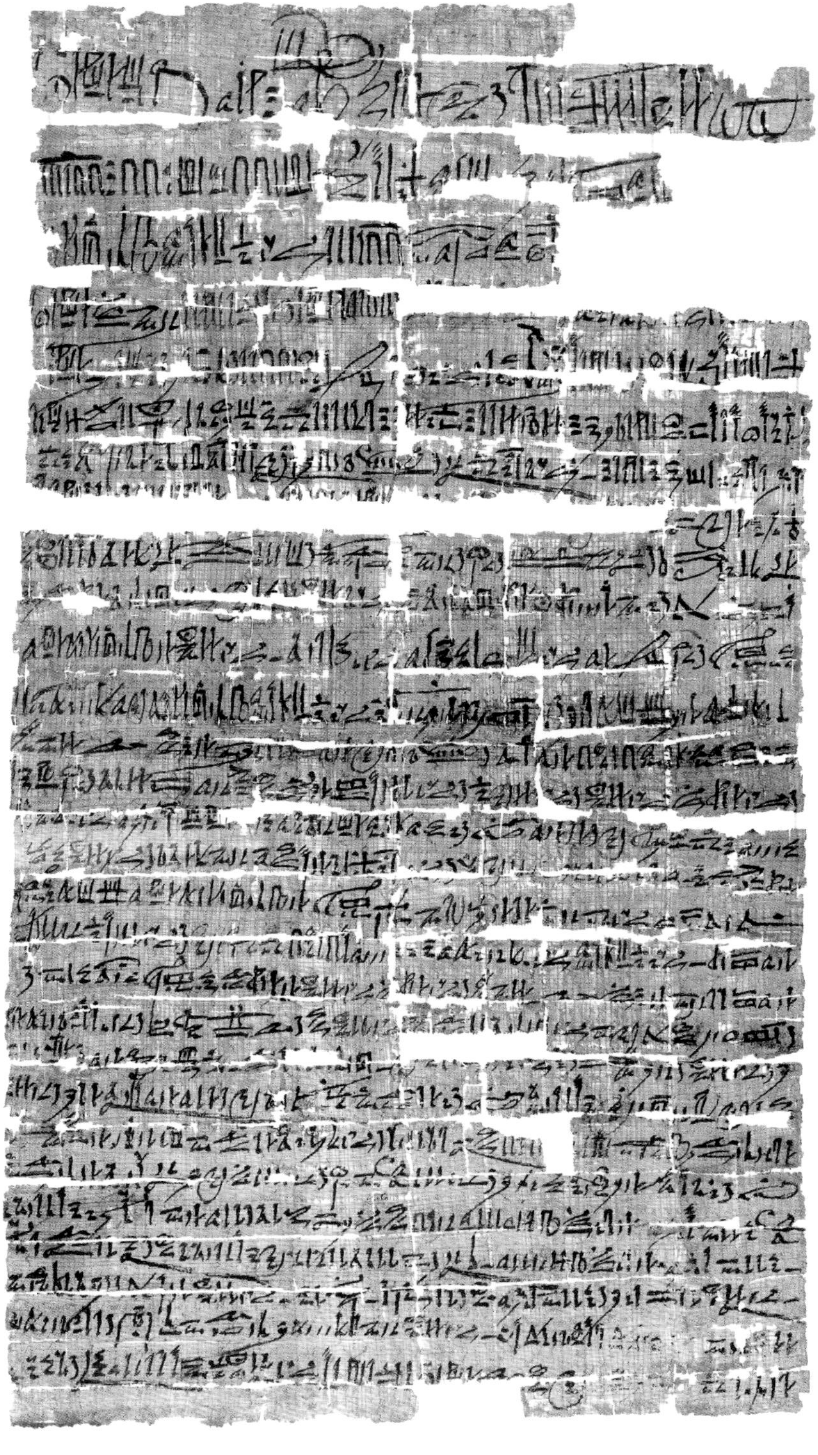

The *Instruction of Amenemopet*

Text: perhaps later New Kingdom.
Papyrus: Third Intermediate Period or
Late Period.

Said to be from Thebes

Acquired in 1888

Papyrus

Length of sheet 1: 54.7 cm

Length of sheet 4: 59.8 cm

Height of both: 30.7 cm

EA 10474

'WISDOM LITERATURE' IS A PROMINENT ELEMENT of surviving ancient Egyptian literature. The genre is best known from the Middle Kingdom, which produced a significant number of texts that were later considered as classics. Fewer texts of this type have survived from the New Kingdom and later, although whether this is chance or reflects a change in literary production is unclear.

The British Museum possesses the complete text of the *Instruction of Amenemopet*; smaller fragments of it have also survived, including a scribal tablet in Turin and an ostrakon in Cairo. Features of the Late Egyptian in which the text was composed suggest that it dates from either the Nineteenth or perhaps more likely the Twentieth Dynasty, although all existing copies are later – this one, for instance, might be as late as the Persian Period.

The work is divided into thirty numbered sections or stanzas, each dealing with one topic. There is no framing story, as with many other texts of the same genre, but only a title naming Amenemopet, an overseer of fields; it is uncertain whether he was the actual author or a fictional wise man. Each section presents a piece of advice that is then refined through a series of similes. Running through the whole text is a concept prominent in the religious thought of the Ramesside Period, now termed 'personal piety'. The author considers the personal relationship between the individual and his god. There are two ways to approach the god: one is to be a 'truly silent one', and rely on the god's free will and action without interfering in his plans. The contrasting approach is that of the 'hot one', who pushes too eagerly on his way to reach the god, speaking with a 'hot mouth'. He shows a strong aggressive inclination and should be avoided, thus producing isolation and even bad luck for his family. The text urges modesty and good behaviour. New Kingdom instructional texts such as *Amenemopet* exhibit a sensitivity which distinguishes them from their Middle Kingdom precursors.

Unusually for an Egyptian composition, each line of verse occupies a separate line of the manuscript, thus revealing the underlying metrical structure. Most literary or poetic Egyptian texts are written continuously, with line breaks dictated by physical constraints, and their metrical structure has to be ascertained by scansion.

The fame of the *Instruction* has been enhanced by the fact that many of its ideas are attested in the Bible. In particular, Proverbs 22 and 23 show similar aspects of thought and expression, and chapter 22, verse 20 actually refers to 'thirty sayings of admonition and knowledge'. The consensus is that the Hebrew text was probably influenced by the Egyptian, although the reverse has occasionally been argued, as has the possibility that both works derive from a now lost Semitic source.

Above: sheet 1. Below: sheet 4.

A mummy-board

Third Intermediate Period, late
Twenty-first Dynasty, *c.* 950 BC

Provenance unknown, but almost
certainly from Thebes

Gift of Arthur F. Wheeler via Mrs
Warwick Hunt in 1889

Wood, plastered and painted

Length: 162 cm

EA 22542

THIS OBJECT IS PERHAPS BEST KNOWN for the strange folkloric history attributed to it: it has acquired the popular nickname of the 'Unlucky Mummy', with a reputation for bringing misfortune. None of these stories has any basis in fact, but from time to time the strength of the rumours has led to a flood of enquiries.

The mummy-board is said to have been bought by one of four young English travellers in Egypt during the 1860s or 1870s. Two died or were seriously injured in shooting incidents, and the other two died in poverty within a short time. The mummy-board was passed to the sister of one of the travellers, but as soon as it had entered her house the occupants suffered a series of misfortunes. The celebrated clairvoyant Madame Helena Blavatsky is alleged to have detected an evil influence, ultimately traced to the mummy-board. She urged the owner to dispose of it and in consequence it was presented to the British Museum. The most remarkable story is that the mummy-board was on board the *SS Titanic* on its maiden voyage in 1912, and that its presence caused the ship to collide with an iceberg and sink!

Needless to say, there is no truth in any of this; the object had never left the Museum until it went to a temporary exhibition in 1990. This mummy-board is both a remarkable ancient object and an example of how Egyptian objects can develop their own modern existence.

Mummy-boards or covers like this were placed on top of the mummy, which would lie inside one or two wooden coffins decorated in a very similar fashion. The mummy to which this board belonged is said to have been left in Egypt. No inscriptions on the board identify the deceased, presumably because that task would have been performed by the outer coffins.

The wooden board was covered in plaster, serving as a painting ground, with many of the decorative elements modelled in the plaster to give the appearance of raised relief. The decoration was executed with great care in red, blue, and light and dark green; the predominantly yellow effect comes either from the use of a yellow ground or from the varnish, applied to the finished object, which has gradually turned yellow. On the shoulders of the mummy-board is a massive coloured collar, below which is a series of complex scenes. They include images of baboons worshipping the sun, figures of Osiris, and many protective deities, including the name of Amenhotep I, the dead king worshipped as a local deity in Thebes. One of the coffin's functions, other than to act as a container for the body, was to serve as a microcosm, setting the deceased within the larger environment of the universe itself; thus the solar and Osirian symbolism essential to assist the person's rebirth figures prominently. The decoration usual in the Twenty-first Dynasty is perhaps the most elaborate example of this.

An oracular shabti decree

Third Intermediate Period,
Twenty-first Dynasty, 1069–945 BC

From Deir el-Bahari

Purchased in 1886; originally acquired
by the Duke of Hamilton in about 1874

Wood

Height: 28.9 cm

EA 16672

TWO ALMOST IDENTICAL wooden tablets were found in Thebes and are now in the British Museum and the Louvre. (Both sides of the British Museum tablet are shown opposite.) They may have come from the cache of mummies in Deir el-Bahari discovered in about 1871. They record an oracular pronouncement of Amun that a set of shabtis (servant figures) should work only for their owner, who is consequently exempt from other tasks, and that the ownership of the shabtis is indeed vested in the woman who bought them. This shows that the power of Amun could be used not just to confirm ownership, but also to control events in the next world. The following is a paraphrased translation:

Amun-Re, king of the gods, the great god, the most ancient one to come into existence, speaks: I shall see to it that the shabtis made for Neskhonsu, daughter of Tenthendjehuty, carry out all duties for Neskhonsu in the sorts of duties which shabtis know how to do in the service of a dead person, who is brought to the necropolis and who has become divine, without any errors. Thus spoke Amun: I shall see to it that they act for Neskhonsu.

Amun-Re, king of the gods, the great god, the most ancient one to come into existence, speaks: I shall see to it that the shabtis made for Neskhonsu carry out every duty for which shabtis are made for the exemption of all the excellent blessed dead, so that they see to it for the exemption of Neskhonsu, so that they see to it for her exemption every year, every month, every ten-day week, every day, and on all the five epagomenal days.

The contents of the writings were placed before Amun, lord of the thrones of the two lands of the mansion of the obelisk, in year 5, fourth month of the *shemu* season, day 2. Amun, lord of the thrones of the two lands of the mansion of the obelisk, the great god, speaks in two copies: with reference to all that which they have paid the faience makers for the shabtis made for Neskhonsu in the form of copper, clothing, bread, cakes, fish, and everything which has been paid them for it and which will be paid: the makers are fully paid by that, it being the value in silver of their value. With reference to everything done in relation to the payment for the shabtis, so that they replace someone at work saying 'I shall do everything they should do', that is the price for which the shabtis act, for replacing Neskhonsu, and so that they might be perfect for her and that they carry out duties for her perfectly.

16672.

Receipt for a set of shabtis

Third Intermediate Period,
Twenty-first/Twenty-third Dynasties,
1069–715 BC

Probably from Thebes

Acquired in 1966

Papyrus

Length: 19 cm

EA 10800

THE PAPYRUS IS WRITTEN in a cursive hieratic script, which bears more than a passing resemblance to abnormal hieratic, the most common daily script of the Twenty-fifth Dynasty until the advent of Demotic. It thus probably dates from the period when this later form of hieratic was developing (*c.* 1069–715 BC).

The main part of the text reads:

Year 14, second month of the *akhet* season, day 8. Padikhonsu, son of Nesupenankh, son of Hor, the chief modeller of amulets of the estate of Amun, has declared to the beloved of the god, the *wab* priest Nespernub, son of Ihafy, son of Iufenkhonsu: 'As Amun the Great God endures, I have received from you the (payment in) silver for these 365 shabtis and their 36 foremen, total 401 to my satisfaction – they are male and female servants. I have received from you their (value in) pure silver, (that is the price of) 401 shabtis. Go to work on behalf of Osiris for the beloved of the god, the *wab* priest Ihafy. Say 'we are ready' whenever he shall summon you to do the service of the day, for I have received from him your (value in) silver.

The text ends with assertions of correctness and the names of witnesses. It shows how, at this time, there was usually one shabti (servant figure) for each day of the year, plus an overseer or foreman for each group of ten. In the Middle Kingdom and earlier New Kingdom, shabtis were found in ones and twos in burials, but a change of emphasis in the Nineteenth and Twentieth Dynasties meant that the number increased to this total of 401.

The only thing missing from the contract is the price paid. The contract was between the maker and son of the man whose name was on the shabtis, presumably indicating that Ihafy was dead, and that Nespernub had these objects made as part of his responsibilities in organizing his father's burial. We have no way of telling whether the specification of the deceased's name is because he was no longer alive to enter into the contract, or whether it is a standard clause. The amulet maker who produced the shabtis belonged to the temple of Amun, which suggests that the production of such items could have been a monopoly enjoyed by the temple administration. The shabtis were probably made of faience, like most amulets of this period.

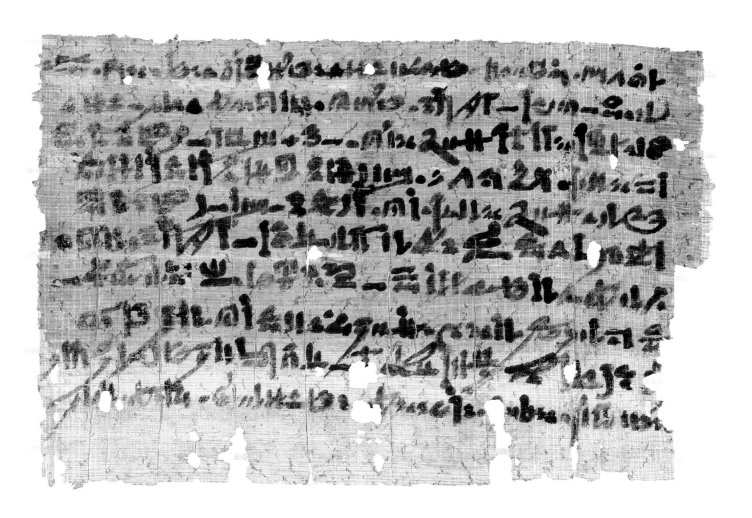

Statue of the Nile god Hapy

Third Intermediate Period, perhaps
Twenty-second Dynasty, *c.* 900 BC

From Karnak

Purchased as part of the first Salt
collection in 1823

Greyish quartzite or sandstone

Height: 220 cm

EA 8

THE STATUE DEPICTS a corpulent figure, male but with somewhat pendulous breasts, presenting an offering table from which hang dead geese and masses of lotus and papyrus flowers. This resembles a three-dimensional version of the series of figures known as 'Nile gods' or 'fecundity figures', frequently found at the lowest level of decoration of temple walls, which represent personifications of Egypt's fertile and bountiful soil. A text on the statue's right side identifies the figure as the Nile god Hapy, with whom such figures are frequently associated. It is not a particularly common type, and the earliest examples seem to be from the Middle Kingdom. They should not be confused with statues of kings presenting offerings, which look similar but are very different in function (compare the statue of Tutankhamun, EA 75, pages 184–5).

The inscriptions indicate that the statue was carved on behalf of Sheshonq, high priest of Amun and chief of the army, for Amun-Re. Sheshonq is shown in a worshipping pose on the left side of the statue, and is described as the son of Osorkon I and Maatkare, daughter of Psusennes II (*c.* 959–945 BC), the last king of the Twenty-second Dynasty. This individual, whose name is written within a cartouche but without the full titles of kingship, is usually referred to as Sheshonq II; the cartouches may perhaps be regarded as 'prospective' in meaning, a reflection of his aspirations to succeed his father on the throne. Without doubt he was appointed as high priest in Thebes, the most powerful position there, to ensure his family's control over Upper Egypt. He seems to have died before his father, although it is likely that Osorkon I made him his co-regent towards the end of his reign in order to smooth the transfer of power, though this was thwarted by Sheshonq's early death.

Little comparable sculpture exists from the Twenty-second Dynasty, and while this statue could be assigned to this period, it may have been made earlier. Sheshonq I removed some Sekhmet statues from Amenhotep III's mortuary temple, took them to Karnak, and added his name to them; since Amenhotep's temple was partly designed to resemble the mound of creation, a statue of a Nile god would not have been out of place there. The arrangement of the mass of offerings is like that of royal offering statues such as EA 75, and although the colour of the stone is not common in Amenhotep III's statuary, there are prominent veins of different colours running through it that are reminiscent of the patterning of the brown quartzite so favoured in other monuments of that date (see, for example, EA 7, pages 154–5, and EA 38, pages 162–3). Thus, the statue might have been reused some 450 years after it was made.

Mummy case of an infant

Third Intermediate Period,
Twenty-second Dynasty, *c.* 945–715 BC

From Speos Artemidos
(south of Beni Hasan)

Acquired in 1905 from the collection of
F. Hilton Price. Originally from the
excavations of John Garstang in
1902-04.

Cartonnage and paint; human remains

Length of mummy case: 73 cm

EA 41603

THIS CARTONNAGE MUMMY case contains the bones of an infant. The style suggests a date in the Twenty-second Dynasty. The deceased is shown with the usual large wig and a feather headdress; around the neck is a broad collar. On the chin is the curly divine beard of the transfigured deceased. Below the arms is a central column of hieroglyphs which gives a conventional prayer for offerings; if the name of the dead child was inscribed, it would have been nearer the foot of the coffin, now lost. Flanking the text are seated funerary deities, interspersed with birds with outspread wings – all intended to protect the body inside the case. The most unusual feature is the double plume on the top of the head. These plumes are typical of the figures of Ptah-Sokar-Osiris (a funerary deity) buried with many interments from the Third Intermediate Period down to Ptolemaic times. Several such figures were discovered by John Garstang in the excavations that yielded this mummy case. It would appear that the mummy case was designed to resemble these figures, though it is not clear why.

The bones of the infant, whose sex is unknown, are so badly deformed that Garstang originally identified them as those of a monkey. In fact, the child suffered from the rare disorder osteogenesis imperfecta, also known as 'brittle bone disease', a condition caused by a genetic defect that reduces or damages the body's production of collagen. The result is inadequate formation of bone tissue, manifest in distortion or breaking of the bones; one form of this condition can develop in the womb. This can be seen clearly in this skull, which has become very low and broad as the bone structure could not support the weight of the cranial vault. Likewise, the bones of the upper arms, thighs, and lower legs have all become curved and would never have been able to bear any weight. The bones are so fragile that they can be fractured while the foetus is still in the womb, and the trauma of birth could have fractured all the bones in the baby's body; it is very unlikely to have survived birth. Today, a baby with this disorder would be delivered by caesarean section.

The site of Speos Artemidos is best-known for the rock temple of Hatshepsut. Garstang found many cemeteries here from the Third Intermediate Period to Roman times; the better-known Eleventh and Twelfth Dynasty cemeteries lie to the north at the main site of Beni Hasan.

Coffin of Denytenamun

Third Intermediate Period, early
Twenty-second Dynasty, *c.* 900 BC

From Thebes

Purchased at the sale of the third Salt
collection in 1835

Sycomore fig wood

Length: 162 cm

EA 6660

DENYTENAMUN WAS A PRIEST OF AMUN in about 900 BC, who presumably lived and died in the Theban area. His anthropoid wooden coffin is of an interesting form, transitional between the styles of the Twenty-first and Twenty-second Dynasties, and bears a number of scenes which are unusual, almost as if the craftsmen were experimenting with the iconography. His fists are shown crossed on his chest. Over his long blue wig is a head-dress of feathers, somewhat more typical of the burials of women. He once had a long beard with a curved end, of the type worn by gods and the dead.

The two straps which cross on his chest over the broad collar are known as *stola* or 'mummy braces', and are associated with Osiris, the god of the dead. These straps, which first appear on images of mummiform deities in the Twelfth Dynasty, and subsequently on images of other gods and the dead, helped identify the deceased with the god and offered protection for the mummy. Actual examples made of leather are often found in burials of the Third Intermediate Period; a pair has been identified on the mummy of Nesperennub (see EA 30720, pages 254–5), and some fine examples are also inscribed with the name of the king reigning at the time of burial. Two crossing linen bands with presumably the same significance are laid over the top of the main wrapping of Denyten-amun's mummy.

On his breast is a standing figure of Osiris, flanked by Isis and Nephthys, with wings spread in a protective gesture. Six vignettes flank a vertical column of hieroglyphs giving his names and titles. The upper register shows Denytenamun worshipping two different manifestations of the necropolis deity Ptah-Sokar-Osiris. In the middle is a unique pair of scenes, showing the mountain of the West and the tomb with more protective deities: a bull (left, also Ptah-Sokar-Osiris) and a cow (right, Isis). At the bottom are the four Sons of Horus, beneath which are two images of Wepwawet, flanked by a winged lion-headed deity.

Denytenamun's mummy shows that he was middle-aged. X-rays have revealed that artificial eyes of stone or glass were placed in his eye-sockets, and that there is a pectoral on his chest in the form of a bird with spread wings, below which is a scarab. His internal organs were embalmed and replaced inside his mummy, as was the practice at this time.

Coffin and mummy-case of Nesperennub

Third Intermediate Period,
Twenty-third Dynasty, *c*. 800 BC

Almost certainly from Thebes

Acquired in 1899

COFFIN

Painted wood

Length: 192 cm

MUMMY-CASE

Painted cartonnage

Length: 173 cm

Both EA 30720

NESPERENNUB WAS A PRIEST in the temple of Khonsu at Karnak in about 800 BC. He held a variety of titles, in particular 'libation-pourer of Khonsu' and 'opener of the doors of heaven in Karnak'. The latter doors were those of the shrine which contained the divine image, which were opened so that the daily rituals could be carried out for the deity. In addition to the inscriptions on his coffin and mummy case, a graffito in the temple of Khonsu belonging to his son gives a date in the reign of king Takelot III of the Twenty-third Dynasty and a genealogy for his family. The location of Nesperennub's tomb is unknown, but many priests in the Third Intermediate Period reused older tombs from the New Kingdom in western Thebes for family burials. They either reused older shafts or cut small new ones, sometimes making minor changes to the internal arrangement of the New Kingdom chapel in the process.

Nesperennub's mummy was enclosed in a close-fitting mummy-case of cartonnage (moulded linen and plaster). This was then placed in a wooden coffin. The mummy case is brightly painted with figures and symbols of gods who would protect his body. An Apis bull is painted on the underside of the foot-case. Later coffins show this bull carrying the mummy of the dead person on its back.

The mummy has been studied with CAT scans. With the aid of high-powered computers, 1,800 sectional scans or slices through the body have been transformed into an interactive three-dimensional image of the mummy, so that it is possible to study it non-invasively, without damaging it. The carefully-made case and mummy can thus be kept intact for further investigations as techniques develop and improve.

Nesperennub died at about the age of 40. He appears to have suffered from a disease which affected his skull, shown by the presence of one or more small holes in the bone, and this might have contributed to his death. Some amulets and rings are visible on his body, and artificial eyes were placed in his eye-sockets. A pair of leather straps, as painted on the coffin of Denytenamun (see EA 6660, pages 252–3), with their Osirian symbolism, were placed on his body. An intriguing dark shape was observed in the 1960s X-rays of his head: the CAT scans revealed that it is a pottery dish, attached to the head. This is most unusual, and the most likely explanation seems to be that it contained resin or a similar material, and was left there, and perhaps forgotten for a while, by the embalmers. When they attempted to remove it, it had become stuck fast to Nesperennub's head, so they simply left it and wrapped it along with the body. Carelessness in embalming was not uncommon, and there are mummies from the Roman Period with the wrong number of limbs, and even one of a child which on examination was shown to contain a cat.

Funerary stela of Deniuenkhonsu

Third Intermediate Period,
Twenty-second Dynasty, *c.* 800 BC

Probably from Thebes

Acquired in 1896

Painted wood

Height: 33 cm

EA 27332

THE SUN-GOD, shown here in his composite form as Re-Horakhty-Atum, is shown receiving offerings from Deniuenkhonsu, who stands at the right with her arms raised in worship. The god is represented in human form, with a falcon's head. The large sun-disc on top of his head, encircled by a serpent, indicates his solar associations. As befits a divine ruler, he grasps royal sceptres in his right hand, while in his left is the *was*-sceptre, signifying 'dominion'. From the top of this the sign of life (*ankh*) faces towards the deceased – an allusion to the new life which she receives from the god. The scene is framed by stylized door-leaves which support the hieroglyph for 'sky'. Within the curved upper zone of the stela the sun is depicted again in two different forms: as a winged disc and as a scarab beetle flanked by jackals.

The ancient Egyptians believed that the sun-god Re was the creator of life on earth, and that he possessed the power to restore the dead to life. In mythological terms, this rebirth took place during the twelve hours of the night, when Re travelled through the subterranean underworld. On this journey he defeated the forces of chaos, experienced rejuvenation himself, and brought light and new life to the dead who lay at rest there. Depicting oneself adoring this deity was thus a very explicit wish for the god to support one in a new life after death. Wooden stelae like this became one of the common, almost mandatory, objects in burials during the Third Intermediate Period and Late Period. At that time few decorated tomb chapels were being constructed, and burials were effected in roughly-cut chambers at the bottom of shafts a few metres deep. The effort for the burial was almost entirely expended on elements placed in the burial chamber: decorative work, text, and motifs expressing wishes for new life were concentrated on the coffins, stelae, and funerary papyri, while shabtis performed the role of images of the deceased and worked on their behalf in the afterlife.

Deniuenkhonsu bears the common titles of 'mistress of the house' and 'singer of Amun-Re' and was married to Ankhenkhonsu. Neither of them is known from other sources.

Coffins of Hor, priest of Montu

Third Intermediate Period,
Twenty-fifth Dynasty, *c.* 700-680 BC

From Thebes

Coffins probably acquired in Egypt by
John Fowler Hull (1801–25), and
purchased at the sale of the collection
of his brother Samuel Hull, 1880 (inner
coffin via W. Cutter)

OUTER COFFIN

Wood, painted

Length: 204.5 cm

EA 15655

INNER COFFIN

Wood, painted; the eyes are of glass

Length: 179 cm

EA 27735

HOR, PRIEST OF MONTU, belonged to a powerful Theban family, and his burial assemblage is typical of those prepared for people of high status during the Twenty-fifth Dynasty. Political decentralization and economic stress had curtailed the construction of new tombs. Burials were deposited in older sepulchres or in temple precincts, and the dead were now provided with only those items considered most essential to ensuring new life – most importantly, a set of coffins richly decorated with religious texts and symbolic images.

The eternal universe in which Hor hoped to dwell was magically created for him by the shape and decoration of his coffins. Two, of a possible three, have survived: a rectangular outer case and an inner one of anthropoid form.

Hor's outer coffin resembles a shrine for the physical body (statue) of a god. The use of this shape for a coffin alludes to the divine status which the occupant hoped to achieve after death. But the coffin is also a model of the universe, the vaulted lid representing the sky, across which the sun god travelled, and the base the earthly realm ruled over by Osiris. To emphasize this link, the lid is painted with scenes depicting the creation of the universe (the separation of the earth god Geb and the sky goddess Nut) and the daily cycle of the sun (Hor is shown piloting Atum, the evening sun, in a barque). The coffin's long sides are arrayed with deities, intended to give eternal protection to the mummy. The spaces between them contain extracts from the *Book of the Dead*. At one end (illustrated on this page, left) Hor is shown sitting before a table of offerings, a scene heavily influenced by Old and Middle Kingdom art.

The inner coffin has been skilfully carved to represent Hor as a divine being. His body is shrouded, leaving only his head exposed, and he stands on a plinth, his back supported by a pillar. The coffin's surfaces are covered with hieroglyphic texts and images, including spells from the *Book of Dead* to ensure food offerings for Hor's spirit and to assist him in passing through the ordeal of judgement.

Hor's burial place seems to have been discovered in the early 1820s, when his funerary objects were acquired by European collectors. The findspot was not recorded, but at around the same time funerary furniture belonging to several relatives of Hor also came to light, suggesting that a communal burial may have been discovered. This was perhaps located at or near Hatshepsut's temple at Deir el-Bahari, where other burials of the priests of Montu were found in the 1850s and 1860s.

The British Museum also has a shabti box of Hor (EA 8525) and another box is in Aberdeen. No actual shabtis of his survive.

J.H.T.

The Shabaka stone

Third Intermediate Period, Twenty-fifth Dynasty, *c.* 716–702 BC

Presumably originally from Memphis

Gift of Earl Spencer in 1805

Conglomerate

Length: 137 cm

EA 498

IN THE TWENTY-FIFTH and Twenty-sixth Dynasties (*c.* 716–525 BC) the Egyptians became extremely interested in using models and styles from earlier periods to enhance their elite culture. Motifs from the Old and Middle Kingdoms were highly favoured for use in monumental decoration, and indications that a text might have come from a much earlier copy gave it a ring of substance and authority. An example of this trend is the so-called 'Shabaka stone', which probably comes from a temple. The beginning of the text claims that it is a copy of a much older document, which was found to be worm-eaten in the reign of king Shabaka (*c.* 716–702 BC) and was therefore reinscribed on this stela. It has indeed been claimed that the text was composed in the Old Kingdom, but its language and orthography, especially the appearance of forms completely alien to Old Egyptian, the language of the Old Kingdom, suggest that it was probably composed in the Twenty-fifth Dynasty. Less certain is the antiquity of the text on which it was based, for which a Nineteenth Dynasty date has been proposed. The hieroglyphs themselves have been damaged in places when the stela was later re-employed as a millstone or a column base. It may have been discovered in Alexandria, whither it could have been taken in the Ptolemaic or Roman Period.

The text is an important document for the study of Egyptian religion, although it is difficult and open to interpretation. It is sometimes termed the 'Memphite theology', since it places Ptah, the principal god of Memphis, better known as the patron deity of craftsmen, at the centre of things. The text is conventionally divided into three sections. The first part concerns many of the gods of Heliopolis and refers to the mythical conflict of Horus and Seth, who are united in the house of Ptah, thus linking the supreme god of Memphis to the Heliopolitan gods. The second part praises Ptah, describing him as a creator god who brought things into being by thinking and speaking. The final part reiterates the unity of all the different deities in Memphis. It can be viewed as a dramatic or ritual text, which might even have been performed in an appropriate context.

Assuming the text to have been a product of the Twenty-fifth Dynasty, it is likely to have served a dual purpose: not just to indicate the importance of Ptah, but also the importance that Shabaka assigned to the god and by inference to his priesthood. The text's political dimension would thus indicate the new dynasty's support for what must have been a powerful priesthood which, it was hoped, would in turn support the new regime. In 715 BC Shabaka was responsible for asserting control of his Nubian ('Kushite') dynasty over the whole of Egypt, the first time the country had been unified since the Twenty-first Dynasty.

Sphinx of king Taharqa

Third Intermediate Period, Twenty-fifth Dynasty, *c.* 680 BC

From Temple T at Kawa, Sudan

Gift of F. Ll. Griffith (the excavator) in 1932 (Oxford Excavations in Nubia)

Granite gneiss

Length: 74.7 cm

EA 1770

FOLLOWING THE EGYPTIAN WITHDRAWAL FROM NUBIA at the end of the New Kingdom, a number of small political entities rapidly established themselves in the ensuing power vacuum. In the course of the three centuries after the Egyptians withdrew, these various small entities were gradually united into the second kingdom of Kush.

The second kingdom of Kush was very Egyptianized, acknowledging Amun as their principal deity, and using Eyptian modes of art and writing. In the eighth century BC they turned the tables on Egypt and acquired control of Upper Egypt, extending full control over the whole of the land at the beginning of the reign of Shabaka (*c.* 716–702 BC).

Kawa in Upper Nubia (Sudan), 100 km south of the third Nile Cataract, was the home of a local form of Amun, and was one of the sites at which the kings of the Kushite Twenty-fifth Dynasty constructed temples. One of their aims was apparently to ensure the prominence of this deity. This statue was found to the south of the central shrine of Temple T at Kawa, in a room at the western end of which was a raised dais, presumably for a throne, on which might have been placed a seated statue of Amun. No such statue survived, though this sphinx and parts of several others did.

Sphinxes represent the immense power of the Egyptian and Kushite king. While the body of this example is conventional, the head in particular looks back to the earlier sculptural forms of the Middle Kingdom, particularly noticeable in the careful depiction of the raised ruff of hair around the animal's neck, which resembles those of the well-known sphinxes of king Amenemhat III from Tanis (Cairo, CG 393, 394). Compare also the now-modified mane of the sphinx of Amenemhat IV, EA 58892, pages 98–9. The features are characteristic of the Twenty-fifth Dynasty, and might be a stylized portrait of king Taharqa (690–664 BC), whose name is incised between the forepaws. The double uraeus cobra on the brow is characteristic of the royal insignia of the kings of Kush. Also highly distinctive of the art of this period are the pronounced furrows flanking the nose.

Kawa was originally founded in the New Kingdom, perhaps even by Akhenaten, which may explain the source of the word *aten* in its Egyptian name, Gematen; the earliest buildings yet discovered date from Tutankhamun's reign. The site rose to prominence during the Kushite period in the eighth century BC, and excavations have revealed the town and temples there. Temple T was constructed of sandstone blocks by Taharqa, starting in the sixth year of his reign; the building work took four years, and was undertaken by architects and builders brought all the way from Memphis in Egypt.

Coffin of king Menkaure

Twenty-fifth or Twenty-sixth Dynasty
(*c.* 700–600 BC)

From the pyramid of Menkaure at Giza

Gift of Colonel Richard William
Howard Vyse in 1838

Wood (*Juniperus* sp., *Abies* sp.,
Cupressus sempervirens, *Ficus
sycomorus*, *Tamarix* sp.)

Length: 166 cm

EA 6647

THIS FRAGMENTARY COFFIN was made to contain the body of king Menkaure (Greek: Mycerinus) of the Fourth Dynasty (*c.* 2532–2503 BC), builder of the third pyramid at Giza. It is of simple form, representing the dead ruler in the shroud and tripartite wig of a transfigured being. The plain surface is relieved only by an inscription carved in two columns down the centre of the lid: 'O the Osiris King of Upper and Lower Egypt Menkaure, living forever, born of the sky, conceived by Nut, heir [of Geb] . . . : Your mother Nut spreads herself over you in her name of "Mystery of Heaven". She has made you a god, [whose enemies do not exist,] King of Upper and Lower Egypt Menkaure, living forever.' This is a version of a much-copied inscription, found as early as the Old Kingdom *Pyramid Texts*, which invokes the maternal sky-goddess Nut to protect the king and ensure his resurrection.

The pieces of the coffin were discovered among debris in the antechamber during the first modern investigation of the pyramid of Menkaure by R.W.H. Vyse in 1837. The excavators also recovered parts of a human body (EA 18212), which radiocarbon dating has dated to the mediaeval period. The coffin was not part of the original funerary equipment of the king, but was made for a later restoration of his burial, as is clear from both stylistic and epigraphic evidence. Anthropoid (human-shaped) coffins did not make their first appearance in Egypt until centuries after Menkaure's reign, and the representation of an integral pedestal supporting the feet does not occur on coffins before the late eighth century BC. The inscription supports a relatively late dating. The phraseology and the spelling of individual words are different from those of Menkaure's own time, being characteristic of funerary texts written in the Twenty-fifth and Twenty-sixth Dynasties. At this period there was a major revival of interest in the great eras of Egypt's past. A cult of Menkaure had been established at Giza at least by the Twenty-sixth Dynasty, and it is conceivable that the pyramid was entered at that time and the supposed remains of the king reinterred in a newly-made coffin.

The coffin is constructed from several different kinds of wood. The larger components are all of juniper and fir, softwoods which were not native to Egypt and must therefore have been imported. Local timbers (sycomore fig and tamarisk) were only used to make some of the dowels and tenons joining the planks. One piece of the wood has been radiocarbon dated to 1212–846 BC – somewhat earlier than the date for the reburial suggested by the stylistic and inscriptional evidence. This discrepancy might be accounted for if the craftsmen who made the coffin recycled old timber, a regular practice in ancient Egypt.

J.H.T.

Sarcophagus lid of Sasobek

Late Period, Twenty-sixth Dynasty,
c. 630 BC

Provenance uncertain

Acquired at the sale of the Anastasi
collection in 1839

Siltstone

Length: 223 cm

EA 17

THE HEYDAY OF THE ANTHROPOID stone sarcophagus was after 700 BC, in the Late Period. Sasobek's sarcophagus is one of the finest examples of its type to have survived. It is of a relatively unusual type – finely detailed false divine beards are uncommon on such sarcophagi. Many other examples of this period display rather exaggerated wide facial features, but Sasobek's face is naturalistic (although not a portrait) and serene. The large ears may hint at some archaizing inspiration from monuments of the Middle Kingdom. The sarcophagus is in a superb state of preservation, having suffered damage only to the tip of the beard and the left side of the wig. Sasobek holds the *djed* pillar of Osiris in his right hand and the knot of Isis in his left. These amuletic symbols would grant him the stability and protection associated with the two deities. A broad collar runs across his shoulders, and below his hands is a kneeling winged figure of the goddess Nut, with her arms spread protectively across the body. Below the goddess are two columns of hieroglyphs, consisting of offering formulae, names, and titles.

The style of the sarcophagus suggests a date in the middle of the seventh century BC or a little later. Sasobek's principal title was that of vizier, and it seems most likely that he served in the reign of Psamtek I (664–610 BC). The provenance of this sarcophagus is less than certain. Thebes has been suggested as one possibility, although very few stone sarcophagi of this date have been unambiguously identified as coming from there, and this seems most unlikely. Similar sarcophagi come from the Memphite necropolis, and Sais, the city from which Psamtek's family came, has also been suggested; one of Sasobek's titles associates him with Neith, the goddess of Sais, although this does not necessarily indicate a Saite provenance. Sasobek's son Horwedja is known from a statue in Baltimore (Walters Art Gallery 154); he bears titles associated with both the Memphite region and with Neith.

A prosthetic toe

Before 600 BC

From Thebes

Acquired in 1881

Cartonnage

Length: 11.8 cm

EA 29996

THIS PROSTHESIS is in the shape of the big toe of the right foot, together with an area where it fitted on the foot, and has a number of holes around the edges through which it could be sewn onto something else (perhaps a sock or a sandal strap). The prosthesis is made of cartonnage, a material more commonly associated with mummy cases and masks, and composed of layers of linen impregnated with animal glue and gesso. This is covered with a tan-coloured layer which analysis has shown to be made of crushed dolomitic limestone with an ochre colourant. There is a space where the toenail might have been; a recess below the surface of the slot suggests that a separate imitation nail might have been inserted there.

It is difficult to assign a date to the object. The cloth used to create the cartonnage is a fine tabby weave, of a style very common in Egypt before Byzantine times; more relevantly, the threads of otherwise single yarn are sometimes doubled or plied, a feature characteristic of the dynastic period. This practice was only superseded by the more familiar draft spun yarns in roughly 600 BC, and suggests that the object was made before then.

Signs of wear and repair might indicate that the artificial toe had been used in life and was then buried with its owner. However, the lack of stiffer attachment options also suggests that it could have been used to repair damage to the body either immediately before death or in some unfortunate accident during the mummification process.

Very little evidence has survived from Egypt of attempts to create artificial limbs following the amputation of parts of the body. However, two other artificial toes have been discovered. The first is visible in an X-ray of a female mummy in the Albany Institute of History, and appears to have been made in two parts. The second was discovered in Theban Tomb 95 in the 1990s, actually attached to a mummy.

Gold cobra wearing the red crown of Lower Egypt

Late Period, after 600 BC

Provenance unknown

Acquired in 1886

Sheet gold

Length: 13.6 cm

EA 16518

THE COBRA was much feared and respected in Egypt. It possessed many different associations, particularly with royalty, and use of the symbol meant that the dangerous power of the cobra was magically turned to the user's benefit. Thus the king's uraeus, worn on his brow, is referred to in some battle texts as destroying his enemies and giving the king power over them. Images of Egyptian gods also bear the rearing cobra. It could be interpreted either as Hathor who, in the guise of the Eye of Re, was sent to destroy mankind for being disrespectful, or as Sekhmet, the fiery weapon of the god Re who could also be sent out to destroy the enemies of the gods. Re bequeathed this gift of potential destruction, represented by the rearing cobra, to his descendants, the kings of Egypt.

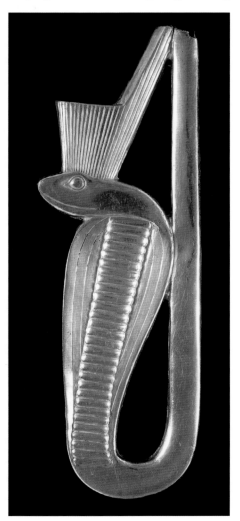

The rearing cobra also represents the goddess Wadjet, patron of the town of Buto. She and the vulture goddess Nekhbet, of el-Kab, represented Lower and Upper Egypt respectively and were shown wearing the appropriate red and white crowns. Together they were the tutelary goddesses of the third name of the king, the so-called 'two ladies' name, placing him under their protection. Hence the uraeus represents both Wadjet and the power immanent in the cobra.

The cobra was used as a decorative element on furniture, vessels, and jewellery. The fact that this cobra wears the red crown of Lower Egypt almost certainly means that it represents Wadjet. The fine workmanship and the material used suggest that it belonged to a piece of elite, perhaps royal, furniture, such as a chair.

Statue of Isis protecting Osiris

Late Period, Twenty-sixth Dynasty,
c. 590 BC

Probably from Karnak

Acquired in 1895

Grey siltstone

Height: 81.3 cm

EA 1162

THIS SMALL YET IMPRESSIVE statue shows Isis protecting a small figure of Osiris with her wings. The goddess wears a *modius*, a crown of uraeus serpents, surmounted by a pair of cows' horns and a sun-disc. The latter combination is worn by many female deities, and it is usually only other iconographical details and texts that allow the specific goddess to be identified. Osiris, as usual, is shown as a mummy wrapped in a tight robe, wearing the *atef* crown with two feathers and carrying a crook and flail, the symbols of kingship. Hieroglyphs in front of his feet give the god's name and epithets and the name of the dedicator of the object, Sheshonq; in front of these is a short recitation by Isis indicating that she protects her brother and defeats his enemies. The longer text running around the base of the statue is a prayer offered by Sheshonq to Isis, requesting a long life and a good burial.

Sheshonq's principal title was 'steward of the divine adoratrice of Amun'. The office of the 'divine adoratrice of Amun', also called 'god's wife of Amun', extends back into the late New Kingdom, but it became particularly important in Thebes during the Third Intermediate Period. At that time, the high priest of Amun was probably more concerned with temporal power, and the Amun cult revolved around a woman appointed to the 'divine adoratrice' post. These women were usually sisters or daughters of kings ruling in the north of Egypt, and their appointment in Thebes allowed these kings to keep a measure of influence there. They did not marry, and 'adopted' their successors under the influence of the current king.

The name Sheshonq is of Libyan origin and belonged to several kings of the Twenty-second and Twenty-third Dynasties (945–715 BC), but became popular among Egyptians from that time onwards. Ring EA 68868 (see page 272) bears the same name and title. Two men named Sheshonq are named as stewards of the divine adoratrices, and the limited information on the ring makes it difficult to know to which to ascribe it. The better-known Sheshonq (perhaps the more likely owner of both the ring and the statue) had an impressive tomb in the Assasif at Thebes, and worked under the divine adoratrice Ankhnesneferibre, daughter of Psamtek II, in the first half of the sixth century BC. The other Sheshonq lived somewhat later, perhaps also in the lifetime of Ankhnesneferibre, but in the second half of the same century. The sarcophagus of Ankhnesneferibre (see EA 32, pages 276–7), along with other material bearing her name, is in the British Museum.

The statue may have come from one of two chapels dedicated to forms of Osiris worshipped at Karnak. These were built and extended by the divine adoratrices and the kings with whom they were associated, and lie to the north of the main temple complex.

Gold ring of Sheshonq

Late Period, Twenty-sixth Dynasty,
early sixth century BC

Provenance unknown, but perhaps
from Thebes

Purchased in 1976

Gold

Diameter: 3.0 cm; length of
bezel: 3.4 cm

EA 68868

THIS MASSIVE GOLD RING is of a shape common for such rings in the Late Period, which more or less replaced the earlier stirrup-shaped type. The lozenge-shaped bezel is so thick that the back had to be cut away to accommodate the wearer's finger; the shank and the bezel were made in separate moulds and joined together. It is incised with the name of Sheshonq and his title, 'chief steward of the divine adoratrice'. The bezel could be pressed into clay to seal documents and objects. Besides having this functional aspect, the ring was no doubt also worn as a mark of Sheshonq's status and wealth.

Sheshonq was one of the most important figures in Thebes in the early sixth century BC. See EA 1162, pages 270–1, for more information.

Leg of a chair, stool or bed

Late Period, probably Twenty-fifth
Dynasty, eighth–seventh centuries BC

Provenance unknown

Acquired in 1893

Wood of the Christ's Thorn tree
(*Ziziphus spina-christi*)

Height: 42.3 cm

EA 24656

THE CENTRAL PART of this object is a human-headed sphinx, or
just possibly a cat, since Egyptian sphinxes are usually recumbent. The eyes were originally inlaid. The hair is represented by
a smooth raised area with a central forelock, a sidelock to left
and right, and long tresses at the back. The element through
which the leg was joined to a piece of furniture is somewhat
oval-shaped, pierced by mortise holes running front to back and
left to right. Below the first hole is a hieroglyph which represents Lower Egypt, with a lily above (a so-called 'lotus'). All the
decoration has been filled with a white pigment. The purpose of
the holes behind the ears and above the legs is unclear.

The leg's base is a rectangular block, with hieroglyphs on the
front for 'all life and dominion' and on the sides for 'all health
and all joy'. These expressions are found primarily in the context
of wishes for the king, suggesting that the leg might have come
from an item of royal furniture. The high quality of the work
would support this. The precise nature of the item of furniture
is uncertain, since chairs, stools, and beds all employ this type of
leg. Beds of this type are known in Nubia from the second
millennium BC to the present day, and frequently appeared in
tombs, supporting the corpse.

The treatment of the head, with its round and fleshy face, is
characteristic of Kushite sculpture of the Twenty-fifth Dynasty.
Similar hairstyles, with the hair gathered in four tufts, are found
on several representations of young Nubian women; they also
occur on a number of figurines in the shape of a cat or sphinx
associated with protection of women in childbirth. Perhaps the
item of furniture was associated with royal childbirth?

Kneeling statue of Wahibre

Late Period, Twenty-sixth Dynasty,
c. 530 BC

Said to be from near Lake Mareotis in
the north-west Delta

Gift of E. Fletcher in 1844

Basalt

Height: 180.3 cm

EA 111

THIS OVER-LIFE-SIZE STATUE of Wahibre shows him kneeling and presenting a small shrine containing a figure of Osiris. He wears a short *shendyt* kilt, in earlier times restricted to royalty. The front of the shrine, the base of the statue, and the back pillar are inscribed with hieroglyphs giving Wahibre's names and titles and the name of his father, Peftjaudineith. The statue exhibits many of the characteristic features of Late Period art. Wahibre's face is rather bland and devoid of expression; he looks straight in front of him, without the slightly upturned gaze seen on some statues of the later Twenty-sixth Dynasty. The stone is highly polished but sparsely decorated, emphasizing the hardness and magnificence of the stone.

Wahibre was a very important official in the Delta during the late Twenty-sixth or Saite Dynasty (so named since Sais – modern Sa el-Hagar – was its capital). One of his main titles was 'overseer of the door of the foreign lands', which presumably meant that he was responsible for the security of Egypt's borders; he was also a general, and other monuments assign him titles concerned with the southern borders of Egypt. It is presumed that his name reflects his birth in the reign of king Apries (589–570 BC), whose second cartouche name was Wahibre (he lived too late to have been named after Psamtek I, who was also called Wahibre). His importance can be judged from the resources to which he must have had access to be able to set up a statue like this. In fact, this is but one of a series of statues known of him, which includes seven in the Egyptian Museum in Cairo. One of these names his mother as Tashebenneith. The British Museum statue was probably set up in a temple, perhaps near a shrine of Osiris. It shows Wahibre demonstrating his piety by making a presentation to Osiris; he would thus expect to partake of the generosity and good fortune of the god, and to receive the offerings enumerated in the formulae on the base and the back pillar. Part of Wahibre's sarcophagus was found in the late nineteenth century in Kawadi, the area north-east of Sa el-Hagar. This might have been where his tomb was sited.

Judging from this statue's stated find spot, it had presumably been transported from its original location. It is reputed to have been found there in 1785, and was at some point brought back to England and deposited in Fletcher's warehouse in London, until he presented it to the Museum in 1844.

Sarcophagus of Ankhnesneferibre

Late Period, Twenty-sixth Dynasty,
c. 525 BC or before

From Thebes, Deir el-Medina

Acquired in 1836

Siltstone

Length: 259 cm

EA 32

THIS IMPRESSIVE SARCOPHAGUS, with its famous representation on the lid, belonged to a 'god's wife of Amun' or 'divine adoratrice of Amun' named Ankhnesneferibre, a daughter of Psamtek II (595–589 BC). Although it was found in a tomb at Deir el-Medina, Ankhnesneferibre and several other women with the same title had tomb chapels at Medinet Habu, in front of the great temple of Ramesses III. It seems that the sarcophagus was moved to a tomb (originally of the New Kingdom) at Deir el-Medina and usurped in the last years of the Ptolemaic Period (*c.* 40 BC) by one Amenhotep Pamontu, whose inscription can be seen in a horizontal line at the top of the sarcophagus base. Considerable modifications had to be made to the original tomb to accommodate the new burial. The sarcophagus of Nitocris, another divine adoratrice, daughter of Psamtek I (664–610 BC), was similarly moved to another tomb at the same site.

The inscriptions represent a range of religious texts, a combination unparalleled elsewhere. They include sections from the *Pyramid Texts*, the *Book of the Dead*, some mythological texts, recitations from funeral rites, magical texts, a hymn to the sun, and hourly rituals for a vigil over the deceased, as well as offering texts. All display the unifying theme of the rebirth of the deceased.

With the Theban high priests of Amun exercising enormous political power from the late New Kingdom onwards, the spiritual focus of the cult of Amun moved to these women. The office of divine adoratrice or 'god's wife' was not new (it is known from the Eighteenth Dynasty), but it now became a focus of power and influence. Ankhnesneferibre was 'adopted' as the successor to Nitocris, probably in the first year of her father's reign, and became the senior 'god's wife' in 584 BC. In turn she adopted another Nitocris, daughter of king Amasis (570–526 BC), as her successor. This mechanism of adoption was used by the northern kings as a way of asserting their influence in Thebes. Ankhnesneferibre's term of office seems to have continued until the Persian invasion in 525 BC.

The sarcophagus has an interesting modern history. The tomb in Deir el-Medina was discovered by officers of the French expedition to Egypt in 1831–3, whose aim was to bring one or both of the Luxor temple obelisks to France. The sarcophagus was taken to France along with the obelisk that is now in the Place de la Concorde in Paris. It was offered to France, but the French government would not pay for it, and it was eventually purchased for the British Museum in 1836. It is said that the remains of a mummy were found in the sarcophagus in 1832, and parts of a woman's body were located in the tomb during excavation in 1928, although it is unknown whether these remains are associated with Ankhnesneferibre.

Lion

Late Period, Twenty-sixth Dynasty
(664–525 BC)

From Akhmim

Acquired in 1888

Ivory on a wooden base

Length 16.5 cm

EA 20763

IT HAS BEEN SUGGESTED that this wonderful small recumbent lion was a decorative element from an item of furniture. Though many chairs have lion heads on the ends of their arms, or other two-dimensional relief elements on their backs and sides, there seem to be no examples of small separate sculptures like this. Two recumbent lions flank the headrest of Tutankhamun, thereby magically protecting the head of the king, but similar examples for non-royal persons are unknown. This might have been just a small free-standing sculpture that would magically protect the owners in whatever context it was made, either domestic or funerary. Comparison of this statuette with the massive Soleb lion of Amen-hotep III made for a temple (EA 2, pages 158–9), illustrates the Egyptians' mastery of animal sculpture of all sizes.

Jar in the shape of a hedgehog

Late Period, perhaps Twenty-sixth
Dynasty, seventh to sixth centuries BC

Provenance unknown

Details of acquisition unknown

Faience

Length: 6.2 cm

EA 58323

THIS SMALL, delicate vessel was probably intended to contain kohl (black eye-paint), as the opening in the back is just large enough for the insertion of a typical kohl stick. Vessels in the shape of hedgehogs are found in the Predynastic Period, but cosmetic containers of this type, with a criss-cross pattern representing the animal's spines, appear to be products of the New Kingdom to the Late Period.

No deity ever took the form of the hedgehog, but this animal must have had some symbolic value. In the Old Kingdom a hedgehog head is shown on the prow of boats making the symbolic passage from this life to the next, and it might be identified with a form of the sun god. The awakening of hedgehogs from hibernation may also be seen as a symbol of rebirth. In several scenes hedgehogs are shown as inhabiting the deserts; by living there, on the edge of the ordered world, they could be seen as triumphing over adversity, and hence as another symbol of continued life.

A selection of amulets

GIRDLE OF ISIS AMULET

This funerary amulet (opposite, left) is known as a *tit*, and takes the shape of an open loop of red jasper; from its bound lower end hangs a long sash flanked by two folded loops. There is a ribbed tube for suspension at the top. The amulet represents the girdle of Isis, the spouse of Osiris, who would protect the deceased. This example bears the name of a man called Nefer.

Chapter 156 of the *Book of the Dead* prescribes that such amulets should be made of red jasper, as here – the colour of the blood of the goddess Isis. Placed on the neck of the mummy, it would afford the body the protection of the goddess. In addition to jasper, other red stones could be used, or indeed glass. After the New Kingdom, examples in faience became more common.

COMPOSITE AMULET

This large amulet (opposite, centre) differs from the others in coming from a temple rather than a tomb. Its size suggests that it was intended to be carried. The benefits it would bestow on its owner or carrier are expressed by the composite set of amuletic images of which it is formed: superimposed on the front of the large *ankh* sign (the hieroglyph for 'life') are the *was* sceptre ('dominion') and the *djed* pillar ('stability'), while on top of the composite of the latter two is the hieroglyph *heh* 'millions (of years of life)'. Such composite amulets may have been associated with the rituals surrounding the celebration of the New Year festival. Gebel Barkal was one of the major religious centres of the Kushite kings.

FUNERARY SCARAB

Egyptian scarabs take several forms, ranging from early examples used as seals, to elaborate heart or commemorative scarabs. At the end of the Third Intermediate Period a medium-sized type of scarab with a flat undecorated base, like this one (opposite, right), began to be used in burials. These scarabs could be sewn onto mummy bandages like other small amulets which were buried with the dead at this time. The scarab amulet symbolized rebirth, as the insect's technique of rolling a dung ball from which its young emerged was seen as a representation both of the sun and of new life.

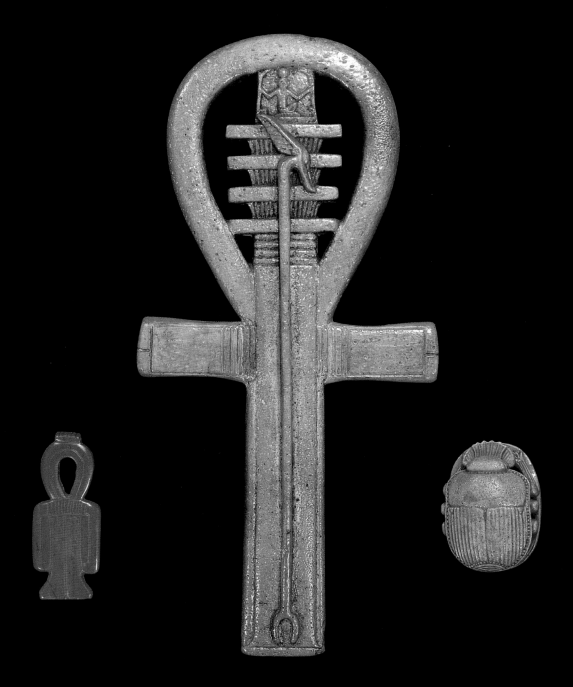

Architectural slab of Nectanebo I

Late Period, Thirtieth Dynasty,
380–362 BC

Found in the Alexandria area, original
provenance unknown

Gift of King George III in 1766 (along
with the similar slab EA 20). Originally
found by Edward Montagu in
Alexandria in 1762/63; his collection
subsequently went to the Earl of Bute
and then to George III.

Greywacke

Height: 122.6 cm

EA 22

THIS SLAB, finely carved from greywacke stone quarried in Wadi Hammammat, combines a number of traditional architectural motifs on both sides, though its precise purpose and original context is unclear. The feet and lower bodies survive from a frieze of birds, probably vultures, carved in high relief above the cornice. The other face of this slab was recut in ancient times, and bears part of a restoration text in Greek, but four similar slabs from the Twenty-sixth and Thirtieth Dynasties (BM EA 20, 998, Bologna 1870 and Vienna ÄS 213) show that this face would have been topped with a frieze of uraei (cobras). The monument thus juxtaposed the goddesses of northern and southern Egypt, Wadjet and Nekhbet.

In the main scene, a kneeling Nectanebo I is shown offering a loaf, delicately balanced in one hand. The king wears a tight-fitting cap adorned with a uraeus. His face, with its somewhat fleshy features, beaked nose, and narrow pursed lips, is one of the more individualistic representations of a pharaoh, but this does not imply that it is a true portrait. An emblematic representation of the goddess Wadjet is paired with the royal titulary in the short inscription in front of the king. The repetition of the royal names behind the king suggest that another image of him followed on an adjacent slab. The other slabs show the king, in various kneeling poses, offering both wine and incense. The recipient of these offerings was clearly a god (or gods), shown on the building's back wall or represented by the statue(s) housed within it.

The other decorated faces on these slabs, probably from the building's exterior, bear a very different type of scene, with the king offering to guardian or demon figures. Such scenes were usually concentrated on the exterior walls of temples, particularly around doorways, to protect the sacred building. The exact form of the original building(s) cannot be ascertained. It may have featured columns, though the surviving slabs did not abut them. Though the inscriptions suggest the building(s) may have been at Heliopolis, the purpose of the structure(s) is unclear. The combination of guardian figures with references to the Nile inundation, set within an apparently unroofed structure, recalls descriptions of New Year festivals in later Ptolemaic temples.

During the Thirtieth Dynasty, an ambitious temple building programme was undertaken. In Ptolemaic times, statuary and architecture of this period was evidently appreciated, and much was moved to Alexandria, including Nectanebo II's sarcophagus (see EA 10, pages 288–9). Were the holes in this piece the result of the slab's reuse in a different type of structure? The slabs arrived at the British Museum in 1766, nearly sixty years before hieroglyphs were first deciphered, and were erroneously described as being 'from the mausoleum of Cleopatra'.

N.A.S.

Torso of Nectanebo I

Late Period, Thirtieth Dynasty,
c. 380–362 BC

From Saft el-Henna

Presented (?) by Edouard Naville in
1885

Granodiorite

Height: 66 cm

EA 1013

THIS FINELY MODELLED torso of grey-green/black granodiorite shows the king standing in the conventional pose, his left foot forward and arms by his side. He wears the usual *shendyt* royal kilt. The back pillar still bears most of its original inscription; the right-hand column contains all the royal names of Nectanebo I apart from his birth name, while the left describes him as beloved of the gods Sopdu and Re-Horakhty. Sopdu is given his common epithet 'lord of the East'; as this indicates, he was associated with the eastern borders, and also protected Egyptian interests in the Sinai. His main cult centre was Saft el-Henna. Re-Horakhty was a combined form of the sun god and Horus of the horizon (and hence also associated with the east).

Egyptian royal sculpture experienced a remarkable revival around 700 BC. Many of the developments looked back to some of the great sculptural products of the Old and Middle Kingdoms, though new and distinctive manners of representation were also developed. Many involved the facial features, but two other aspects are important: the first is the characteristic manner of modelling the torso, generally referred to as tripartition, whereby the sculptor makes distinctions between the chest, rib cage, and abdominal regions. This contrasts with the previous bipartite division into two halves. The tripartite manner developed in the Twenty-sixth Dynasty. A feature of the sculpture of Nectanebo I is what might be termed 'restrained tripartition', as here. The other noteworthy feature is that this statue, like others made after 700 BC, was highly polished.

The Thirtieth Dynasty is the last period in which 'native' Egyptians sat on the throne of the Two Lands. Nectanebo I (380–362 BC, Egyptian name: Nakhtnebef) was the first and greatest ruler of the dynasty. He came from Sebennytos (modern Samannud) in the centre of the Delta, and undertook building and sculptural programmes on a scale not seen since the heyday of the Twenty-sixth Dynasty in the sixth century BC. Nectanebo constructed a temple at Saft el-Henna, in the south-eastern Delta, from which this statue must have come.

It is not clear how this statue came to be in the British Museum. Edouard Naville worked at Saft el-Henna in the winter of 1885, during his survey of Delta sites, and in his May 1887 publication he states that the statue was already in the British Museum. Unpublished correspondence with the Egypt Exploration Fund (now held at the Egypt Exploration Society), for which Naville was working, indicates that he was given the torso by the son of a local dignitary; in the publication he says it was purchased 'from a reluctant fellah'. The head of the Antiquities Service, Gaston Maspero, permitted Naville to keep the object, and it thus seems most likely that he presented it to the British Museum on his return.

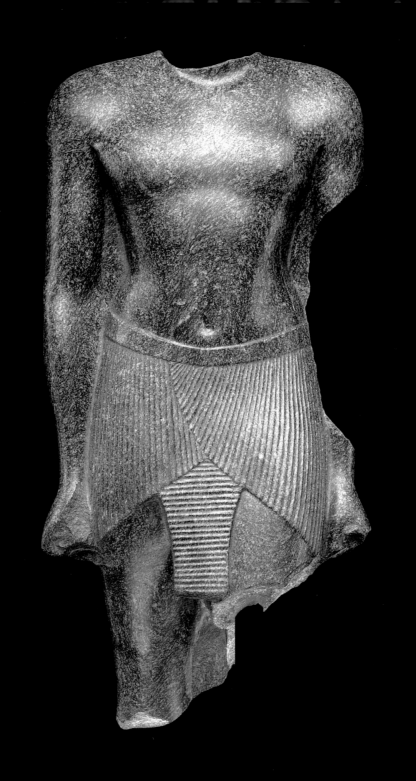

Two obelisks of Nectanebo II

Late Period, Thirtieth Dynasty,
c. 360–343 BC

Found in Cairo, but probably from
Hermopolis in Middle Egypt

Gift of King George III in 1802

Siltstone

EA 524

Height: 256 cm

EA 523

Height: 274 cm

EGYPTIAN OBELISKS were solar symbols and were a very prominent feature of temples, particularly in the New Kingdom. They were usually erected in pairs, in front of an entrance gateway or pylon. Many are massive, like the well-known 'Cleopatra's Needles' in London and New York, but there were also many smaller examples, such as those shown here, which may have stood at the entrance to a ramp into a temple. These obelisks, probably originally about 5.5 m high, were dedicated by Nectanebo II (*c.* 360–343 BC) to the Egyptian god Thoth, usually depicted as an ibis-headed man, here called 'Lord of Hermopolis, who dwells in Hesret and who dwells in the Mansion of the Net'. This inscription provides the clue to their original provenance: Hermopolis, one of the major cult centres of Thoth, is modern el-Ashmunein in Middle Egypt, and the other names in the inscription refer to sections and temples of that city specifically concerned with Thoth. Most of the remains of the site now visible date from the Ptolemaic or Roman Period, but a British Museum expedition which worked there from 1980 to 1990 found many remains of older temples. The inscription describes the obelisks as being topped with precious metal.

The obelisks have an interesting modern history. One of them (EA 523) was first spotted reused in a window-sill in the Citadel in Cairo by Richard Pococke, one of the first British travellers to Egypt, in 1737, while the other was spotted in 1762 in the same area by the Danish mathematician Carsten Niebuhr. Both fragments were seen again by the *savants* who accompanied Napoleon Bonaparte's 1798 expedition to Egypt. They were recorded for the later *Description de l'Egypte* and were taken to Alexandria, in preparation for transport to France in 1801. Following the surrender of the French expedition to the British in the same year, these two obelisks, along with other objects, the most famous of which was the Rosetta Stone, came to Britain as a result of the Treaty of Alexandria, and were presented to the British Museum by George III. Another fragment of the upper part of EA 524 is in the Egyptian Museum in Cairo (CG 17030).

The Thirtieth Dynasty came from Sebennytos (modern Samannud) in the Delta, and was the last Egyptian-born political dynasty to rule the country until the 1952 revolution; Nectanebo II was its last ruler. In the nearly forty years of the dynasty's rule, Egypt witnessed the last great native flowering of artistic and architectural creativity before the second Persian conquest and the arrival of Alexander the Great. Many temples were rebuilt or expanded, and there can be no doubt that these obelisks were set up as part of these building programmes. See EA 10, pages 288–9, for the sarcophagus of Nectanebo II, whose Egyptian name is Nakhthorheb.

Sarcophagus of Nectanebo II

Late Period, Thirtieth Dynasty,
c. 360–343 BC

Found in the Attarin mosque in
Alexandria

Gift of King George III in 1802

Conglomerate

Length: 313.5 cm

EA 10

NECTANEBO II was the last native king of Egypt, the great-grandson of Nectanebo I. His reign (360–343 BC) was ended by the second Persian occupation of Egypt, and it is said that he fled to Ethiopia. It is thus uncertain where he died, or whether his body was brought back to Egypt for burial. This sarcophagus was almost certainly prepared before his flight and may never have been used. If it was, it might have been buried in his dynasty's home town of Sebennytos (modern Samannud in the Delta). Alternatively, it has been suggested that it may have come from some pharaonic settlement near Alexandria, but this remains unproven. Like the Rosetta Stone (EA 24, pages 298–9) and the obelisks (EA 523/4, pages 286–7), it was collected by the Napoleonic expedition to Egypt, and came to the British Museum in 1802 as a result of the Treaty of Alexandria.

The sarcophagus was found in the Attarin Mosque at Alexandria, formerly the church of St Athanasius. At some time it was clearly used as a water container, bath, or tank for ablutions, as shown by the twelve holes drilled around the base to let water out. A myth grew up that it was the sarcophagus of Alexander the Great. This story probably does not antedate the Arab conquest, and seems to have changed subtly in the nineteenth century, after the hieroglyphs were translated. At that point it was realized that the texts did not name Alexander, and the story changed to the site of the mosque being the original location of Alexander's tomb. There seems to be no support for either of these ideas; to this day, his burial place remains undiscovered.

The decoration on the sarcophagus consists of six sections of the funerary text known as the *Amduat*, or 'what is in the netherworld'. This text is primarily known from inscriptions in the New Kingdom tombs of the Valley of the Kings, but after the New Kingdom it began to be written on coffins and on papyri (see the papyrus of Anhai, EA 10472, pages 236–7). In the Thirtieth Dynasty and early Ptolemaic Period many sarcophagi were decorated with this religious text, and it was still occasionally mentioned in papyri of the Roman Period. The *Amduat* charts the nightly passage of the sun god through the underworld; hence it is divided into the twelve hours of the night and illustrates the environment of each hour and what happens in that hour. For example, the third hour of the night is primarily water, while the fourth hour is a fiery desert; in the seventh hour the sun-god meets his primary opponent, the serpent Apophis, who is then dismembered by the sun-god's assistants. The central feature of each hour is of course the barque of the sun-god. In the twelfth hour the sun is reborn.

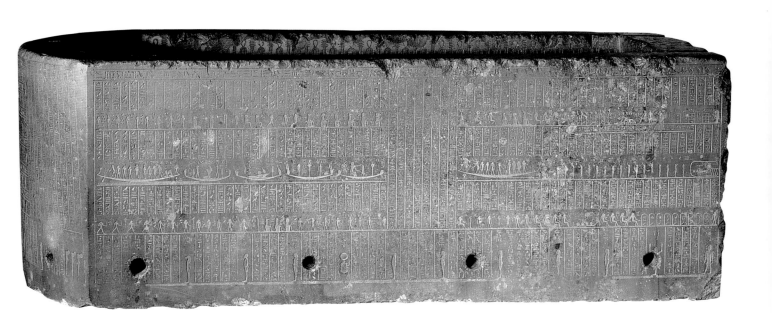

Bronze figure of a seated cat

Late Period, 664–332 BC

Said to be from Saqqara

Gift of Major R.G. Gayer-Anderson
in 1939

Bronze

Height: 42 cm

EA 64391

IN THE POPULAR IMAGINATION the domesticated cat is associated more with ancient Egypt than with any other culture. This bronze statue is probably the finest example of the many such seated figures of cats. It wears gold earrings, and has a silvered collar round its neck and a silver *wedjat* eye amulet over the collar. Below the collar and *wedjat* eye is an incised winged scarab beetle, pushing a silver sun disc. A second scarab is modelled in the bronze on the cat's forehead. The *wedjat* eye symbolizes protection and regeneration, and the scarab, symbolizing the sun, is also a metaphor of rebirth as exemplified in the daily solar cycle. Recent microscopic examinations have shown that the bronze has oxidized to red-brown in many places, and was given an artificial 'patina' by the addition of a modern coat of green paint. X rays reveal possible core material (used to model the statue) in the head area, and also considerable modern repairs.

Feline deities played an important role in the pantheon of ancient Egypt. The cat came to be primarily identified with the goddess Bastet, whose cult centre was at Bubastis in the Nile Delta. Depictions of her with a feline head are known from the Old Kingdom, but the association between the cat and Bastet is probably linked to the rise of Bubastis, when its rulers became the kings of Egypt, forming the Twenty-second Dynasty, sometimes known as the 'Libyan Dynasty'.

Bastet's popularity in these later periods may be tied in with various aspects of feline behaviour, such as the cat's fertility and its motherly and aggressive instincts in protecting its young. As with other creatures sacred to particular deities, it became very popular in the Late Period (664–332 BC) to bury mummies of cats in special cemeteries as a sign of devotion to the goddess. Several cat cemeteries are known from Egypt, and the British Museum has a number of cat mummies. The animals were bred not just as sacred cats but also as ready subjects for mummification: X-ray examination shows that many of the necks of mummified cats were deliberately broken.

This bronze is popularly known as the Gayer-Anderson cat, after its donor. Major Gayer-Anderson lived in Cairo for many years after retiring from the army in 1920, and when he returned to Britain he left his house near the Ibn Tulun mosque to Egypt, to be opened as a museum in his name. The museum still exists. Gayer-Anderson presented most of his collection to the Fitzwilliam Museum in Cambridge in 1943.

A late first-millennium BC king

Perhaps Thirtieth Dynasty or early
Ptolemaic Period, *c.* 360–246 BC

Provenance unknown

Donated in 1854 by Queen Victoria,
who had received it as a gift from the
British Consul-General in Egypt

Egyptian alabaster

Height: 61 cm

EA 941

THIS HIGHLY ATTRACTIVE STATUE, made from a block of beautifully veined Egyptian alabaster, depicts a king with a *nemes* headdress surmounted by a uraeus. Somewhat unusually, the *nemes* lies on a separate layer and is not shown directly on the chest, as would be normal. The reverse of the headdress tapers into a rather more pointed shape than usual; underneath it the layer referred to above is extremely broad. The king's left arm is held at his side, and his right arm crosses his chest. He has a long false beard. The statue may not have been finished, to judge from the ears.

The date of this object has been the subject of some debate (it has even been suggested that it is a forgery, but this is dismissed by art historians). The shallow, very almond-shaped eyes and the general appearance of the face are characteristic of the period from the Twenty-sixth Dynasty to the early Ptolemaic Period. The two preferred dates for the statue are the reign of Nectanebo II (360–343 BC) or that of Ptolemy II (284–246 BC).

The most unusual features of this statue are the use of alabaster (almost uniquely at this time), the long beard, the pose, and the layer under the headdress. An intriguing solution has been proposed to explain them, suggesting that the piece was carved in a strongly archaizing style, based on the famous statue of Netjerikhet (Djoser) of the Third Dynasty from the Step Pyramid at Saqqara, which probably represents the king as a deified being. A similar beard, the position of the right arm, and a double headdress are seen on that statue, but are otherwise unknown during the first millennium BC – beards themselves are rare, and are usually much shorter. While later periods of Egyptian history are known for their archaizing tendencies, artists did not usually look as far back as the Third Dynasty. However, at Saqqara in the Late Period, there was so much interest in the Step Pyramid that a new entrance was cut into its interior (usually referred to as the 'Saite Entrance') from the south; it is possible that the famous statue of Netjerikhet, or one very like it but now lost, was discovered in the course of this or other clearance works undertaken at this time. The impression made by such a statue may have inspired the creation of this piece; although we do not know its provenance, it might have been set up in some enclosure at Saqqara, to give ancient authority to the cult of a more recent ruler.

Burial assemblage of Hornedjtyitif

Early Ptolemaic Period,
mid–late third century BC

From Thebes

Purchased at the sale of the third Salt
collection in 1835

INNER COFFIN

Wood, gessoed and gilded

Length: 194.5 cm

EA 6678

THE PRESUMABLY INTACT TOMB of Hornedjtyitif was discovered by local diggers in Thebes, probably in the Assasif area in the 1820s. The owner was a priest of Amun at Karnak, who seems to have died in the reign of Ptolemy III (246–221 BC). He held an impressive set of titles, and one of the cults with which he was associated was that of the deified queen Arsinoe II, mother of Ptolemy III, as well as those of Ptolemy III himself and his wife Berenike II.

A range of objects was recovered from the burial and acquired by Henry Salt's agent Giovanni d'Athanasi. A massive wooden outer coffin contained a wooden inner coffin, inside which was the mummy. Other objects which form part of the assemblage are a hypocephalus, two papyrus *Books of the Dead*, a Ptah-Sokar-Osiris figure, and a canopic chest. All these objects, apart from one papyrus and the canopic chest (P Amherst 35, Pierpont Morgan Library, New York and Leiden AH 215 respectively), are in the British Museum.

The massive outer coffin (illustrated on page 297) is decorated in yellow outline on a black background. The decoration consists of a broad collar with a pectoral showing the owner before deities, and funerary texts. On the interior of the base is the sky goddess Nut. The inner coffin (opposite, left) also has a broad collar and a very similar pectoral, depictions of deities, and funerary texts, but this is all painted in polychrome on the natural wooden surface. The outstanding feature of this coffin is the striking gilded face and divine beard, emphasizing the deceased's identification with a divine being. Equally remarkable is the lid's underside (opposite, right), decorated with another figure of Nut, surrounded by astronomical representations of decans (the 36 groups of stars into which Egyptians divided the night sky), constellations, and protective deities.

Hornedjtyitif's mummy (not illustrated) is enclosed in a cartonnage covering from the shoulders to the feet, with a separate mask for the head. The covering bears numerous images of funerary deities and demons, and the mask, like the inner coffin, has a gilded face. A pair of sandals is painted on the bottom of the foot case, with a foreign captive, representing the deceased's triumph over the forces of evil and chaos, on the sole of each sandal. One of the papyri was found inside the inner coffin. The papyri bear chapters from the *Book of the Dead*, written in hieratic and accompanied by vignettes. Sheet 1 of papyrus EA 10037 is shown on page 296. The hypocephalus (shown on page 297) is a disc of painted and inscribed cartonnage. Its function was amuletic, and it was placed under the head of the mummy to ensure the rebirth of the deceased. The texts on it relate to Spell 162 of *The Book of the Dead*.

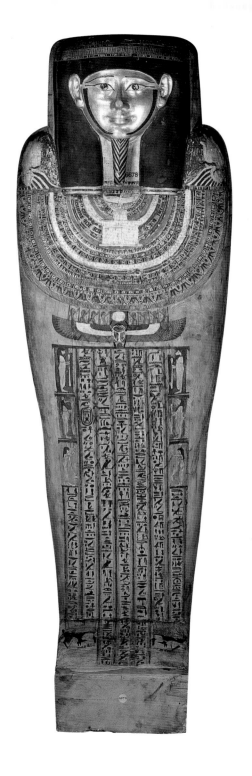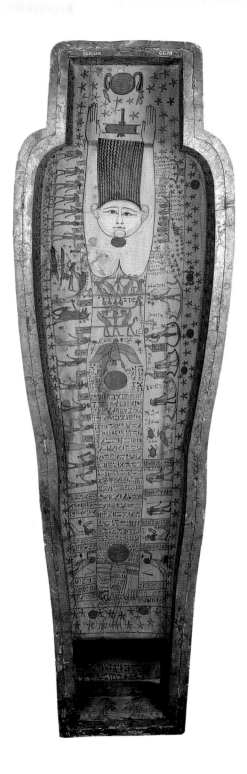

Ptah-Sokar-Osiris figures (opposite, top right) developed from the Osiride figures which originated in the New Kingdom (see the Osiris figure of Anhai, EA 20868, pages 236–7). In the Third Intermediate Period, they developed into mummiform figures of the deity Ptah-Sokar-Osiris, a syncretistic amalgam of two deities associated with resurrection: Osiris, originally from Abydos, and Ptah-Sokar, from Memphis. Under the small falcon in front of the figure was usually a cavity, which often held a corn-mummy, another symbol of Osiris' resurrection.

Inside the canopic chest were wrapped bundles, but examination has shown that these contain only potsherds; radiological examination of the mummy shows four packages inside the body which are probably the embalmed internal organs. It seems likely that the canopic chest was provided purely because Hornedjtyitif and/or those who were assembling the burial goods felt the need to pay their respects to a tradition which went back to the Old Kingdom, but which was dying out in early Ptolemaic times.

The Rosetta Stone

Ptolemaic Period, reign of Ptolemy V,
196 BC

From Fort St Julien, el-Rashid (Rosetta)

Gift of King George III in 1802

Granodiorite

Height: 112.3 cm

EA 24

SOLDIERS OF THE ARMY sent to Egypt in 1798 by Napoleon Bonaparte discovered the Rosetta Stone in 1799 while digging foundations for an addition to a fort near el-Rashid (Rosetta). On Napoleon's defeat, the stone was surrendered to the British under the terms of the Treaty of Alexandria (1801), along with other antiquities. These were given to the British Museum by King George III.

This irregularly-shaped stone is part of an inscribed stela with a text in three different scripts. It had been set up in a temple at Sais, but was probably re-used as a building block and moved to Rosetta in the mediaeval period. At the top are 14 lines of hieroglyphs, followed by 32 lines of the cursive Egyptian script known as Demotic; at the bottom are 54 lines of Greek. Although now famous for its role in the decipherment of hieroglyphs, the Rosetta Stone was primarily a political and religious document. In the years preceding its erection, the Ptolemaic Dynasty, who had ruled Egypt since its occupation by Alexander the Great in 332 BC, had lost control of parts of Egypt. It took some time to crush opposition in the Delta; parts of southern Upper Egypt, particularly Thebes, were not yet under government control. In 196 BC, it was decided to re-emphasize the traditional royal credentials and legitimacy of the 13-year-old Ptolemy V in the eyes of the Egyptian elite with a coronation ceremony in Memphis, and to affirm his royal cult throughout Egypt. This second aim was commemorated through a series of decrees issued by the Egyptian priests, of which the Rosetta Stone is by far the best-known example. Ptolemy had in fact been king since his father died unexpectedly in 205 BC, and was only six at his accession.

In earlier times, such decrees were issued by the king, but this one was issued by the native Egyptian priests, who maintained the native pharaonic culture, including the traditional hieroglyphic script, in an increasingly multicultural country. The agreement between the court and the priests is a part of the complex cultural fusion of the country at this period. The scripts on the decree reflect the different levels at which it functioned: the hieroglyphs made it suitable for a priestly temple decree and are thus at the top; the Demotic reflected the native daily script; and Greek was the language of the administration.

The importance of this inscription to Egyptology is immense. Soon after the end of the fourth century AD, knowledge of how to read and write hieroglyphs disappeared. When the stone was discovered, it was realized that the Greek text, which was comprehensible, might give clues for the decipherment of the other two scripts. Thomas Young, an English physicist, was the first to understand some aspects of the ancient scripts, but it was the work of the French scholar, Jean-François Champollion, which ultimately led to the decipherment of hieroglyphs in 1824.

A naos of Ptolemy VIII

Ptolemaic Period, reign of Ptolemy VIII,
c. 150 BC

From Philae

Gift of the government of the British
Protectorate of Egypt in 1886 or 1887

Red granite

Height: 251.5 cm

EA 1134

'NAOS' MEANS 'SHRINE', and is most commonly used by Egyptologists to describe the central shrine of a temple, in which the cult image would be housed. Naoi, to use the plural, are usually made from single pieces of very hard stone. Numerous examples still exist; perhaps the best-preserved is that in the temple of Edfu, built by Nectanebo II of the Thirtieth Dynasty. Earlier shrines may also have been monolithic, or could have taken the form of a small wooden construction on a stone base.

This naos is surmounted by a cornice of uraei (serpents) with three winged sun-discs beneath. Flanking the central void are columns of hieroglyphs giving the names and titles of Ptolemy VIII and his wife Cleopatra II, flanked in turn by a papyrus column on each side. Beneath the void are two winged sun-discs and two opposed representations of a king, his arms upraised to support a large sky hieroglyph. Adjacent texts include a dedication to Isis. Extensive traces of red colouring survive; they may have been added after the shrine's original use as the red hue is rather bright for ancient Egyptian paint.

The central feature is the large void in which the image of the god would have been placed. The interior is undecorated, and the space would have been closed off by a pair of wooden doors. A number of small recesses in the stone surrounding the space indicate that the doors pivoted between the top of the space and the top of the small granite jamb that runs from the bottom to roughly half-way up, thus giving the doors something of an L shape. Four other recesses show that bolts to hold the doors closed operated at the sides, top, and bottom of the doors.

This naos, with various other blocks, was found reused in a Coptic church on the island of Philae, a major centre of the cult of Isis in Ptolemaic and Roman times. Judging from the dedication to Isis, it is likely that it held an image of that goddess. Two other larger naoi, now in Florence and the Louvre, are known from Philae, both of which were seen in 1828–9 by Champollion and Rosellini in either the main sanctuary of the temple or one of the adjacent rooms. Both were also dedicated by Ptolemy VIII. Perhaps the British Museum naos came from a smaller sanctuary in the temple. The great temple of Isis was moved during the 1970s to a higher site on the nearby Agilika island, to save it from the rising waters behind the Aswan dam.

It seems that this object came to London as the result of an accommodation between the British Museum and Egypt. For many years the British Museum had claimed the fallen colossus of Ramesses II at Memphis. In 1886–7 Budge relates that this naos was offered to the Museum instead to end the claim.

Stela of Taimhotep

Late Ptolemaic Period, 43/42 BC

From Saqqara or Memphis

Purchased as part of the first Salt collection in 1823

Limestone

Height: 90.2 cm

EA 147

SEVERAL FINE PTOLEMAIC STELAE come from the Memphite region; this example is perhaps one of the most accomplished and certainly among the most interesting. At the top, under a large winged sun-disc with two pendant uraei, Taimhotep is shown on the right, adoring and making offerings to a series of deities: the necropolis god Sokar-Osiris, the Apis bull, Isis, Nephthys, Horus avenger of his father, Anubis, and the personification of the West. Below are twenty-one lines of hieroglyphs.

This text is a sophisticated example of the tomb autobiography genre. It begins with a series of epithets praising Taimhotep, and then invites visitors to the tomb to listen to her story. She was born in year 9 of Ptolemy XII (73 BC), and in his year 23, at the age of 14, she was married to Pasherenptah, the high priest of Memphis. She gave birth to three daughters but no son, and they appealed to the god Imhotep (a deified form of the architect of the Third Dynasty Step Pyramid, regarded as a healing deity and often identified with the Greek Asklepios) for a male child. Imhotep appeared to Pasherenptah in a dream, asking him to carry out a 'great work' in his sanctuary in Memphis, in return for which he would give him a son.

This work was duly carried out, Taimhotep became pregnant, and her son was born in year 6 of Cleopatra VII (46 BC). He was named Imhotep and Padibastet; later he became high priest of Memphis. Four years later, she died at the age of 31 and was buried by her husband, who set up this stela for her.

In the last part of the text, the deceased Taimhotep paints a pessimistic view of death and urges her husband to 'eat, drink, and be merry'. There is of course no proof that this was her wish, and was not added to the stela by her husband. This lyric presents a very traditional Egyptian concept, which can be traced back at least to the so-called 'Song of the Harper', known from the New Kingdom, and to Middle Kingdom poetry.

A stela of Pasherenptah is also in the British Museum's collection (EA 886). He too is shown before a row of deities, and the accompanying text includes an informative although perhaps more conventional biographical text, indicating that he became high priest of Ptah at the age of 14, and in 76 BC crowned Ptolemy XII (father of the famous Cleopatra). He died a year after Taimhotep.

Mummy of Artemidorus

Roman Period, AD 100–20

From Hawara

Gift of H. Martyn Kennard in 1888

Stucco with portrait in encaustic
on limewood

Length: 171 cm

EA 21810

IN 30 BC, EGYPT BECAME A ROMAN PROVINCE. Earlier funerary traditions were maintained, but the influence of the classical world gradually became more visible. One of the innovations of this period was the mummy portrait.

The body of Artemidorus is enclosed in a red-painted stucco casing into which a portrait panel has been inserted, showing the face of a young man in three-quarter view; the lower edges of the frame of the portrait are cut to resemble the shape of contemporary busts.

Below the portrait is a falcon-collar of gold leaf with hawk-headed terminals representing Horus. The identity of the deceased is preserved in a short, misspelled Greek inscription across the breast, which reads 'Farewell, Artemidorus'. Below the collar is a range of Egyptian funerary scenes, applied in gold leaf in six registers. The largest of these shows the god Anubis attending the mummy, which lies on a lion-shaped bier flanked by goddesses (probably Isis and Nephthys). Below this, Thoth and Re-Horakhty stand either side of a symbol of Osiris that represents his cult-centre at Abydos, while below that, Osiris himself is depicted on a bier, awakening to new life. Over the feet, gilded sandals are shown flanking the *atef* crown of Osiris. This mummy represents an excellent example of the merging of cultural influences: a Greek personal name and a Romanized portrait together with traditional Egyptian funerary deities protecting the deceased.

CAT scans of this mummy reveal evidence of damage to bones in the area of the nose. There are no signs of healing and, while it is possible that they are as a result of rough post-mortem treatment, it is conceivable that these injuries were the result of an assault and may have been the cause of death. There are also some cracks on the back of the skull, which could also be from ante-mortem injury or post-mortem treatment. Artemidorus was probably between 18 and 21 when he died, in keeping with the age suggested by the portrait. His hairstyle is typical of the period of the Roman emperor Trajan.

Artemidorus' mummy was found during W.M.F. Petrie's excavations of the Roman cemetery at Hawara in the Faiyum. This cemetery was a great source of Roman portrait mummies, and that of Artemidorus was discovered in a brick-lined tomb with that of another Artemidorus, perhaps his father (now in Manchester, 1775), and a woman named Thermoutharin (now in Cairo, JE 33231). The style of all three is extremely similar and they must have come from the same workshop. An interesting entry from Petrie's diary records that they were discovered on the day that Heinrich Schliemann, the excavator of Troy, was Petrie's lunch guest.

Mask of a woman

Roman Period, *c.* AD 100-120

Provenance unknown

Acquired in 1897

Cartonnage, plaster, paint

Height: 68 cm

EA 29476

THE BEST-KNOWN FUNERARY representations from Roman Egypt are the so-called 'mummy portraits' (see EA 21810, pages 304–5, and EA 65346, pages 312–13) but plaster masks, often extending over the upper body, were also popular, and are found from the earliest years of the Roman occupation.

The face of this mask was shaped separately by pressing the plaster onto a mould; on some examples this method of manufacture is clearly indicated by finger-marks on the interior. This face was subsequently attached to the headdress and torso, and the somewhat unusual orientation of the head is probably due to a rather awkward join with the other parts.

The anonymous woman wears a yellow tunic, leaving her breasts exposed. A band of cloth runs from the tunic between the breasts onto a colourful collar, at the bottom of which is a winged scarab beetle. In her hair is a garland of rosebuds. Her sleeves bear the protective wings of Isis and Nephthys, and images of other deities appear on the area of the mask behind her hair. These include Anubis and Re-Horakhty. The woman wears earrings, gold bracelets on both wrists, and two rings on the fingers of her left hand. She holds a sprig of leaves, perhaps myrtle.

The style of the earrings, bracelets, and rings suggests a date in the early second century AD; around that time this hairstyle, based on a traditional Egyptian one, became popular in funerary portraits. The style of the facial representation, the hair, and elements of the dress show strong classical influence, but the religious iconographical elements show that the fundamental concepts of the Egyptian way of death were still to be found well into the Roman era, with the scarab symbolizing both the solar cycle and the regeneration of life, and Isis, Nephthys, and the other deities protecting the owner.

Little is known about the specific findspots of such masks, although they seem to have been particularly popular in Middle Egypt. This object is unprovenanced, but it has been argued that it may be associated with the types of mask that covered a considerable part of the upper body, and which have been found from the Roman Period, in particular the later second and third centuries AD, at Deir el-Medina and Deir el-Bahari in the Theban region.

The burials of the Soter family

Roman Period, early second century AD

From Thebes, probably TT32

Purchased as part of the first Salt collection in 1823

IN JANUARY 1820 a tomb was found in the Theban necropolis belonging to members of the family of Soter; the coffins and mummies are now in various European museums. The findspot has been plausibly identified as Theban Tomb 32 of Djehutymose, constructed in Ramesses II's reign. Other material from this group was located in Theban Tomb 317, and in debris surrounding the Deir el-Bahari temple. Epigraphic evidence allows deaths in the family group to be dated to specific years of the reigns of Trajan, Hadrian, and Antoninus Pius, in the first half of the second century AD. These dates match the stylistic indications of motifs on the coffins. The inscriptions are in hieroglyphic and Greek, the hieroglyphic ones being of a religious nature, and those in Greek providing genealogical data about the occupants, including ages at death. Soter himself was an official in Thebes, probably more prominent within the local native Egyptian rather than the Greek community.

COFFIN OF SOTER

Painted wood

Length: 213 cm

EA 6705

LID OF THE COFFIN OF SOTER
The exterior decoration of Soter's coffin comes from the traditional Egyptian repertoire. It includes the judgement of the dead and the presentation of the deceased to Osiris, plus scenes with the sun-god and other deities essential to the deceased's welfare. Inside (opposite, left) is a large figure of the sky-goddess Nut, stretched above the mummy. Her dress is overlaid by a stylized bead net, symbolizing her role as sky goddess, though this garment also has connections with Osiris dating back to the New Kingdom. Twelve female figures on each side personify the hours of day and night, and the morning and evening sun in barques frame the goddess' head. Flanking Nut's body are the signs of the zodiac, Leo to Capricorn on the left and Aquarius to Cancer on the right. These zodiacal signs use Egyptian forms, like those on the famous example from Dendera now in the Louvre, rather than Greek forms, seen in some Roman tombs in Egypt. The zodiac inside the coffin (found on all coffins in the group) stresses that the space enclosing the body should be equated with the area of rebirth and renewal, which is both the tomb and the temple.

A shroud of Soter is also in the Museum's collection (EA 6705A).

MUMMY OF CLEOPATRA

Length: 161 cm

EA 6707

MUMMY AND COFFIN OF CLEOPATRA
Cleopatra was a daughter of Soter and his wife Cleopatra Candace. According to a hieroglyphic inscription on her coffin (EA 6706), she died at the age of perhaps 17 years. This would have been in the second century AD, probably in the reign of the emperor Trajan. For many years her age was read as 11 years, but examination of the mummy with CAT

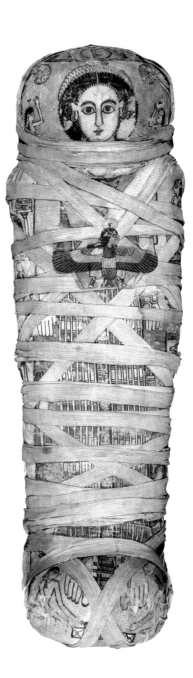

COFFIN OF CLEOPATRA

Painted wood

Length: 183 cm

EA 6706

scans has suggested she was more mature, prompting a re-reading of the text.

A cloth or shroud was placed over the mummy (page 309, right) after the principal wrapping had taken place, and several individual bandages were then wound round it. The shroud bears a painted image of a young woman, with hair and jewellery in the typical style of the period. Roman victory figures also appear on the shroud. Cleopatra is shown as the goddess Hathor, victorious over death and proceeding into the afterlife. On the mummy's breast is a small human-headed bird made of cartonnage.

Cleopatra's coffin (below) is essentially the same shape as the outer coffin of Hor (see EA 15655, pages 258–9), with a post at each corner and a vaulted lid. This design of coffin appeared in about 750 BC and is believed to represent a shrine for the body of a god, in this case the divine transfigured dead Cleopatra. Unlike Hor, Cleopatra's mummy was placed directly inside the coffin, and a large deposit of black resin, with scraps of linen adhering, marks the outline of the mummy. The coffin is decorated inside and out; on the base was an image of (probably) Nut, with another image of the goddess on the vault of the lid. On the side shown below, the daily voyage of the boat of the sun-god (shown as a sun-disc in which is a figure of the god) is depicted. On the lid at this point is a series of winged deities with their arms raised in adoration.

Mummy of a man

Roman Period

Provenance unknown

Acquired at the sale of the third Salt
collection in 1835

Length: 162 cm

EA 6704

A LARGE NUMBER of mummies from the Roman Period has survived. Many are very elaborately decorated on the exterior, suggesting that the external appearance was perhaps
paramount at this time, rather as it had been in the Old Kingdom. The quality of the
mummification inside the wrappings was frequently poor, and examples are known of
incomplete bodies or even of animal parts substituted for human remains.

This is the mummy of an anonymous adult man, and is among the best-preserved
examples known. The external preparation has been carried out with great care and skill
by the embalmer, and the contours of a living body have been skilfully imitated. The arms
are extended at the sides of the body, and the fingers are extended, touching the thighs.
The facial features, including eyes and a stylized beard, are painted on the outermost
wrappings, and the crown of the head was deliberately left uncovered so as to reveal the
natural hair of the deceased. The fingers and toes are each wrapped separately, and the
forearms have a series of bandages applied in geometric patterns. The nipples, fingernails,
and toenails are all gilded; a lotus flower has been painted on each knee. A waistband,
armlets, and anklets are decorated with plaited cordage, and cross-straps of similar material pass behind the neck and across the abdomen and thighs.

X-ray examination suggests that the brain was removed through the nostrils. The face
and nose have been modelled in resin-soaked linen, and the nose unusually assumes its
prominent form. Part of the skull is obscured but there are obvious fractures, and the cer-
vical spine is intact. The upper part of the chest has been packed with a mass of what
seems to be sand, mud, and resin, as has the pelvis. Several other mummies in this style
are known, and they may all have come from the same workshop.

The mummy came to the British Museum in a coffin of Ramesside date belonging to a
woman named Mutemmenu (EA 6703). Rather than this being an example of Roman
reuse of an earlier coffin, it is far more likely that the nineteenth-century finders of the
mummy placed it inside a coffin which they had already acquired, in an attempt to obtain
a higher price for the objects.

Mummy portrait of a woman

Roman Period, *c.* AD 160–170

Probably from el-Rubayat

Bequest of Sir Robert Mond, 1939

Encaustic on limewood

Height: 44.3 cm

EA 65346

THE WOMAN, whose hair is arranged in the manner of the mid-second century AD, wears a gold wreath of leaves, an unusual purple tunic with gold bands, and a white mantle. Her earrings are made of emeralds set in gold, with suspended pearls. Her necklace is composed of a large emerald and a red stone (perhaps carnelian) in gold mounts, with the jewelled mounts separated by gold plaques. The gold of the jewellery settings is actually made of gold leaf. The large brown eyes have individually painted lashes, and the complexion is delicately tinted with pink and ochre. The quality of the portrait and the lavishness of the lady's dress shows that she belonged to the highly Romanized elite.

The mummy portrait is a phenomenon unique to the Roman Period in Egypt. Most examples come from the area in and around the Faiyum, where there was a large Egyptian and Greek community, many aspects of whose activities are well known from the large number of Greek papyri which have been recovered from the area. Other examples have now come to light from Marina el-Alamein, Thebes, and elsewhere. There can be little doubt that the paintings were intended to represent the deceased as they looked when alive, under the influence of portraiture as an expression of Romanization, of loyalty to the emperor and his world. However, given the Egyptianizing context of portraits still attached to their mummies (like that of Artemidorus, EA 21810, pages 304–5), portraiture can only have helped to add identity to the mummy, given the lack of the texts so common in the pharaonic period and the fact that these mummies were usually buried in unmarked grave pits with no other trappings. An interesting and disputed issue is whether these portraits were painted at death or during the subject's life and later attached to mummies. Some scholars believe that the mummies resided in the houses of the living for a time as a sort of ancestor cult before being placed in the ground, while others think they were buried immediately.

Most surviving mummy portraits have unfortunately become separated from the mummies to which they were attached, and we rarely know the identities of the subjects. This portrait is one of the finest of those attributed to the cemetery of el-Rubayat in the Faiyum, and differs from most panels from that site in its use of encaustic technique (paint mixed with beeswax) and limewood. Most panels from el-Rubayat are not as well executed as this example.

Textile with figures in a boat

Late Roman Period, early fourth century AD

From Akhmim

Acquired in 1889

Linen and wool

Length: 128.5 cm

EA 20717

THE DESIGN on these two fragments of a textile is drawn from Greek rather than Egyptian mythology. It shows two *putti* or Erotes (male winged childlike figures who were associated with Eros, the Greek god of love, comparable to the later Roman Cupids) in a very small boat. One of them steers the boat, while the other may be holding a fishing net, below which a fish can be seen in the water. On the fragment to the right is the prow of another boat, indicating that at least one other similar boat and pair of *putti* appeared as part of the design. The background is filled with flower petals; another interpretation of the fishes is that they form part of this background. The whole scene is framed by a border composed of laurel leaves and floral garlands. In the corners are masks, on the bottom left that of a satyr and on the right that of a maenad (a female follower of the god Dionysus).

A hanging like this might have decorated the dining room of a wealthy person. It is executed in the illusionistic style characteristic of a particular group of fourth-century AD paintings and mosaics. Comparable figures of this date have been noted in ceiling panels at the Piazza Armerina in Sicily and in the ceiling panels of a palace in Trier. Art of this period commonly employs such figures in water settings. The meaning of *putti*/Erotes can be complex, and is very dependent on the context. While they are attractive decorative motifs above all, their significance can vary from religious to funerary. The presence of the fish and floral motifs might also have a function beyond the decorative: as in pharaonic times, they may have been considered as allegories of regeneration and new life.

The textile was made using the 'weft-loop pile' technique, in which designs are woven into a plain linen cloth using colourful woollen yarns. The use of colour to show modelling and the naturalistic tones employed are characteristic of this period, and give what has been termed a 'painterly' effect. The way in which the coloured yarns are used to indicate shading is clearly related to techniques used in contemporary mosaics.

other side: HIST OF SELF PORTRAIT T78

from BM "Masterpieces of Ancient Egypt"

Wall from a chapel of queen Shanakdakhete

Meroitic Period, *c.* 150 BC

From Shanakdakhete's pyramid chapel at Meroe

Gift of the Sudanese Government in 1905

Sandstone

Length 455.5 cm

EA 719

THE TERM 'KUSH' was used long before the eighth century BC to refer to Nubia. The most long-lasting phase of the Kushite kingdom began in the ninth century BC; kings, known in Egypt as the Twenty-fifth Dynasty, put an end to the fragmented state of Egypt by 715 BC. They did not last long in Egypt, and their last rulers, Taharqa and Tanutamun, fled to Nubia from the Assyrians. There, they and their descendants held sway until the fourth century AD, being buried at el-Kurru, Nuri, Gebel Barkal, and Meroe. The latter location has given the name 'Meroitic' to the culture's later stages and to their script and language, still not fully understood. The rulers were buried beneath small, very steep-sided pyramids with chapels.

This wall comes from the south side of a pyramid chapel at Meroe, Tomb Beg. N. 11, of Queen Shanakdakhete, the first female ruler (reigned *c.* 170–150 BC). She appears here enthroned with a prince (?) seated behind her, protected by a winged Isis, with several registers of scenes in front. At the top the queen adores a row of deities, while other registers show her and the prince leading four sacred bulls. Deities and offering scenes abound, but the most recognizable motif to the Egyptological eye is the miniature weighing of the heart before Anubis, just in front of the seated queen's knees. Four rows of women complete the remainder of the scene. The style of the reliefs is visibly Egyptian in origin, but Kushite art took on its own characteristics through several centuries of independent development. For example, there was an increased use of figures in conventional profile, such as Isis here, and of squat, heavy figures.

No texts are preserved in the scenes; the cartouches for the royal names are left empty. There are, however, remains of two Meroitic additions to the scene. A few almost illegible characters appear in front of the man holding four bulls, while in front of a woman in one of the lower rows is an inscription which may be interpreted as a woman's name, Bkelo/Bake, and a title, which is repeated on the north wall of the same chapel, now in the Sudan National Museum, Khartoum.

The tomb complex was one of those excavated by G.A. Reisner in 1921–2, but this wall relief had been removed previously. The superstructure consisted of a sandstone masonry pyramid filled with rubble, with a three-roomed chapel to the east from which came this relief and the one now in Khartoum. The burial chambers were located beneath this chapel, and were reached from a staircase in front of the gateway or pylon that served as the entrance to the chapel. The burial had been ransacked, and all that greeted the modern excavator were fragments of faience and pottery, plus some beads and some indeterminate bones.

Meroitic stela

Meroitic Period, *c.* 24 BC

From Hamadab

Gift of John Garstang in 1914

Sandstone

Height: 236.5 cm

EA 1650

IN 1909 JOHN GARSTANG of the University of Liverpool began excavations in Sudan at Meroe, the capital of the kingdom of Kush; during the 1914 season he also excavated at Hamadab, 2 km to the south. There his team unearthed the remains of a small temple with a doorway flanked by two stelae, both *in situ*. The stela standing on the left of the doorway was given to the British Museum, while the other was left in place.

The stela consists of a single block of ferruginous sandstone that tapers a little towards the base. The lower part is only very roughly dressed and was set into the ground. Above this is an inscription on the front face, topped by a lunette relief panel, only the lower part of which remains. The panel depicts Queen Amanirenas and Prince Akinidad facing a god, probably Amun, on the left; on the right the same individuals appear before a goddess, perhaps Mut, who holds an *ankh* (the hieroglyph denoting 'life'). Beneath the base line is a narrow frieze depicting bound prisoners.

The lower part of the block is divided by horizontal incised lines framing the inscription, forty-two lines of text in what is known as Meroitic cursive script (although the script is not actually cursive, since the letters are not joined). The Meroitic alphabet consists of fifteen consonants, four vowels and four syllabic characters. Although the sound equivalents of the characters are known and one can therefore 'read' the text, its meaning is far from clear. Meroitic, the indigenous language of the kingdom of Kush at least from the early first millennium BC until the fourth century AD, is one of the few ancient languages which cannot be deciphered. Close relations to the language are lacking, as are bilingual inscriptions, apart from a few very short texts.

This is particularly unfortunate in the case of this inscription. We know from Roman sources that in 24 BC the Kushites invaded Egypt, incorporated only six years earlier into the Roman empire, and carried off imperial statues from Syene (Aswan), probably including the famous head of Augustus in the British Museum (GR 1911,0901,1). Roman historians provide a detailed account of the aftermath of the raid, the defeat of the Kushite army, its flight, and ultimately the sacking of the Kushite religious centre at Napata near the Fourth Nile Cataract. Many scholars think that this inscription records the campaign. The names of Amanirenas and Akinidad can be read, and are thought to be contemporary with these events. Among the words on the inscription is 'Areme', thought by most experts to be the Meroitic term for Rome. This inscription may hence be of immense interest and might allow us to reevaluate this first clash between two of the major powers of the ancient world, known for over 2,000 years solely from Roman imperial propaganda. The decipherment of Meroitic is eagerly awaited.

D.A.W.

Meroitic pottery

CUP

Meroitic Period, perhaps first/second
centuries AD

From Faras, burial 786

Gift of the University of Oxford in 1912

Ceramic

Height: 8.9 cm

EA 51615

AMPHORA

Meroitic Period, perhaps first/second
centuries AD

From Faras, burial 1226

Gift of the University of Oxford in 1912

Ceramic

Height: 43 cm

EA 51500

THE SO-CALLED 'MEROITIC PERIOD' was the last major phase of the history of the kingdom of Kush in Nubia. The term is used to cover the approximate period 300 BC–AD 350. The earlier date roughly marks the date when the kings began to be buried at Meroe, which had already been functioning as a capital city for some time. The highpoint of this phase was in the first century BC and first century AD, and pottery was one of its most outstanding products. There is definite variation in products from various parts of the kingdom, suggesting the existence of local ceramic centres, particularly in the north (Faras and Karanog). However, the range of types and decoration has made the creation of an internal chronology rather difficult. Two examples are given here to illustrate two of the principal types: those with mostly figured decoration in red and black on white, and a decorative style mostly in black on an orangeish ground, with floral and some figured decoration.

CUP
The decoration on this vessel consists of a mythical winged animal and a number of lily-like motifs, in red and black on a white ground.

AMPHORA
This vessel is decorated in black with floral-based designs on an orange ground, with numerous birds at the bottom. This sort of design may have been inspired by products of the Ptolemaic and Roman Periods in Egypt, but it seems to be a Nubian production, since nothing quite like it has been discovered in Egypt.

Two bronzes from X-Group tombs

LAMP

Perhaps first/second centuries AD

From Tumulus 192.23 at Qasr Ibrim

Gift of the Egypt Exploration Society in 1962

Bronze

Length: 17.5 cm

EA 66576

PATERA

Perhaps fourth/sixth centuries AD

From the Podium at Qasr Ibrim

Gift of the Egypt Exploration Society in 1969

Bronze

Length: 29.1 cm; diameter: 15.7 cm

EA 67163

THE TERM 'X-GROUP' was first coined by G.A. Reisner when surveying Nubia in the early twentieth century. It is also known as the Ballana culture, after the site at which several opulent royal tombs were found in the 1930s. This culture appears in Nubia at the time of the collapse of the Kushite state in the mid-fourth century AD and tombs, and to a lesser extent, habitation remains typical of the Ballana culture are found into the sixth century, when the arrival of Christianity brought profound changes. People of this cultural group are probably to be identified with the Nobates of classical texts.

LAMP

This bronze lamp has an elongated body, a long, fluted nozzle, a rounded tip, and a flat sunken top. The handle has a D-shaped stem at the end of which is a horse's head and neck. The design is common in the early Roman imperial period, and it seems probable that this product was made in the Roman empire and found its way to Nubia, where it was buried in a tomb of the X-Group or Ballana culture.

The object was one of many items of pottery, glass, and metalwork found in Tumulus Tomb 192.23 to the north of the main site of Qasr Ibrim. This tomb contained the burials of twenty-three adults and two children, although this very high number suggests a mass burial made after the original interment.

PATERA

A *patera* is a dish used for libations. This example is decorated in the centre with a number of concentric circles, with blobs of bronze around the edges. The flourishes at the join of the handle and bowl may represent dolphins, and the handle terminates in what is possibly a grotesque mask. Similar objects are known from the royal burials at Ballana from the X-Group or Ballana culture and from other Nubian and Egyptian contexts; there is also an example with no precise provenance in the collection of the British Museum's Department of Prehistory and Europe (1859, 5-10.1). It is unknown whether these objects were made in Egypt or Nubia; the original models could have come from the Roman world. The elaborate nature of the metalwork bears witness to the high standards of craftsmanship at the time.

The object was found in a deposit of windblown material just above the original floor of the 'Podium', below the Christian levels and associated with some X-Group pottery. The Podium is a stone platform, originally built in perhaps the first century BC and modified later in the Meroitic Period.

Wall painting of the martyrdom of saints

Coptic/Byzantine Period,
sixth century AD

From a building at Wadi Sarga, Egypt

Gift of the Byzantine Research and
Publication Fund in 1919

Painted plaster

Length: 144.5 cm

EA 73139

THE PERSECUTION OF CHRISTIANS IN EGYPT reached its peak in the reign of the emperor Diocletian (AD 284–35), and yet in the reign of Constantine (AD 307–337) Christianity became the official creed of the Roman empire.

This wall painting is composed of two distinct elements. In the centre is a panel executed in red paint, consisting of a scene and a Coptic inscription. The figures with raised arms are the saints Ananias, Azarias, and Misael, also known as 'the three children in the furnace' (see the story in the Book of Daniel, chapters 1 and 3, where they are given the names Shadrach, Meshach, and Abednego). They are accompanied by an angel.

Below this is an inscription in three lines: 'The sixty martyrs of Samalut; their day the twelfth of (the month of) Mekheir. Hourkene the younger, my brother Mena the younger. (In the name of) Jesus Christ.' These martyrs are otherwise unknown; the date referred to is presumably that of their martyrdom. As for the two men named, they might have been monks who commissioned the work or to whom it was dedicated. The overall context of this text eludes us.

Arranged around this panel are large, polychrome figures of saints Damian (left) and Cosmas (right); below it are smaller figures of their brothers Leontios, Eupredios, and Anthinmos. These five individuals, together with their mother Theodote, were martyred at Aegae in Cilicia during the persecution of the emperor Diocletian (late third century AD). According to accounts of their martyrdom, they were subjected to various tortures, including being placed on a burning pyre; they remained untouched by the flames, and thus the iconographic parallel from the Book of Daniel is very appropriate. The palm-like fronds around their feet probably represent flames. The miraculous preservation of the three biblical figures – sometimes called the 'three Hebrew children' – from burning was used frequently in Christian art as an illustration of the triumph of the faithful over death. It was particularly popular in Egypt and Nubia.

The difference in style and use of colour between the two scenes suggests that the inner and outer scenes were executed by different artists. It is likely that the central panel was the original, with the outer figures added later; the quality of its drawing is freer and perhaps somewhat superior to the coloured figures.

The settlement of Wadi Sarga is briefly described on page 326. The house in which this painting was found was located some 3 km to the north of the main monastic site.

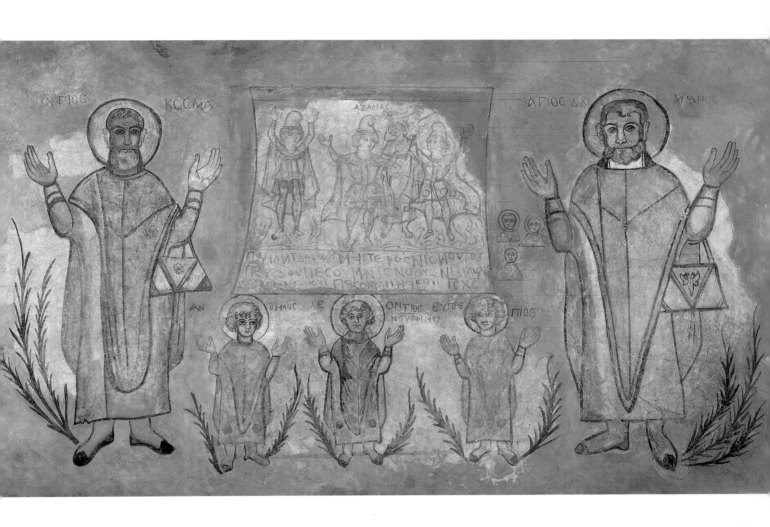

Pottery jug with a human face

Coptic/Byzantine Period, fifth/seventh
centuries AD

From Wadi Sarga

Gift of the Byzantine Research Fund
in 1919

Marl clay

Height: 29.6 cm

EA 73196

THE PALE COLOUR of this anthropomorphic vessel shows that it was made from the marl clays of the desert rather than the silts of the Nile Valley. Like most pottery of the Coptic Period, it was wheel-made, with the decoration applied after the basic form was constructed. Although fairly coarse, this vessel would have been a suitable, if a little eccentric, item for household use.

The vessel's decoration is unusual in combining applied, incised, and painted techniques. Its neck has a face on either side. Clay has been added to the surface of the vessel and moulded to depict a stylized male face. Details of the eyelids and hair have been painted in black, using a striped and cross-hatched design. The edges of the face, brows, mouth, and nose are highlighted in red. These colours are often used together in the decoration of Coptic pottery.

The surface of the vessel's body is covered with incised decoration, both above and below the undulating 'pie-crust' shoulder. These patterns would have been made with a knife. The geometric pattern focuses on a concentric rhomboidal design in the centre, below the face, flanked by long diagonal lines. Four orange bands were added around the circumference of the vessel after the incisions had been made.

Usually, vessels made of the finer clays were incised, and the rougher wares were painted. The decorative range of expression on Coptic pottery is far wider than that seen in pharaonic times, and the styles used have a good measure of originality.

The settlement of Wadi Sarga, located about 24 km south of Asyut, was excavated by the Byzantine Research and Publication Fund in 1913–14, and the interruption caused by World War I effectively prevented publication of the site. It was a monastic settlement of some type, either a collection of hermit's cells or (more likely) a more centralized community. The cemeteries for the site were located outside the wadi.

The Shenoute Codex

Coptic/Byzantine Period, seventh century AD

Provenance unknown

From the collection of John Lee; presented to the British Museum in 1935 by the law firm of Warwick, Williams, and Marchant

Papyrus

Height: 20.2 cm

EA 71005

SHENOUTE (*c.* AD 348-466) is regarded as one of the great figures and authors of the Coptic Church, whose writings were read for many generations after his death. He became abbot of the White Monastery near Sohag in about AD 385, and under him this institution became a powerful religious centre in Middle Egypt and attracted many monks. This papyrus sheet is a page from a codex with an account of some episodes in his life. The writing dates it to the seventh century AD, or just possibly the sixth; it was thus copied over two centuries after Shenoute lived. This papyrus is written in the Sahidic dialect of Coptic.

The page illustrated opposite is sheet 3. The whole text contains parts of six episodes, and is described as a 'discourse' by Shenoute in its title: during a famine, prayer brings the monks enough wheat for six months' baking; Shenoute's clairvoyance puts to shame a man who had disparaged him during a trip to the monastery; a magistrate pursues one of his stewards for a debt, which the latter is miraculously able to repay; a hardhearted rich man dies and is resuscitated by Shenoute, and then gives his wealth to the poor and becomes a monk; and a sign from God permits grain to appear miraculously in the granary when there is no more bread for visitors. The ending of the final story is missing, but it concerns a man in the previous story who took home some bread to his family.

A series of other texts exists based on the life of this important figure in the Coptic Church, who was later canonized. The best-known account of Shenoute's life and miracles is written in the Bohairic dialect of Coptic, and is somewhat later in date, although there are also some fragments of a similar text in Sahidic. The most recent editors of this text suggest that, in spite of the title citing Shenoute as the author, it was written by one of his followers and ascribed to the great man. Such hagiographies are well known for great figures of the early Church, and there is no greater figure in the Coptic communion than Shenoute.

The former owner of the text, John Lee of Aylesbury (1783-1866), was a lawyer, landowner, and antiquary who amassed a variegated collection, including Coptic papyri. Most are now in the British Library. This manuscript is known to have been in his collection at least since 1837.

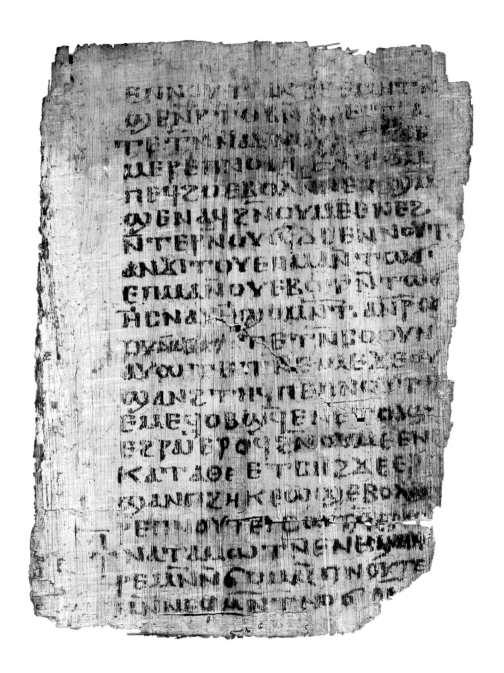

Limestone gravestone of Mary

Perhaps eighth century AD

Provenance unknown

Acquired in 1903

Limestone

Height: 134 cm

EA 618

COPTIC GRAVESTONES vary widely in size, and this is one of the larger ones. It consists of two panels. The upper panel is square, and in its centre is a Coptic cross within a wreath: in the spandrels (the space between a curved figure and a rectangular boundary – in the present case, between the wreath and the corners of the square) are foliated ornaments. The lower panel bears three areas of decoration. At the top is a Coptic inscription in five lines naming the deceased: 'Young Mary. She entered into rest the tenth of Tobe.' Below, in the centre, is a dove with outstretched wings, with a medallion hanging from its neck. Below it is a triple guilloche scroll (a type of running ornament, consisting of a decoration of interlaced bands, forming a pattern of circles or loops); within each of the six circles thus formed is a foliated cross, and in the inner spandrels are small discs, each incised with a plain diagonal cross. The entire lower panel is enclosed within a rectangular border of leaves on a central stalk. Both panels are contained within a larger border of vine scrolls.

In the present Coptic calendar, the date of the deceased's death would have been in the middle of the Gregorian month of January, as the month of Tobe runs from early January to early February. The object has been assigned an eighth-century date on stylistic grounds. The dove is a common image on such stelae, and, together with the foliage, forms a symbol of the paradise into which the deceased was to pass.

Limestone is the most common material for Coptic gravestones. These stones, which are mostly either rectangular, as here, or have rounded or triangular tops, were laid upon the grave or against a tomb wall, or even stood independently. Most stelae which have come down to us have unfortunately lost their context, as has the present example.

Old Nubian text

Perhaps twelfth century AD

From the cathedral at Qasr Ibrim

Gift of the Egypt Exploration Society in 1988

Parchment

Height: 25 cm

EA 71304

IN THE COURSE of the Nubian Rescue Campaign (to save monuments from the rising waters of Lake Nasser after the construction of the Aswan dam), work by the Egypt Exploration Society in the cathedral of St Mary the Virgin at Qasr Ibrim in 1963-4 revealed a number of fragments of parchment, bearing mostly biblical texts, which are now in the British Museum. They were located in a few centimetres of dust, and were probably part of the cathedral library. Different handwritings indicate that they came from a range of books, and the fact that they are all isolated passages of text suggest that they were deposited in the course of an attack upon the site. The exact historical event cannot be identified, although Shams ed-Dowla, the brother of Saladin, captured the site in AD 1173, after which the cathedral became a mosque for a while.

The texts are a mixture of the psalms, New Testament texts (John, Revelations, Philippians, Corinthians) and two non-biblical texts, all translated into Old Nubian. The example illustrated here has a number of similarities in content with a homily on the Archangel Raphael attributed to St John Chrysostom; another text in the group is part of the so-called *Liber institutionis michaelis*, relating to the Archangel Michael. The texts are written in black ink on both sides of the parchment; the names of Raphael and Michael are emphasized by being written in red.

The Old Nubian language (so called to distinguish it from the languages now spoken in Nubia) belongs to a Nilo-Saharan linguistic family and is related to tribal languages of southern Sudan and Uganda. It may have been spoken as early as the second millennium BC, although the earliest written forms date from the eighth century AD. The alphabet it employs is largely borrowed from Coptic, with a number of letters taken from Meroitic; the latter language gave way to Greek and Coptic, which were then complemented by written Old Nubian. It is quite likely that there was a period after AD 600 when people of this area could read and speak Meroitic and wrote in Old Nubian. The latest text known in Old Nubian dates from AD 1485.

ⲉ̄ⲡⲡⲓⲧⲟⲩⲛⲁⲧⲁⲗⲗⲱ ⲕⲁ
ⲁⲗⲗⲟ ⲉ̄ⲛⲁⲅⲅⲉⲗⲟⲥ ⲟⲩⲣⲁ ⲫⲁⲏ
ⲛ ⲥⲁⲉⲡⲡⲓⲕⲁ ⲟⲩⲓⲥⲟⲩⲇⲁ ⲟⲛⲉⲓⲡⲟⲛ
ⲕⲁⲧⲧⲟⲩ ⲧ̄ⲅⲉⲟⲛⲟⲥⲓⲟ̄ⲉ̄ⲛⲓⲕⲁ ⲡ̄ⲗⲁⲓ̈ⲗ̄ⲗⲉ
ⲁ ⲓ̈ⲥⲉⲛⲟⲁ ⲅ̄ⲟⲓⲕⲟⲩⲇⲁⲩⲉⲧⲓⲥⲟⲛ ⲧⲉⲓⲥ
ⲧ̄ⲇⲇⲟⲗ ⲟⲩⲉⲣⲟⲩⲉⲓⲥⲕⲁ ⲁ̄ⲗⲁⲥⲣⲁⲅⲁⲣⲁ
ⲓⲕⲁ ⲟⲩⲉⲁⲗⲉⲇⲟⲩⲙ ⲇⲁⲩⲉⲁ̄ⲧ̄ⲣ̄ⲙⲉⲛⲛⲁ
ⲉⲛⲛⲁ ⲇⲟⲩⲉⲥⲛ̄ ⲧⲁⲩⲓⲥⲁⲙⲓⲩⲩⲁⲛⲛⲟ
ⲛ ⲟⲩⲉⲣⲟⲩⲉⲗⲁⲁ ⲅ̄ⲧⲁⲥⲥⲁⲛⲁ ⲁⲓ̈ⲟⲩ
ⲛⲓⲥⲙⲙⲉ ⲡⲗⲁⲛ̄ ⲣⲓⲕⲁⲛⲉⲗⲁ ⲟⲩⲉⲣⲟⲩ
ⲁ ⲡⲁⲇⲓⲛⲧⲓⲙⲉⲛⲁ̄ⲛⲛⲁⲗⲟⲉⲓⲁ̄ ⲉⲗⲟⲛⲉ̄
ⲩⲣⲟⲩⲁ̄ ⲟⲛⲛⲟⲣⲓⲟⲥⲓ ⲉⲓⲥⲟⲩ ⲁⲅⲅⲉⲗⲟⲥ ⲟⲩⲣ
ⲣⲁⲫⲁⲏⲗⲓⲛ ⲓ̄ⲥ̄ⲉⲓⲥⲁ ⲉⲓⲥⲡⲗⲁⲛ ⲅⲟⲩⲣⲓⲥⲁ
ⲁⲛⲓⲥⲕⲉⲣⲁⲥⲓ ⲧⲁⲓⲥⲕⲉⲧⲁⲁ ⲍⲁⲣⲱⲓⲓⲟⲩⲛ ⲣⲓⲥⲁ
ⲛⲉⲗⲁⲗⲟ ⲉ̄ⲧⲥⲓⲕⲁ ⲇⲟⲩⲉⲣⲓⲥⲕⲁ ⲙⲉⲁⲗⲗ̄ⲣⲁ̄
ⲉⲁⲓⲛⲁ ⲉ̄ⲛⲁⲛⲓⲱⲧ̄ⲛⲁ̄ ⲉⲗⲁⲉⲛⲧⲟⲩⲗⲟ ⲓ̄ⲥ̄
ⲗⲟ ⲇⲟⲩⲁⲁⲉⲛⲧⲟⲩⲗⲗⲱ ⲉ̄ⲛⲥⲉⲩⲉⲓⲥⲛⲁ̄ ⲉⲓ
ⲙⲉⲛⲁⲉⲛⲧⲟⲩⲗⲁ ⲧⲁⲛⲅⲟⲓⲕⲛⲁ ⲓ̈ⲥⲟⲥⲉⲛ
ⲛⲓⲙⲉⲛⲟⲩ ⲅⲟⲇⲉⲛ ⲕⲁⲡⲁⲗⲁⲛ̄ⲧ̄ⲣ̄ⲙⲉⲛⲟⲩ
ⲗⲁ ⲉⲗⲁⲉⲛⲧⲩⲗⲱ ⲓ̄ⲥ̄ⲕⲁⲗⲱ ⲉⲧⲥⲓⲟⲛ ⲉⲓⲁ̄
ⲁⲣⲉⲥⲛ̄ ⲅⲟⲓⲕⲕⲟⲣ ⲁⲓⲁⲱ ⲁⲩⲟⲩⲧ̄ⲕⲟⲓⲕⲁ
ⲩⲣⲟⲩⲁ̄ ⲁⲓⲟⲩ ⲉⲛⲙⲉⲁⲇⲟⲩ ⲓ̈ⲱⲁⲛⲉⲓⲟ̄ ⲙⲉ
ⲟⲩⲓⲉⲣⲉⲛⲛⲓⲛⲛⲁⲗⲟ ⲓ̈ⲱⲉⲕⲟⲩ ⲣⲁⲫⲁⲏ
ⲁⲓⲟⲩ ⲓ̈ⲕⲟⲛⲥ̄ⲧⲁⲛⲧⲓⲛⲟⲩ ⲁ̄

Benedictional cross

Fourteenth century AD

From the burial of Bishop Timotheus at Qasr Ibrim

Gift of the Egypt Exploration Society in 1971

Iron

Height: 54 cm

EA 71955

EXCAVATIONS by the Egypt Exploration Society in the cathedral at Qasr Ibrim in 1964 revealed a small crypt. On the debris in this crypt lay a corpse, which was identified as that of someone in holy orders. This cross lay on the body's breast, suggesting that the deceased was a bishop; underneath the body lay two scrolls (now in Cairo, JE 90223-4), in Coptic and Arabic, which were letters testimonial from the Coptic Patriarch Gabriel (IV) announcing the appointment of a new bishop, Timotheus, to the See of Nubia. His consecration in Cairo took place on 19 November AD 1371. The cross is referred to in the Coptic scroll as a 'rod of iron' and a 'staff' in the Arabic; it was Timotheus' symbol of authority.

The cliff on which Qasr Ibrim stands served in the New Kingdom mainly as a place for the construction of shrines, probably for important officials associated with the fortress at Aniba on the opposite bank of the Nile, where many of the viceroys of Nubia resided. A temple was erected on the site by king Taharqa, but the earliest fortifications at the site date from the late New Kingdom or immediately thereafter. The site was then occupied for a short time by the Romans, and in mediaeval times became the centre of an important bishopric. Bishop Timotheus' grave in the cathedral church has all the appearances of a hasty burial, but nonetheless shows that Christianity was still flourishing in Nubia in the later fourteenth century AD. In the mediaeval period Qasr Ibrim was frequently caught up in conflicts in the area between the Muslim rulers of Egypt and the Christian rulers of the kingdoms of Makuria and Dotawo.

Glossary

ANKH: Egyptian hieroglyph, meaning 'life'. Frequently held in the hands of statues and images of deities.

ATEF CROWN: similar to the **white crown** (see below), but flanked by feathers; a pair of ram's horns often appears at the base.

BA: one of the spirits of the deceased, the means by which the dead were empowered to leave the tomb and travel, for example, to the world of the living or to join the sun god in his barque. Commonly shown as a human-headed bird.

BOOK OF THE DEAD: known in Egyptian as the *Book of Coming Forth by Day*, this is a standard funerary text, written on papyrus and placed in elite burials from the New Kingdom to the Roman Period. It is composed of a variable set of spells, and has its origin in the Pyramid Texts and the Coffin Texts.

CARTONNAGE: a material composed of layers of linen soaked in either glue or plaster. Cartonnage was used for a variety of purposes, particularly for mummy cases in the Third Intermediate Period.

CARTOUCHE: oval ring placed around the hieroglyphs for royal names, particularly those of kings. From the French word for a cartridge.

COPTIC: the last form of the Egyptian language, essentially a late form of **Demotic** written in Greek letters, with six additional signs to represent characters from Demotic. It is overwhelmingly associated with Christian texts, but its origins predate the spread of Christianity in Egypt.

DEMOTIC: A more cursive version of the **hieratic** script which developed in the Third Intermediate Period. The term is also used to describe the late form of the Egyptian language written in the script. It became the standard script for administrative texts until the second century AD, when its place was largely taken by Greek. Later religious and literary texts were also written in Demotic.

DJED PILLAR: hieroglyph for 'stability', probably a stylized form of the backbone of Osiris.

CANOPIC JARS/CONTAINER: containers for the embalmed internal organs of the deceased (excluding the heart). So named from an early confusion between these jars and the mythological Greek pilot Canopus who was worshipped in the form of a human-headed jar.

EPAGOMENAL DAYS: the Egyptian civil calendar had 12 months of 30 days (360 days). The extra five days inserted to make up the 365 days of the solar year are called the epagomenal days. (The Egyptians called them the 'days upon the year'.)

FALSE DOOR: the central offering place in tombs from the Old Kingdom. It developed out of the offering niche, embellished by multiple text-inscribed jambs and architraves. Although primarily associated with the Old Kingdom, false doors continued to be made until the New Kingdom.

HIERATIC: Originally a cursive form of **hieroglyphs**, written in ink with a reed pen. It was the principal form of writing for administrative and literary texts on papyri and ostraca from the Old Kingdom to the Third Intermediate Period. It is better suited than hieroglyphs to rapid writing with a brush.

HIEROGLYPHS: the sacred picture writing of Egypt, reserved during most of the historical periods for monumental inscriptions.

'HORUS NAME': one of the king's five names, identifying the ruler with Horus, the son of Osiris, the embodiment of the ruler. Typically written within a *serekh*.

KA: a spirit of the deceased, something of a 'double', which lived in the tomb with the mummy. By providing the *ka* with sustenance, the individual was kept alive after death. Most commonly represented by a pair of upraised arms.

LOWER EGYPT: term used to describe the northern part of Egypt, roughly from ancient Memphis northwards. In pharaonic times it was divided into 22 nomes (provinces).

MAAT: a concept represented by a feather, embodied by a goddess with a feather on her head. It represents the established order of the world, which the king had to protect at all costs. Sometimes imprecisely translated as 'right' or 'justice'.

MASTABA: flat-topped, stone or brick freestanding tomb, with rooms inside the superstructure. The term comes from the Arabic word for 'bench'.

NEMES HEADDRESS: the headcloth with two long lappets and a tail at the rear worn by the Egyptian king.

NOME, NOMARCH: 'Nome' is used in Egyptology to describe the individual provinces of ancient Egypt, 22 in Lower Egypt and 22 in Upper Egypt. The word derives from the Greek *nomos*, 'province'. A ruler of a nome is typically termed a 'nomarch'.

OFFERING FORMULA: a complex prayer found on almost every funerary monument, requesting the king and the gods to give offerings to the deceased.

OSTRAKON: a flake of stone or a potsherd used for writing notes, letters, and so on. Since papyrus was expensive, ostraka were the standard medium for the keeping of daily records.

RED CROWN: the distinctive crown of Lower Egypt. It was combined with the **white crown** to produce the characteristic crown of Upper and Lower Egypt.

RISHI: Arabic word for 'feather', used to describe a feather-pattern decoration found on coffins and masks from the Seventeenth to the early Eighteenth Dynasties.

SARCOPHAGUS: a stone container for the body, or for coffins containing the body.

SED FESTIVAL: a celebration of the renewal of royal powers. It is often claimed that this festival was first performed after 30 years of the king's reign, but there are numerous exceptions to this 'rule', and it is probably more accurate to suggest that a *sed* festival could take place at almost any time when it was felt the king wished to renew his powers.

SERDAB: a concealed statue chamber, particularly common in Old Kingdom tombs. From the Arabic word for 'cellar'.

SEREKH: a rectangular container for the royal Horus name, believed to be based on the shape of the panelling of early palace exteriors.

SHABTI: a funerary figure, originally a small substitute statue-like representation of the deceased. They gradually multiplied in numbers, and there were 401 of them in burials from the late New Kingdom onwards. At this time these figures were expected to perform tasks asked of the deceased in the afterlife.

SISTRUM: a rattle-like musical instrument, particularly associated with the goddess Hathor, and principally played by women.

STELA: an upright stone slab, inscribed with images and text. It could be used for a com-memorative inscription or as part of the equipment or decoration of a tomb or burial.

UPPER EGYPT: term used to describe the southern part of Egypt, roughly from ancient Memphis southwards. In pharaonic times it was divided into 22 nomes (provinces).

URAEUS: the serpent on the king's headdress. It represents the identification of the king with the power of the serpent. Often associated with Wadjet, the cobra goddess of Lower Egypt.

WEDJAT EYE: A stylized representation of the Eye of Horus, the son of Osiris. It has several meanings: as an amulet, it represented the healed eye of the god, after it had been torn apart by the god Seth; it can also represent offerings.

WHITE CROWN: the distinctive crown of Upper Egypt. It was combined with the **red crown** to produce the characteristic crown of Upper and Lower Egypt.

Further reading

GENERAL INTRODUCTORY BOOKS
J. Baines and J. Malek, *Cultural Atlas of Ancient Egypt*, New York, 2000.
R. Schulz and M. Seidel (eds), *Egypt : The World of the Pharaohs*, Cologne, 1998.
A.J. Spencer and S. Quirke, *The British Museum Book of Ancient Egypt*, London, 1992.

GENERAL REFERENCE WORKS
D.B. Redford (ed.), *The Oxford Encyclopedia of Ancient Egypt*, 3 vols, Oxford, 2001.
W. Helck and E. Otto (eds), *Lexikon der Ägyptologie*, 7 vols, Wiesbaden, 1975–92.

HISTORY OF EGYPT
I. Shaw (ed.), *The Oxford History of Ancient Egypt*, Oxford, 2000.

ARCHITECTURE
D. Arnold, *The Encyclopaedia of Ancient Egyptian Architecture*, London, 2002.

ART
G. Robins, *The Art of Ancient Egypt*, London, 1997.
G. Robins, *Proportion and Style in Ancient Egyptian Art*, London, 1994.

GEOGRAPHY
J. Baines and J. Malek, *Cultural Atlas of Ancient Egypt*, New York, 2000.

RELIGION
G. Hart, *The Routledge Dictionary of Egyptian Gods and Goddesses*, London, 2005.
E. Hornung, *Conceptions of God in Ancient Egypt: The One and the Many*, Ithaca, 1983.
S. Quirke, *Ancient Egyptian Religion*, London, 1992.

FUNERARY BELIEFS
J. Assmann, *Death and Salvation in Ancient Egypt*, Ithaca, NY, 2005.
E. Hornung, *The Ancient Egyptian Books of the Afterlife*, Ithaca, NY, 1999.
W. Grajetzki, *Burial Customs in Ancient Egypt: Life in Death for Rich and Poor*, London, 2003.
A.J. Spencer, *Death in Ancient Egypt*, Harmondsworth, 1982.
J.H. Taylor, *Death and the Afterlife in Ancient Egypt*, London, 2001.

HISTORY OF THE EGYPTIAN COLLECTIONS OF THE BRITISH MUSEUM
T.G.H. James, 'The formation and growth of the Egyptian collections of the British Museum' in E.R. Russmann, *Eternal Egypt: Masterworks of Ancient Art from the British Museum*, London, Berkeley, CA, 2001, 46–63.

HISTORY OF THE BRITISH MUSEUM
D.M. Wilson, *The British Museum: A History*, London, 2002.

Bibliography for the objects

ABBREVIATIONS

Andrews, *Jewellery I*	C.A.R. Andrews, *Catalogue of Egyptian Antiquities in the British Museum VI: Jewellery I,* London, 1981.
Arnold *et al., Egyptian Art*	D. Arnold, C. Ziegler and C.H. Roehrig, *Egyptian Art in the Age of the Pyramids,* New York, 1999.
ASAE	*Annales du Service des Antiquités d'Egypte.*
Belzoni, *Narrative*	G. Belzoni, *Narrative of the Operations and Recent Discoveries in Egypt and Nubia,* ed. A. Siliotti, London, 2001.
BIFAO	*Bulletin de l'Institute Française d'Archéologie Orientale.*
BSEG	*Bulletin de la Société d'Egyptologie de Genève.*
BSFE	*Bulletin de la Société Française d'Egyptologie.*
CdE	*Chronique d'Egypte.*
Dawson and Gray, *Mummies*	W.R. Dawson and P.H.K. Gray, *Catalogue of Egyptian Antiquities in the British Museum. I. Mummies and Human Remains,* London, 1968.
Freed, *Pharaohs of the Sun*	R.E. Freed *et al.* (eds), *Pharaohs of the Sun: Akhenaten, Nefertiti, Tutankhamen,* Boston, 1999.
HTBM	*Hieroglyphic Texts from Egyptian Stelae, &c. in the British Museum,* 13 vols, London, 1911–93.
JARCE	*Journal of the American Research Center in Egypt.*
JEA	*Journal of Egyptian Archaeology.*
JNES	*Journal of Near Eastern Studies.*
Kozloff and Bryan, *Egypt's Dazzling Sun*	A.P. Kozloff and B.M. Bryan, *Egypt's Dazzling Sun: Amenhotep III and his World,* Cleveland, 1992.
KRI	K.A. Kitchen, *Ramesside Inscriptions: Historical and Biographical,* 8 vols, Oxford, 1975–89, plus *Translations* and *Notes and Comments.*
LÄ	W. Helck and E. Otto (eds), *Lexikon der Ägyptologie,* 7 vols, Wiesbaden, 1975–92.
MDAIK	*Mitteilungen des Deutschen Archäologischen Instituts, Abteilung Kairo.*
Nicholson and Shaw, *Ancient Egyptian Materials*	P.T. Nicholson and I. Shaw (eds), *Ancient Egyptian Materials and Technology,* Cambridge, 2000.
Parkinson, *Cracking Codes*	R. Parkinson, *Cracking Codes: the Rosetta Stone and Decipherment,* London, 1999.
Phillips, *Africa*	T. Phillips (ed.), *Africa, the Art of a Continent,* London, 1995.
PM	B. Porter and R.L.B. Moss, assisted by E.W. Burney, *Topographical Bibliography of Ancient Egyptian Hieroglyphic Texts, Statues, Reliefs, and Paintings,* 8 vols, Oxford, 1927-2000, ongoing.
Roehrig, *Hatshepsut*	C.H. Roehrig (ed.), *Hatshepsut: From Queen to Pharaoh,* New Haven, 2005.
Russmann, *Eternal Egypt*	E.R. Russmann, *Eternal Egypt: Masterworks of Ancient Art from the British Museum,* London, Berkeley, CA, 2001.
SAK	*Studien zur altägyptischen Kultur.*
Spencer, *Early Dynastic Objects*	A.J. Spencer, *Catalogue of Egyptian Antiquities in the British Museum V: Early Dynastic Objects,* London, 1980.
Spencer, *Early Egypt*	A.J. Spencer, *Early Egypt, The Rise of Civilisation in the Nile Valley,* London, 1993.
Taylor, *Death and the Afterlife*	J.H. Taylor, *Death and the Afterlife in Ancient Egypt,* London, 2001.
Walker and Bierbrier, *Ancient Faces*	S. Walker and M.L. Bierbrier, *Ancient Faces,* London, 1997.

Predynastic Period

EA 59648: G. Brunton and G. Caton-Thompson, *The Badarian Civilisation and Predynastic Remains*, London, 1928, 28–9, pls XXIV (2), XXV (3, 4); Phillips, *Africa*, 52, fig. 1.1. See Spencer, *Early Egypt*, 22–7 and B. Midant-Reynes, *The Prehistory of Egypt*, Oxford, 2000, 152–66 for the Badarian culture.

EA 32751: Dawson and Gray, *Mummies*, 1, pl. Ia, XXIIa, b. Budge's account of uncovering the body appears in his book *By Nile and Tigris*, London, 1920, II, 360–1. Early mummification from Hierakonpolis is illustrated in Taylor, *Death and the Afterlife*, 47.

EA 35502: R.D. MacIver and A.C. Mace, *El Amrah and Abydos*, London, 1902, 42, pl. XIV (D46); J. Aksamit, *Cahiers de la Ceramique Egyptienne 3* (1992), 17–22; S. Hendrickx, *Cahiers Caribéens d'Egyptologie* 3–4 (2002), 29–50. See also G. Graff in S. Hendrickx, R.F. Friedman, K.M. Cialowicz and M. Chlodnicki (eds), *Egypt at its Origins*, Leuven, 2004, 765–78.

A-Group: General: H. Nordström in D.B. Redford (ed.), *The Oxford Encyclopedia of Ancient Egypt*, Oxford, 2001, I, 44–6; W.Y. Adams, *Nubia: Corridor to Africa*, London, 1997, chap. 5; D.N. Edwards, *The Nubian Past*, London, 2004, 68–74. For the burial in Tomb 31, see F.L. Griffith, *Liverpool Annals 8* (1921), 14–15, pl. II.

EA 51157: Spencer, *Early Dynastic Objects*, 103 (766); F.Ll. Griffith, *Liverpool Annals 8* (1921), 14. See *LÄ* 6, 77–8 for ostrich eggs; for examples of A-Group graves with decorated eggs, see C.M. Firth, *Archaeological Survey of Nubia 1909–10*, Cairo, 1915, pl. 11.

EA 51168: Spencer, *Early Dynastic Objects*, 50, pl. 44 (346, q); F.Ll. Griffith, *Liverpool Annals 8* (1921), 14–15.

EA 68512: Not formally published: Spencer, *Early Egypt*, 41–4 describes the production of flint blades. For the carved handles, see G. Bénédite, *JEA 5* (1918), 1–15, 225–41; H.J. Kantor, *JNES 3* (1944), 127–31; A.L. Kelley, *Ancient World* 6 (1984), 95–102. For examples excavated from Abydos, see G. Dreyer *et al.*, *MDAIK* 49 (1993), 27, pl. 6 and *MDAIK* 54 (1998), 99.

EA 20791: Spencer, *Early Dynastic Objects*, 79–80 (576), pl. 64; Phillips, *Africa*, 64–5 (1.18); A. Roveri and F. Tiradritti (eds), *Kemet: Alle Sorgenti del Tempo*, Milan, 1998, 206–7 (165). The Ashmolean fragment usually appears with the BM one; the Luzern fragment is in H.W. Müller, *Ägyptische Kunstwerke, Kleinfunde und Glas in der Sammlung E. und M. Kofler-Truniger*, Berlin, 1964, 12–13 (A3). For an overview of the main palettes, see B. Midant-Reynes, *The Prehistory of Egypt*, Oxford, 2000, 240–6; the most recent discussion is D. O'Connor, *JARCE* 39 (2002), 5–25.

Early Dynastic Period

EA 37996: Spencer, *Early Dynastic Objects*, 67 (483), pl. 55; A. Roveri and F. Tiradritti (eds), *Kemet: Alle Sorgenti del Tempo*, Milan, 1998, 223 (185); Russmann, *Eternal Egypt*, 66–7 (1).

EA 32650: W.M.F. Petrie, *Royal Tombs of the Earliest Dynasties*, London, 1901, 22 (14), 40–1, pls XI (14), XV (16); Spencer, *Early Dynastic Objects*, 64 (45a), pls 49, 53. See also Spencer, *Early Egypt*, 78, fig. 55; the recent work in the tomb is reported on by G. Dreyer *et al.*, *MDAIK* 54 (1998), 141–64.

EA 67153: W.B. Emery, *Great Tombs of the First Dynasty* III, London, 1958, 84, pls 97–8; Spencer, *Early Dynastic Objects*, 16 (16), pls 8, 9.

EA 35597: W.M.F. Petrie, *Royal Tombs of the Earliest Dynasties*, London, 1901, 33, pl. XXXI; Spencer, *Early Dynastic Objects*, 16 (15), pls 8, 9. See Spencer, *Early Egypt*, 82 for a reconstruction of a tomb with stelae of the First Dynasty. For a comparison of the royal stelae see H.G. Fischer, *Artibus Asiae* 24 (1961), 53–6.

EA 35571–2: W.M.F. Petrie, *Royal Tombs of the Earliest Dynasties* II, London, 1901, 27, pl. IX (13); Spencer, *Early Dynastic Objects*, 596, 597, pls 67, 68; id., *Early Egypt*, 88–9, fig. 68.

Old Kingdom

EA 691: A.H. Gardiner, T.E. Peet and J. Cerny, *The Inscriptions of Sinai* I, London, 1952–5, pl. I; vol. II, 56 (4); Spencer, *Early Dynastic Objects*, 16 (18), pl. 8; Arnold *et al.*, *Egyptian Art*, 176–7. See G. Dreyer in H. Guksch and D. Polz (eds), *Stationen: Beiträge zur Kulturgeschichte Ägyptens*, Mainz, 1995, 31–4 for a consideration of Zanakht's place in the dynasty.

EA 171: Spencer, *Early Dynastic Objects*, 13 (1), pl. 1; Russmann, *Eternal Egypt*, 69–70 (4). A number of other Third Dynasty statues are collected together in Arnold *et al.*, *Egyptian Art*, 178–87; see M. Eaton-Krauss in N. Grimal (ed.), *Les critères de datation stylistiques à l'ancien Empire*, Cairo, 1998, 209–25 for 'pre-canonical' statuary.

EA 69014–5: W.M.F. Petrie, *Medum*, London, 1892, 27–8, pl. XXVIII (2, 3); Y. Harpur, *The Tombs of Nefermaat and Rahotep at Maidum*, Cheltenham, 2001, 191, 193, figs 80–1, pls 12, 18; Spencer, *Early Egypt*, 110–11. See Harpur, *op.cit.* for recent consideration of all aspects of this tomb.

EA 1181: Arnold *et al.*, *Egyptian Art*, 290–1; for a study of the other chapel fragments, see H.G. Fischer, *Egyptian Studies I. Varia*, New York, 1976, 33–7.

EA 682: *HTBM* I², 17, pl. XVII. Chicago block and translation of whole in P.F. Dorman, *JEA* 88 (2002), 95–110; translation: N.C. Strudwick, *Texts from the Pyramid Age*, Atlanta, GA, 2005, 303–5 (226).

EA 1324: *HTBM* I², 10, pl. X. Translation of dedication text: N.C. Strudwick, *Texts from the Pyramid Age*, Atlanta, GA, 2005, 243–4 (162). Photograph *in situ*: J. de Morgan, *Fouilles à Dahchour en 1894–1895*, Vienna, 1903, pl. XXVI. Discussions of date most recently summarized in M. Baud, *Famille royale et pouvoir sous l'Ancien Empire égyptien*, Cairo, 1999, 83–92, 592.

EA 1239: W.M.F. Petrie, *Deshasheh*, London, 1898, pls xxx (1), xxxii (1–3); see PM IV, 123 and T.G.H. James and W.V. Davies, *Egyptian Sculpture*, London, 1983, 21–3; date of the coffin, G. Lapp, *Typologie der Särge und Sargkammern*, Heidelberg, 1993, 33. For discussion of the number of men with the same name see N. Kanawati and A. McFarlane, *Deshasha*, Sydney, 1993, 71–4.

EA 10735: P. Posener-Kriéger and J.-L. de Cenival, *Hieratic Papyri in the BM: Fifth Series, The Abu Sir Papyri*, 1, pl. II (sheet 10); 2, pl. III–IV (sheet 7 recto); P. Posener-Kriéger, *Les archives du temple funéraire de Néferirkarê-Kakaï*, Cairo, 1976, 22–41, 324–6; translation: N.C. Strudwick, *Texts from the Pyramid Age*, Atlanta, GA, 2005, 165–71 (90).

EA 55722: Arnold *et al.*, *Egyptian Art*, 460–61; Russmann, *Eternal Egypt*, 76–8, (9); J. C. Harvey, *Wooden Statues of the Old Kingdom*, Leiden, 2001, 206–7 (A47).

EA 1848: G.T. Martin, *The Tomb of Hetepka*, London, 1979, 20–1, pl. 21; A. Roveri and F. Tiradritti (eds), *Kemet: Alle Sorgenti del Tempo*, Milan, 1998, 295 (300); tomb location, Martin, *op. cit.*, pl. 2, square F6; see H.G. Fischer, *Egyptian Studies I. Varia*, New York, 1976, 13–16 for the unusual title.

First Intermediate Period

C-Group: General: D.A. Welsby in D.B. Redford (ed.), *The Oxford Encyclopedia of Ancient Egypt*, Oxford, 2001, I, 258–9; W.Y. Adams, *Nubia: Corridor to Africa*, London, 1977, chap. 6; D.N. Edwards, *The Nubian Past*, London, 2004, chap. 4; H. Hafsaas, *Cattle Pastoralists in a Multicultural Setting*, Ramallah, 2006.

EA 51245: None. C-Group pottery is discussed as part of M. Bietak, *Studien zur Chronologie der nubischen C-Gruppe*, Vienna, 1968.

EA 51225: None, but see F.Ll. Griffith, *Liverpool Annals* 8 (1921), 76.

EA 51220: Andrews, *Jewellery I*, 58, pl. 27 (374); F.Ll. Griffith, *Liverpool Annals* 8 (1921), 75.

EA 1203: *HTBM* I, pl. 53; PM I², 596; Russmann, *Eternal Egypt*, 81–2 (12). Text: J.J. Clère and J. Vandier, *Textes de la première période intermédiaire et de la XIème dynastie*, Brussels, 1948, 19; translation (German): W. Schenkel, *Memphis. Herakleopolis. Theben*, Wiesbaden, 1965, 226–8.

EA 41668: Andrews, *Jewellery I*, 60 (395). See E. Naville, *The XIth Dynasty Temple at Deir el-Bahari* I, London, 1907, 45–6 for information about the remainder of the burial. For notes on the 'wives' of Mentuhotep, see L.K. Sabbahy, *JARCE* 34 (1997), 163–6.

EA 40915: Tomb 3 and this model are described in E. Naville, *The XIth Dynasty Temple at Deir el-Bahari* I, London, 1907, 44–5; see also *Aliments sagrats–Alimentos sagrados–Sacred Foods*, Barcelona, 2001, 179–80 (36). The human remains are in Dawson and Gray, *Mummies*, 5, pl. IIIc (10). See D. Samuel in Nicholson and Shaw, *Ancient Egyptian Materials*, 537–76 for a consideration of brewing and baking in the light of scientific study.

EA 6459: None. The dress patterns are considered in E. Riefstahl, *Patterned Textiles in Pharaonic Egypt*, New York, 1944, 11–12. A similar object is shown in J. Bourriau, *Pharaohs and Mortals*, Cambridge, 1988, 126–7 (121). See G. Pinch, *Magic in Ancient Egypt*, 2nd edn, London, 2006, chap. 9 for a consideration of fertility magic.

Middle Kingdom

EA 963: *HTBM* 4, pl. 1; image at top: H.G. Fischer, *Egyptian Studies* II. *The Orientation of Hieroglyphs. Part 1. Reversals*, New York, 1977, fig. 91; D. Franke, in P.D. Manuelian (ed.), *Studies in Honour of William Kelly Simpson I*, Boston, 1996, 287–9.

Djehutyhotep: P.E. Newberry, *el Bersheh* I, London, 1894, pls XXIV, XXIX, XXX; Russmann, *Eternal Egypt*, 93–5 (223). See A. Middleton in W.V. Davies (ed.), *Studies in Egyptian Antiquities: a Tribute to T.G.H. James*, London, 1999, 37–44 for the pigments, and E. Brovarski *et al.*, *Bersheh Reports* I, Boston, 1992 for survey information on the site. Information on current work at Bersha is at http://millennium.arts.kuleuven.ac.be/bersha/

Gua: H. Willems, *Chests of Life*, Leiden, 1988, 76–7 for information on the discovery of the tomb; for other burials see G. Daressy, *ASAE* 1 (1900), 22–43. See E. Hornung, *Ancient Egyptian Books of the Afterlife*, New York, 1999, 7–12, for the Coffin Texts and the *Book of the Two Ways*.

EA 9524: S.R.K. Glanville and R.O. Faulkner, *Catalogue of Egyptian Antiquities in the British Museum II: Wooden Model Boats,* London, 1972, 10–13, frontispiece, pl. IIIa (8); W. Seipel, *Ägypten: Götter, Gräber und die Kunst* I, Linz, 1989, 116 (83). For general literature on boats, see D. Jones, *Boats*, London, 1995; see also Taylor, *Death and the Afterlife*, 103–5.

EA 579: *HTBM* 2, pl. 15; J. Bourriau, *Pharaohs and Mortals*, Cambridge, 1988, 29–31 (20); Russmann, *Eternal Egypt*, 99–100 (27). See G. Robins, *Proportion and Style in Ancient Egyptian Art*, London, 1994 for grids in Egyptian art.

EA 828: *HTBM* 2, pl. 21; transliteration, translation, notes: C. Obsomer, *Sesostris Ier: étude chronologique et historique du règne*, Brussels, 1995, 539–42, doc. 32, with full bibliography. For comments on the possible stela workshop, see R.E. Freed in P.D. Manuelian (ed.), *Studies in Honour of William Kelly Simpson I*, Boston, 1996, 327–34.

EA 684: Russmann, *Eternal Egypt*, 101–04 (29); on pp 35–6 Russmann considers the distinctive facial features of this king. For a description of the find, see E. Naville, *The XIth Dynasty Temple at Deir el-Bahari* I, London, 1907, 57–8, pl. XIX.

EA 1063: E. Naville, *Bubastis*, London, 1891, 26–7, pls I, X; Russmann, *Eternal Egypt*, 105–7 (31). Illustration of the Cairo statue, B. Fay, *MDAIK* 44 (1988), pl. 27b. For sculpture of Senwosret III and Amenemhat III see F. Polz, *MDAIK* 51 (1995), 227–54.

EA 101: *HTBM* 2, pls 1–2; A.M. Blackman, *JEA* 21 (1935), 1–9, pl. I. Translation: M. Lichtheim, *Ancient Egyptian Autobiographies Chiefly of the Middle Kingdom*, Freiburg, 1988, 122–4 (56). Abydos offering chapels: W.K. Simpson, *The Terrace of the Great God at Abydos*, New Haven, CT, 1974; D. O'Connor in P. Posener-Kriéger (ed.), *Mélanges Gamal Eddin Mokhtar*, Cairo, 1985, II, 161–77.

EA 59194: Andrews, *Jewellery I*, 76, pls 30, 31 (554); Russmann, *Eternal Egypt*, 109 (34).

EA 54460: Andrews, *Jewellery I*, 75–6, pls 30–1 (554); Parkinson, *Cracking Codes*, 107 (29).

EA 58892: H.R. Hall, *British Museum Quarterly* 2 (1927–8), 87–8, pl. LVIIIa; PM VII, 384–5; B. Fay, *The Louvre Sphinx and Royal Sculpture from the Reign of Amenemhat II*, Mainz, 1996,

68 (54), pl. 94a–b. Fay includes images of many later Middle Kingdom sphinxes. G. Daressy, *ASAE* 5 (1904), 105–12, describes some objects from Heliopolis in Alexandria.

EA 54678: J. Garstang, *JEA* 14 (1928), 46–7; J. Bourriau, *Pharaohs and Mortals*, Cambridge, 1988, 136–8 (138), with full bibliography; Phillips, *Africa*, 78 (1.35); C. Ziegler, *The Pharaohs*, Milan, 2002, 426 (97).

Ramesseum Papyri: A.H. Gardiner, *The Ramesseum Papyri*, Oxford, 1955; J.W.B. Barns, *Five Ramesseum Papyri*, Oxford, 1956; R.B. Parkinson, *The Tale of the Eloquent Peasant*, Oxford, 1991, xi–xiii; id., *Poetry and Culture in Middle Kingdom Egypt: A Dark Side to Perfection*, London, 2002, 71–2. Translations of some of the literary texts are in R.B. Parkinson, *Tale of Sinuhe and Other Ancient Egyptian Poems 1940–1640 BC*, Oxford, 1997. The papyri are the subject of an ongoing international research project co-ordinated by the Museum.

EA 37097: *Egyptian Treasures*, Santa Ana, CA, 2000, 240–1. For the Matariya group see particularly L. Keimer, *BIFAO* 28 (Cairo 1929), 49–50; B.J. Kemp and R.S. Merrillees, *Minoan Pottery in Second Millennium Egypt*, Mainz, 1980, 163–4; J. Bourriau, *Pharaohs and Mortals*, Cambridge, 1988, 120–1.

EA 1785: No formal publication; see PM VIII, 378.

EA 41748: W.M.F. Petrie, *Researches in Sinai*, London, 1906, 129, fig. 141; Parkinson, *Cracking Codes*, 181–2, pl. 31; B. Sass, *Genesis of the Alphabet*, Wiesbaden, 1988, 12–14 . For a recent consideration of the Proto-Sinaitic script see Sass, *op. cit.*, 8–50.

Second Intermediate Period

EA 7876: I.E.S. Edwards, in P. Posener-Kriéger (ed.) *Mélanges Gamal Eddin Mokhtar*, Cairo, 1985, I, 239–45; *Egyptian Treasures*, Santa Ana, CA, 2000, 106–7; C. Ziegler (ed.), *The Pharaohs*, Milan, 2002, 479 (240). See J. Capart *et al.*, *JEA* 22 (1936), 169–93 for the Leopold-Amherst Papyrus.

EA 6652: PM I², 602; *Pharaonen und Fremde* , Vienna, 1994, 275–6 (383); D. Polz, *Die Pyramidenanlage des Königs Nub-Cheper-Re Intef in Dra' Abu el-Naga*, Mainz, 2003. For *rishi* coffins see Taylor, *Death and the Afterlife*, 223–4.

EA 871: W.V. Davies, *A Royal Statue Reattributed*, London, 1981; Roehrig, *Hatshepsut*, 23–4. See K.S.B. Ryholt, *The Political Situation During the Second Intermediate Period*, Copenhagen, 1997 for a recent view of the historical background.

EA 55424: Phillips, *Africa*, 106. For publication of original burial, see G.A. Reisner, *Excavations at Kerma parts I–III*, Cambridge, MA, 1923, 239. See D.A. Welsby and J.R. Anderson (eds), *Sudan: Ancient Treasures*, London, 2004, 78–89 and D.N. Edwards, *The Nubian Past*, London, 2004, chap. 4 for summaries of Kerma and its cultures.

EA 10057/58: T.E. Peet, *The Rhind Mathematical Papyrus*, Liverpool, 1923. Edition and commentary by mathematicians: A.B. Chace, L.S. Bull, H.P. Manning and R.C. Archibald, *The Rhind Mathematical Papyrus*, Ohio, 1927–9. For a more accessible account, see G. Robins and C. Shute, *The Rhind Mathematical Papyrus*, London, 1987 and, generally, R.J. Gillings, *Mathematics in the Time of the Pharaohs*, Massachusetts, 1972.

New Kingdom

EA 32191: Russmann, *Eternal Egypt*, 210–11 (110); Roehrig (ed.), *Hatshepsut*, 33–4 (12), with more references, and discussion of early Eighteenth Dynasty statuary on pp 23–7. The other statues of Ahmose are in J.F. Romano, *JARCE* 13 (1976), 103–5 and D.A. Welsby and J.R. Anderson (eds), *Sudan: Ancient Treasures*, London, 2004, 103. See Taylor, *Death and the Afterlife*, chap. 4 and H. Schneider, *Shabtis*, Leiden, 1977, for the meaning and development of the shabti.

EA 29770: J.H. Taylor, *British Museum Magazine* 21 (1995), 8–10; J.H. Taylor, *Apollo* (July 1996), 33–8; Russmann, *Eternal Egypt*, 204–6 (106). For other coffins and masks of this date and the identity of various Satdjehutys, see A. Grimm and S. Schoske, *Im Zeichen des Mondes*, Munich, 1999.

EA 52831: N.C. Strudwick, *Legacy of Lord Carnarvon*, Laramie, WY, 2001, 26 (6), pl. III with bibliography. See J. Bourriau, *Pharaohs and Mortals*, Cambridge, 1988, 113 (100) for the serpent in Cambridge.

EA 683: I. Lindblad, *Royal Sculpture of the Early Eighteenth Dynasty in Egypt*, Stockholm, 1984, 26–7, pl. II with bibliography. Discussed and illustrated in R. Tefnin, *Annuaire de l'institute de philologie et d'histoire orientales et slaves* 20, Brussels, 1968–72, 433–4, pl. II; J.F. Romano, *JARCE* 13 (1976), 97–8, pl. XXVI. See C. Leblanc, *BIFAO* 80 (1980) for a typology of this type of figure. Early Eighteenth Dynasty statuary is considered in Roehrig, *Hatshepsut*, 23–7. Another statue of Amenhotep I has been found at Sai in the Sudan: D.A. Welsby and J.R. Anderson (eds), *Sudan: Ancient Treasures*, London, 2004, 102–3.

EA 93: R. Tefnin, JEA 69 (1983), 96–107; I. Lindblad, *Royal Sculpture of the Early Eighteenth Dynasty in Egypt*, Stockholm, 1984, 32–3, pl. 16. See Belzoni, *Narrative*, 166 for his account of the find.

EA 174: Russmann, *Eternal Egypt*, 120–1 (44); Roehrig, *Hatshepsut*, 114–15; C. Meyer, *Senenmut. Eine prosopographische Untersuchung*, Hamburg, 1982, 30, pl. 3; P.F. Dorman, *The Monuments of Senenmut*, London, 1988, 118–19, 188–9. See Dorman, *op. cit.* for consideration of the dates of the damage to monuments of Hatshepsut and Senenmut. See the bibliography for EA 480 for the circumstances of the find.

EA 12: PM II², 296. D. Laboury, *La statuaire de Thoutmosis III*, Liège, 1998, 186–9 (C46); texts: *HTBM* 8, pl. VI. For the French discovery and illustration, see *Description de l'Egypte. Antiquités* III, pl. 31 and *Text* II, 477–8; see also Belzoni, *Narrative*, 147, 181. The parallel at Karnak features in P. Barguet, *Le temple d'Amon-Rê à Karnak*, Cairo, 1962, 126 n. 1, pl. XLa, and that at Armant in R. Mond and O. Myers, *The Temples of Armant*, London, 1940, 51, 190, pl. XX.

EA 48: PM II², 454; *HTBM* 8, pl.V; R. Schulz, *Die Entwicklung und Bedeutung des kuboiden Statuentypus I*, Hildesheim, 1992, 365–6, pl. 94; Russmann, *Eternal Egypt*, 122–4 (46), with bibliography.

EA 708: *HTBM* 5, pls 32–3. See P.F. Dorman, in J. Assmann et al., *Thebanischen Beamtennekropolen*, Heidelberg, 1995, 148–54 for the identity of Menkheperresoneb.

EA 1103: E.H. Naville, *Bubastis*, London, 1891, 30, pls XXVI A, XXXV D; *HTBM* 10, pl. 12; *KRI* 1, 227; S. Grallert, *Bauen-Stiften-Weihen*, Berlin, 2001, 531, 637–8. M. Bietak, *Egyptian Archaeology* 26 (2005), 13–17, and Roehrig, *Hatshepsut*, 80–1, discusses the location of Perunefer.

EA 56929–30: Taylor, *Death and the Afterlife*, 133–5 with notes on extra-sepulchral shabtis; see F. Pumpenmeier, *Eine Gunstgabe von seiten des Königs*, Heidelberg, 1997 for the figures of Qenamun from Abydos (in particular) and elsewhere. See N. de G. Davies, *The Tomb of Ken-Amun*, New York, 1930 for TT93.

EA 64564: Russmann, *Eternal Egypt*, 128–9 (50); M. Hill, *Royal Bronze Statuary from Ancient Egypt*, Leiden, 2004, 151, pl. 3. For research into the decoration of the bronze see S. La Niece, F. Shearman, J. Taylor and C. Simpson, *Studies in Conservation* 47 (2003), 95–108, with fig. 1. See B.M. Bryan, *The Reign of Thutmose IV*, Baltimore, MD, 1991 for more about his king and his sculpture.

EA 43: PM II², 102; text, *HTBM* 7, 5, pl. 6. On the use of

emblematic hieroglyphs, see H.G. Fischer, *MMJ* 5 (1972), 5–23, especially pp 21–2. For Mutemwia, see B.M. Bryan, *The Reign of Thutmose IV*, Baltimore, MD, 1991, 113–15. For the king merged with a falcon, see H. Sourouzian in M. Eldamaty and M. Trad (eds), *Egyptian Museum Collections around the World* II, Cairo, 2002, 1123–32. For a description of the discovery, see R. Richardson, *Travels along the Mediterranean* II, London, 1822, 91; J.-J. Fiechter, *La moisson des dieux*, Paris, 1994, 114.

Sebekhotep: E. Dziobek and M. Abdel-Raziq, *Das Grab des Sobekhotep*, Mainz, 1990, especially pls 3, 6 (photos), 33, 35 (reconstructions), with bibliography.

EA 3, 5, 7: General bibliography on the statues and building programmes of the reign: Kozloff and Bryan, *Egypt's Dazzling Sun*, 125–84; papers by W.R. Johnson and D. O'Connor in D. O'Connor and E.H. Cline, *Amenhotep III: Perspectives on His Reign*, Ann Arbor, MI, 1998, 63–94 and 125–72; B.M. Bryan in S. Quirke (ed.), *The Temple in Ancient Egypt*, London, 1997, 57–81. See H. Sourouzian and R. Stadelmann, *MDAIK* 57 (2001), 271–80 and *MDAIK* 59 (2003), 425–46 for the most recent work in the temple of Kom el-Hitan.

EA 7: Russmann, *Eternal Egypt*, 132–3 (52); Kozloff and Bryan, *Egypt's Dazzling Sun*, 156–8, pl. 7.

Sekhmets: J. Yoyotte, *BSFE* 87–8 (1980), 47–75; B.M. Bryan in S. Quirke (ed.), *The Temple in Ancient Egypt*, London, 1997, 57–81. See G. Haeny, *Untersuchungen im Totentempel Amenophis' III*, Wiesbaden, 1981, 90–99 for statues of Sekhmet found at Kom el-Hitan in the 1960s. More statues were found as this book went to press.

EA 2: Kozloff and Bryan, *Egypt's Dazzling Sun*, 219–20; Russmann, *Eternal Egypt*, 130–1 (51). See J. Ruffle, *Sudan and Nubia* 2 (1998), 82–7, for notes on Prudhoe's travels and how the lions came to London.

EA 15: T.G.H. James and W.V. Davies, *Egyptian Sculpture*, London, 1983, 32; photo of body of statue on p. 13. For an account of its discovery, see Belzoni, *Narrative*, 180, pl. 28. For photo and comments on the recutting of statues of Amenhotep III, see Kozloff and Bryan, *Egypt's Dazzling Sun*, 172–5.

EA 38: S.R.K. Glanville, *JEA* 15 (1929), 6, pl. II; Kozloff and Bryan, *Egypt's Dazzling Sun*, 227–8; text: *HTBM* 8, pls 10–11, pl. XI. For statuary in the mortuary temple of Amenhotep III, see B.M. Bryan in S. Quirke (ed.), *The Temple in Ancient Egypt*, London, 1997, 57–81.

EA 657: *HTBM* 8, pl. 20; W. Helck, *Urkunden der 18.*

Dynastie, Leipzig, 1957, 1659–61. Translation: B.G. Davies, *Egyptian Historical Records of the Later Eighteenth Dynasty* IV, Warminster, 1992, 5–6. See Z. Topozada, *BIFAO* 88 (1988), 153–64 for Amenhotep III's campaigns in Nubia.

EA 480: Freed, *Pharaohs of the Sun*, 200 (2). Texts: *HTBM* 5, pl. XXXIX. For the possible identification with the Ramesside individual see L. Habachi, *MDAIK* 14 (1956), 52–62, especially p. 61 n. 5. For the circumstances of the find, see T.G.H. James, *BSFE* 75 (1976), 7–30; M. Dewachter, *CdE* 54 (1979), 22–5; and M. Eaton-Krauss, *JEA* 85 (1999), 113–29.

EA 1001: *HTBM* 8, pls XVI–XVII; Kozloff and Bryan, *Egypt's Dazzling Sun*, 319–21, with bibliography for all three sarcophagi. See A. Varille, *ASAE* 45 (1947), 1–15 for TT383.

Nebamun: There is no systematic publication of the fragments, but all apart from the Lyons fragments are discussed and the reconstruction considered in L. Manniche, *Lost Tombs*, London, 1988, chap. 11; R.B. Parkinson, *The Tomb-Chapel of Nebamun* is in preparation. For the Lyons fragments see G. Galliano, *Guide des collections: les antiquités: l'Égypte, le Proche et Moyen-Orient, la Grèce, l'Italie. Musée des beaux-arts de Lyon*, Paris, 1997, 43. They are frequently illustrated, for example, T.G.H. James, *Egyptian Painting*, London, 1985, 26–33 and M. Hooper, *The Tomb of Nebamun*, Cambridge, 1997. See also PM I², 817–18. See L. Manniche in N. Strudwick and J.H. Taylor, *The Theban Necropolis. Past, Present and Future*, London, 2003, 42–5 for a consideration of the meaning of scenes in private tombs.

Fowling: E. Miller and R.B. Parkinson in W.V. Davies (ed.), *Colour and Painting in Ancient Egypt*, London, 2001, 49–52.

Banquet: For the meaning of the banquet, see L. Manniche in R. Tefnin (ed.), *La peinture égyptienne ancienne. Un monde de signes à préserver*, Brussels, 1997, 29–36.

Inspecting cattle and geese: Parkinson, *Cracking Codes*, 122–3.

Field scene: this and other examples are discussed in N. Strudwick, *The Tomb of Amenemopet called Tjanefer at Thebes* (TT 297), Berlin, 2003, 49–56.

EA 935: F.Ll. Griffith, *JEA* 17 (1931), 179–81; *HTBM* 8, 29, pl. XXVI; M. Müller, *Die Kunst Amenophis' III und Echnatons*, Basel, 1988, IV, 123; Freed, *Pharaohs of the Sun*, 231 (88). See E. Hornung, *Akhenaten and the Religion of Light*, Ithaca, NY, 1999 for the theology of the Amarna Period and pp 34, 76–7 for the name changes of the Aten.

EA 57399: F.Ll. Griffith, *JEA* 12 (1926), 1–2; Kozloff and

Bryan, *Egypt's Dazzling Sun*, 213–14; Freed, *Pharaohs of the Sun*, 254; Russmann, *Eternal Egypt*, 143–4 (59). For the other residence of Panehsy, J.D.S. Pendlebury, *The City of Akhenaten* III, London, 1951, 26–7.

EA 55193: T.E. Peet and C.L. Woolley, *The City of Akhenaten* I, London, 1923, 24; B. Nolte, *Die Glasgefässe im alten Ägypten*, Berlin, 1968, 70, pl. XXIX (2); J.D. Cooney, *Catalogue of Egyptian Antiquities in the British Museum IV: Glass*, London, 1976, 146 (1753); Kozloff and Bryan, *Egypt's Dazzling Sun*, 386–8; Freed, *Pharaohs of the Sun*, 265 (212); Russmann, *Eternal Egypt*, 164 (76). See Nicholson and Shaw, *Ancient Egyptian Materials and Technology*, 195–224 and Kozloff and Bryan, *Egypt's Dazzling Sun*, 373–82 for the production and uses of glass.

EA 75: Russmann, *Eternal Egypt*, 148–50 (63); text: *HTBM* 9, 6, pl. III. Painting in the tomb of Rekhmire: N. de G. Davies, *The Tomb of Rekh-mi-re at Thebes*, New York, 1943, 37, pl. XXXVI; context of the Thutmose III parallel, C. E. Loeben, *Beobachtungen zu Kontext und Funktion königlicher Statuen im Amun-Tempel von Karnak*, Leipzig, 2001, 88–92.

EA 551: G.T. Martin, *The Memphite Tomb of Horemheb* I, London, 1989, 29–31, pls 21–2. For general information on the tombs, see G.T. Martin, *The Hidden Tombs of Memphis*, London, 1991. On temple tombs, see K.J. Seyfried in J. Assmann, G. Burkard, and W. V. Davies (eds), *Problems and Priorities in Egyptian Archaeology*, London, 1987, 219–53.

Protective figures: EA 50703: Russmann, *Eternal Egypt*, 159–61 (71); **EA 61283**: *Il Senso dell'arte nell'Antico Egitto* Milan, 1990, 147–8 (97). See generally A. Wiese and A. Brodbeck (eds), *Tutankhamun: the Golden Beyond*, Basel, 2004, 106–9; N. Reeves and R.H. Wilkinson, *The Complete Valley of the Kings*, London, 1996, 132–3; W. Waitkus, *GM* 99 (1987), 51–82. See T.M. Davis, *The Tombs of Harmhabi and Touatânkhamanou*, London, 1912, pl. LXIII for *in situ* images of two parallel objects in the tomb of Horemheb.

EA 20865: R.D. Anderson, *Catalogue of Egyptian Antiquities in the British Museum III: Musical Instruments*, London, 1976, 3, fig. 2. See V. Dasen, *Dwarfs in Ancient Egypt and Greece*, Oxford, 1993, 55–83 for general discussion of Bes; see pp 77–80 in relation to music and the tambourine; also Kozloff and Bryan, *Egypt's Dazzling Sun*, 226–7, and L. Manniche, *Music and Musicians in Ancient Egypt*, London, 1991, 118–19.

EA 36: Unpublished; PM I², 790. For tombs in the New Kingdom necropolis at Saqqara, see G.T. Martin, *The*

Hidden Tombs of Memphis, London, 1991; a photograph of the Maya statue appears in Freed, *Pharaohs of the Sun*, 279 (256).

EA 2560: J. Stevens Cox, *JEA* 63 (1977), 67–70, pl. X. Survey of wigs: Nicholson and Shaw, *Ancient Egyptian Materials*, 495–501; G. Robins, *JARCE* 36 (1999), 55–69 examines the role of hair in the construction of identity. P. Derchain, *SAK* 2 (1975), 55–74 considers links between wigs and sexual activity.

EA 2472: G. Killen, *Ancient Egyptian Furniture* I, Warminster, 1980, 49–50, pls 82–3; *Egyptian Treasures from the British Museum*, Santa Ana, CA, 2000, 172–3; *Egypt's Golden Age: the Art of Living in the New Kingdom*, Boston, 1982, 69–70 (40). For a discussion of wood-turning, see Nicholson and Shaw, *Ancient Egyptian Materials*, 357–8. The Turin examples mentioned are illustrated in A.M. Donaldoni Roveri (ed.), *Egyptian Civilization: Daily Life*, Milan, 1988, 144, 157.

EA 10059: C. Leitz, *Hieratic Papyri in the British Museum 7: Magical and Medical Papyri of the New Kingdom*, London, 1999, 51–84, pls 26–46; the section translated is on p. 73, pls 35–6. For the sections in Cretan and Northwest Semitic, see E. Kyriakidis, *Ägypten und Levante* 12 (2002), 213–16 and R.C. Steiner, *JNES* 51 (1992), 191–200. For Egyptian medicine see J.F. Nunn, *Ancient Egyptian Medicine*, London, 1996; for magic in medicine, G. Pinch, *Magic in Ancient Egypt*, 2nd edn, London, 2006, 133–46.

EA 60006: Russmann, *Eternal Egypt*, 172–3 (82). For the discovery, see G. d'Athanasi, *A Brief Account of the Researches and Discoveries in Upper Egypt*, London, 1836, 67. See C. Aldred, *JEA* 42 (1956), 3–7 for the New York statuette, and *Ancient Art from the Shumei Family Collection*, New York, 1996, 4–7 for the statuette in Kyoto.

EA 19: Texts: *KRI* II, 667; *HTBM* 9, pl. V. For an account of the retrieval of the statue, see Belzoni, *Narrative*, e.g. pp 154–5. For the history of the statue and restoration of the parts in Egypt, see C. Leblanc and D. Esmoingt, *Memnonia* 10 (1999), 79–100, including a photomontage of EA19 on its base in the Ramesseum.

EA 117: *HTBM* 9, pl VIII; *KRI* II, 539–41. King-lists in general are examined in D.B. Redford, *Pharaonic King-Lists, Annals and Day-Books*, Mississauga, Ont., 1986. J. von Beckerath, *Handbuch der ägyptischen Königsnamen*, 2nd edn, Mainz, 1999 lists royal names from all periods in Egypt.

EA 5634: R.J. Demarée, *Ramesside Ostraca*, London, 2002, 18, pls 25–8; Parkinson, *Cracking Codes*, 164 (76); *KRI* III,

515–24. See particularly J.J. Janssen, *SAK* 8 (1980), 127–52 for the subject of the attendance records of workmen.

EA 43071: G. Pinch, *Votive Offerings to Hathor*, Oxford, 1993, 108–9 (3.6), pl. 20 and more general information in chap. 2.2 and pp 179–82. For examples of textiles found at Deir el-Bahari, see E. Naville and H. R. Hall, *The XIth Dynasty Temple at Deir el-Bahari* III, London, 1913, 15, 30, pls XXX–XXXI.

EA 947: A. Shorter in *Studies Presented to F. Ll. Griffith*, London, 1932, 128–32; *HTBM* 10, 18, pls 33–5; F. Gomaà, *Chaemwese, Sohn Ramses' II. und Hoherpriester von Memphis*, Wiesbaden, 1973, 86 (60); C. Chadefaud, *Les statues porte-enseignes de l'Egypte ancienne*, Paris, 1982, 112. The early photograph is in F. Teynard, *Egypte et Nubie*, Paris, 1858, 7, pl. 18. See Gomaà, *Chaemwese* for discussions of the life and monuments of Khaemwaset, and K.A. Kitchen, *Pharaoh Triumphant*, Warminster 1983, 103–9 for an English account of the man.

EA 705: No formal publication. The discovery is related by R. Richardson, *Travels along the Mediterranean* II, London, 1822, 2–3.

Henutmehyt: J.H. Taylor in W.V. Davies (ed.), *Studies in Egyptian Antiquities: A Tribute to T.G.H. James*, London, 1999, 59–72 with more references.

EA 10470: Budge's account of the find is in his book *By Nile and Tigris* I, London, 1920, 136–8. The papyrus has been published several times, from original editions by Le Page Renouf and Budge in 1890 and 1894 to the edition with commentary based around Faulkner's translation, O. Goelet (ed.), *The Egyptian Book of the Dead*, New York, 1994. Sheets with individual recent publications: Sheet 3: Russmann, *Eternal Egypt*, 198–9 (102); Sheet 35: Russmann, *Eternal Egypt*, 199–202 (103). Introduction to funerary literature, E. Hornung, *The Ancient Egyptian Books of the Afterlife*, Ithaca, NY, 1999.

EA 81: R. Schulz, *Die Entwicklung und Bedeutung des kuboiden Statuentypus*, Hildesheim, 1992, 367–8, pl. 95a; texts: *HTBM* 9, 20–1, pl. XVI. Other monuments of Roy are mentioned by L. Bell, *MDAIK* 37 (1981), 60–1.

EA 26: Russmann, *Eternal Egypt*, 178–9 (90); texts: *HTBM* 9, 14–15, pls IX–XIA. See Belzoni, *Narrative*, 147 for the discovery.

EA 9999: P. Grandet, *Papyrus Harris* I, 3 vols, Cairo, 1994–9, with many more references.

EA 140: C. Aldred in J. Ruffle, G.A. Gaballa and K.A. Kitchen, *Glimpses of Ancient Egypt*, Warminster, 1979,

96–8, pl. II. Web pages relating to the restoration of the sarcophagus: http://www.arce.org/conservation/Ramesses-Brochure.html

EA 5620: R.J. Demarée, *Ramesside Ostraca*, London, 2002, 15, pl.1; W.H. Peck, *Drawings from Ancient Egypt*, London, 1978, 114, with a photograph of the Medinet Habu parallel; the latter is published in The Epigraphic Survey, *Medinet Habu* II, Chicago, 1930–70, pl. 75. See also id., *Ramses III's Temple within the Great Inclosure of Amon*, Part II, Chicago, 1936, pl. 122: F, G, and a more fragmentary parallel in pl. 123:A; for translations of the parallel text in Medinet Habu see W.F. Edgerton and J.A. Wilson, *Historical Records of Ramses III*, Chicago, 1936, 64–5.

Tomb robbery papyri: EA 10221: T.E. Peet, *The Great Tomb-Robberies of the Twentieth Egyptian Dynasty*, Oxford, 1930, 28–45, pls I–IV. See H.E. Winlock, *JEA* 10 (1924), 217–77 for an examination of the Seventeenth Dynasty tombs, and D. Polz, *Die Pyramidenanlage des Königs Nub-Cheper-Re Intef in Dra' Abu el-Naga*, Mainz, 2003 for the rediscovery of one of the tombs.

EA 10054: Peet, *op. cit.*, 52–71, pls VI–VIII; *KRI* VI, 489; A. Gasse, *JEA* 87 (2001), 81–92.

EA 10068: Peet, *op. cit.*, 79–102, pls IX–XVI; for comments on the house list, see B. Kemp, *Ancient Egypt: Anatomy of a Civilization*, London, 1989, 306–8; J.J. Janssen, *Altorientalische Forschungen* 19 (1992), 8–23.

EA 20868/10472: See C.A.R. Andrews, *JEA* 64 (1978), 88–98 for the possible family and date of Anhai; for the *Book of Gates*, see E. Hornung, *The Ancient Egyptian Books of the Afterlife*, Ithaca, NY, 1999, 55–77.

EA 10375: Text: J. Cerny, *Late Ramesside Letters*, Brussels, 1939, 44–8, no 28. Translation: E.F. Wente, *Late Ramesside Letters*, Chicago, 1967, 59–65; id., *Letters from Ancient Egypt*, Atlanta, GA, 1990, 194–5. Part with comments: C.N. Reeves and R.H. Wilkinson, *The Complete Valley of the Kings*, London, 1996, 204–5.

Third Intermediate Period

EA 10474: Translation: M. Lichtheim, *Ancient Egyptian Literature* II, Berkeley, CA, 1976, 146–63, with references to other works, in particular, I. Grumach, *Untersuchungen zur Lebenslehre des Amenope*, Munich, 1972. A good English article about the text is H.-W. Fischer-Elfert in D.B. Redford (ed.), *The Oxford Encyclopedia of Ancient Egypt*, Oxford, 2001, II, 171–2. A full new publication and study is under way.

EA 22542: Not fully published; see PM I², 827–8; A. Niwinski, *21st Dynasty Coffins from Thebes: Chronological and Typological Studies*, Mainz, 1988, 151 (260) with earlier bibliography. See J.H. Taylor in W.V. Davies (ed.), *Colour and Painting in Ancient Egypt,* London, 2001, 164–81 for comments on the colours of coffins. The strange stories attributed to the object are summarized in more detail in the online leaflet http://www.thebritishmuseum.ac.uk/aes/faqs/unlucky.html

EA 16672: J. Cerny, *BIFAO* 41 (1942), 105–18; translation and comment: H.D. Schneider, *Shabtis* I, Leiden, 1977, 323–5.

EA 10800: I.E.S. Edwards, *JEA* 57 (1971), 120–24; translation and comment: H.D. Schneider, *Shabtis* I, Leiden, 1977, 329–30. See Taylor, *Death and the Afterlife*, chap. 4, for the development of the shabti.

EA 8: Texts: J. Liebovitch, *JNES* 12 (1953), 79–81 (25), 113, cf. K. Mysliwiec, *Royal Portraiture of the Dynasties XXI–XXX*, Mainz, 1988, 16, 22, 102. See K.A. Kitchen, *The Third Intermediate Period in Egypt*, Warminster, 1986, for the history and relationships of the period. See J. Baines, *Fecundity Figures*, Warminster, 1985 for this genre of representation, and B.M. Bryan in S. Quirke (ed.), *The Temple in Ancient Egypt*, London, 1997, 57–81, for statuary from the Amenhotep III temple.

EA 41603: J. Garstang, *The Burial Customs of Ancient Egypt,* London, 1907, 204, 207, fig. 219; Dawson and Gray, *Mummies*, 13–14, pl. VIIb; J. Filer, *Disease,* London, 1995, 63, pl. VI.

EA 6660: Dawson and Gray, *Mummies*, 10, frontispiece a and pl. Vd. For the *stola* motif, see R. van Walsem, *The Coffin of Djedmonthuiufankh,* Leiden, 1997, 116–19.

EA 30720: J.H. Taylor, *Mummy: The Inside Story,* London, 2004; Dawson and Gray, *Mummies*, 8–9, pls Vb, XXV.

EA 27332: *HTBM* 11, pls 18/1, 19/1; Russmann, *Eternal Egypt,* 221–2 (118).

Coffins of Hor: Taylor, *Death and the Afterlife*, 30 (fig 14), 239 (fig 176); J.H. Taylor in W.V. Davies (ed.), *Colour and Painting in Ancient Egypt*, London, 2001, colour pls 55 (3), 56 (3); J.H. Taylor in N. Strudwick and J.H. Taylor (eds), *The Theban Necropolis: Past, Present and Future*, London, 2003, pls 69, 73; C.M. Sheikholeslami, in Strudwick and Taylor, *op.cit.*, 132, pl. 91; M. J. Raven, *Oudheidkundige Mededelingen uit het Rijksmuseum van Oudheden* 62 (1981), 10, 14–17, pls 3, 7A.

Late Period

EA 498: translation, M. Lichtheim, *Ancient Egyptian Literature* I, Berkeley, CA, 1973, 51–7, with bibliography; analysis of the text, *LÄ* I (1975), 1065–9; language and dating, F. Junge, *MDAIK* 29 (1973), 195–204. See PM III², 873 for more bibliography. The BM is grateful for permission to mention some of the conclusions of Amr El Hawary in his unpublished dissertation *Das (Er)finden der Vergangenheit. Das Denkmal Memphitischer Theologie, eine pluralistische Untersuchung.*

EA 1770: M.F. Laming Macadam, *The Temples of Kawa* II, London, 1949, 97, 139 (0732), pl. LXXIV; S. Wenig, *Africa in Antiquity* II, Brooklyn, 1978, 50–1, 168 [fig. 24, cat. 77]. See K. Mysliwiec, *Royal Portraiture of the Dynasties XXI–XXX*, Mainz, 1988, 33, 40. For the history of Kawa, see D.A. Welsby and J.R. Anderson (eds), *Sudan: Ancient Treasures*, London, 2004, 148–50.

EA 6647: PM III², 34; R.W.H. Vyse, *Operations Carried on at the Pyramids of Gizeh in 1837*, London, 1840–2, II, 86, 87, 93–6, pl. opp. 94; S. Birch, *ZÄS* 7 (1869), 49–50; K. Sethe, *ZÄS* 30 (1892), 94–8; British Museum, *A Handbook to the Egyptian Mummies and Coffins*, London, 1938, 21–3, pl VIII; T.G. Allen, *Occurrences of Pyramid Texts*, Chicago, 1950, 28–9; C.M. Zivie-Coche, *Giza au premier millenaire*, Boston, 1991, 97–101.

EA 17: M.L. Buhl, *The Late Egyptian Anthropoid Stone Sarcophagi*, Copenhagen, 1959, 120–1. See also B.V. Bothmer et al., *Egyptian Sculpture of the Late Period, 700 BC to AD 100*, New York, 1969, 44; R. el-Sayed, *Documents relatifs à Sais et ses divinités*, Cairo, 1975, 269 (67).

EA 29996: N. Reeves, in W.V. Davies (ed.), *Studies in Egyptian Antiquities: A Tribute to T.G.H. James*, London, 1999, 73–7. The example from Thebes is illustrated in Z. Hawass, *Hidden Treasures of the Egyptian Museum*, Washington, DC, 2004, xxvi and published in A.G. Nerlich, A. Zink, U. Sziemies, and H.G. Hagedorn, *The Lancet*, 356 (Dec. 23/30, 2000), 2176–9.

EA 16518: J.H. Taylor and N.C. Strudwick, *Mummies: Death and the Afterlife in Ancient Egypt*, Santa Ana, CA, 2005, 174–5.

EA 1162: J.H. Taylor and N.C. Strudwick, *Mummies: Death and the Afterlife in Ancient Egypt*, Santa Ana, CA, 2005, 13; E. Graefe, *Untersuchungen zur Verwaltung und Geschichte der Institution der Gottesgemahlin*, Wiesbaden, 1981, 219–21, (P20), pls 8*, 16b, 17.

EA 68868: J.H. Taylor and N.C. Strudwick, *Mummies:*

Death and the Afterlife in Ancient Egypt, Santa Ana, CA, 2005, 192–3; see earlier entry for EA 1162.

EA 24656: Phillips, *Africa*, 107. See J. Bulté, *Talismans Egyptiens d'heureuse maternité*, Paris, 1991, 83–4, pls 27–8 for small figurines in this style.

EA 111: PM IV, 6; H. Gauthier, *ASAE* 22 (1922), 85–8, with other objects of the same man in the remainder of the article; for a collection of monuments, family and names and titles, see R. el-Sayed, *Documents relatifs à Sais et ses divinités*, Cairo, 1975, 228–30.

EA 32: Texts: C.E. Sander-Hansen, *Die religiösen Texte auf dem Sarg der Anchnesneferibre*, Copenhagen, 1937. For comments on the find-spot see G. Nagel, *Fouilles de Deir el-Médineh (Nord) [1928]*, Cairo, 1929, 15–22. See N. and H. Strudwick, *Thebes in Egypt*, London, 1999, 136–8.

EA 20763: None.

EA 58323: None. Hedgehogs are discussed in V. von Droste zu Hülshoff, *Der Igel im alten Ägypten*, Hildesheim, 1980. H. Altenmüller, *SAK* 28 (2000), 1–26 discusses the boat with the hedgehog prow.

Amulets: General, C.A.R. Andrews, *Amulets of Ancient Egypt*, London, 1994.

EA 20639: J.H. Taylor and N.C. Strudwick, *Mummies: Death and the Afterlife in Ancient Egypt*, Santa Ana, CA, 2005, 104–5.

EA 54412: F.D. Friedman, *Gifts of the Nile*, London, 1998, 131, 226 (119). See J. Berlandini, *BSEG* 18 (1994), 5–22 for comments on this composite motif.

EA 64659: C.A.R. Andrews, *Amulets of Ancient Egypt*, Austin, 1994, 58.

EA 22: F. Arundale and J. Bonomi, *Gallery of Antiquities*, London, 1842, 110, pl.45 [fig.165]; K. Mysliwiec, *Royal Portraiture*, Mainz, 1988, 69, 79, pl.86c; J. Yoyotte in F. Goddio, *Alexandrie. Les quartiers royaux submergés*, London, 1998, 199–224; Russmann, *Eternal Egypt*, 244–7 (134); J. Yoyotte, *RdE* 54 (2003), 219–53.

EA 1013: E.H. Naville, *The Shrine of Saft el Henneh and the Land of Goshen*, London, 1887, 5, pl. 8; B.P. Davoli, *Saft el-Henna*, Imola, Italy, 2001, 20, 43–4, pl. XV.

EA 523 and 524: E. Iversen, *Obelisks in Exile* II, Copenhagen, 1968, 51–61; L. Habachi, *The Obelisks of Egypt*, New York, 1977, 102–3. See P. Boylan, *Thoth, the Hermes of Egypt*, London, 1922 for information about the deity. The Cairo fragment of EA 524 appears in C. Kuentz, *Obélisques*, Cairo, 1932, 61, pl.15

EA 10: For some of the recent history of the object, see P.M. Fraser, *Ptolemaic Alexandria* II, Oxford, 1972, 39–40 (§2). See E. Hornung, *The Ancient Egyptian Books of the Afterlife*, Ithaca, NY, 1999, 27–53 for the Amduat.

EA 64391: Frequently illustrated; see J. Malek, *The Cat in Ancient Egypt*, 2nd edn, London, 2006 on the Egyptian cat.

Ptolemaic Period

EA 941: J. Josephson, *Egyptian Royal Sculpture of the Late Period*, Mainz, 1997, 30, pl.11a; S. Walker and P. Higgs (eds), *Cleopatra of Egypt*, London, 2001, 42–3 [5]; S.-A. Ashton, *Ptolemaic Royal Sculpture from Egypt*, Oxford, 2001, 84–5, [4]. For the possible relationship to the Djoser statue, see J. Baines and C. Riggs, *JEA* 87 (2001), 103–18.

Hornedjtyitif: Walker and Bierbrier, *Ancient Faces*, 29–30. On the date of the assemblage, see J. Quaegebeur in S.P. Vleeming (ed), *Hundred-Gated Thebes*, Leiden, 1995, 142–4. For the mummy see Dawson and Gray, *Mummies*, 26–7, pls XIIIb, XXXIId; J. Filer in A. Leahy and J. Tait (eds), *Studies in Ancient Egypt in Honour of H. S. Smith*, London, 1999, 97–100. J. Filer, *The Mystery of the Egyptian Mummy*, London, 2003 is a popular book focusing on this burial.

EA 24: R.B. Parkinson, *The Rosetta Stone*, London, 2005, including translation of the demotic text on pp 57–60; C.A.R. Andrews and S. Quirke, *The Rosetta Stone: Facsimile Drawing*, London, 1988. For the background to the decipherment see Parkinson, *Cracking Codes*, 12–69; L. and R. Adkins, *The Keys of Egypt*, London, 2000.

EA 1134: Not formally published; see PM VI, 253. Budge's reference to the acquisition of the naos is in his book *By Nile and Tigris* I, London, 1920, 102–4.

EA 147: S. Walker and P. Higgs (eds), *Cleopatra of Egypt*, London, 2001, 186–7 (193); *Cleopatra's Egypt*, Mainz, 1988, 230–1 (122). Translation: M. Lichtheim: *Ancient Egyptian Literature* III, Berkeley, CA, 1980, 59–65; C. Maystre, *Les grands pretres de Ptah de Memphis*, Göttingen/Freiburg, 1992, 414–22; E.A.E. Reymond, *From the Records of a Priestly Family from Memphis*, Wiesbaden, 1981, 165–77. All of these references contain further bibliographies. The 'song of the harper' is translated in M. Lichtheim, *Ancient Egyptian Literature* I, Berkeley, CA, 1973, 194–7.

Roman Period

EA 21810: Walker and Bierbrier, *Ancient Faces*, 56–7; Dawson and Gray, *Mummies*, 35, pls XVIId, XXXVI a–c. See EA 65346 for further information on mummy-portraits.

EA 29476: G. Grimm, *Die römischen Mumienmasken aus Ägypten*, Wiesbaden, 1974, 36, 94–5, pl. 111 (1); Walker and Bierbrier, *Ancient Faces*, 136–8. For more on the later masks and their owners, see C. Riggs in N. Strudwick and J.H. Taylor, *The Theban Necropolis*, London, 2003, 195–9 and *JEA* 86 (2000), 121–44.

Soter: For the Soter family, tomb and notes on other objects, see: L. Kákosy, in S.P. Vleeming (ed.), *Hundred Gated Thebes*, Leiden, 1995, 61–7; K. van Landuyt in Vleeming (ed.), *op. cit.*, 69–82; Walker and Bierbrier, *Ancient Faces*, 149–50; C. Riggs in N. Strudwick and J.H. Taylor, *The Theban Necropolis*, London, 2003, 193–5; F.R. Herbin, *Padiimenipet fils de Sôter*, Paris, 2002; C. Riggs, *The Beautiful Burial in Roman Egypt*, Oxford, 2005, 182-205, 280-2. For the mummy **EA 6707** see Dawson and Gray, *Mummies*, 33, pl. XVIIa and J. Filer in M.L. Bierbrier (ed.), *Portraits and Masks*, London, 1997, especially pp 124–5.

EA 6704: Dawson and Gray, *Mummies*, 33–4, pls XVIIb, XXXVc, d; Taylor, *Death and the Afterlife*, 90–1.

EA 65346: Walker and Bierbrier, *Ancient Faces*, 95–6; Russmann, *Eternal Egypt*, 209–10 (109). For general material on mummy portraits and related issues, see E. Doxiadis, *The Mysterious Fayum Portraits*, London, 1995; Walker and Bierbrier, *Ancient Faces*; M.L. Bierbrier (ed), *Portraits and Masks*, London, 1997, esp. papers by S. Walker (pp 1–6) and B. Borg (pp 26–32); K. Parlasca, *Mumienporträts*, Wiesbaden, 1966; B. Borg, *Mumienporträts*, Mainz, 1996.

EA 20717: F.D. Friedman, *Beyond the Pharaohs*, Providence, RI, 1989, 126 (36). See D.L. Carroll, *Looms and Textiles of the Copts*, San Francisco, CA, 1988 for background information to weaving and textiles in this period.

Meroitic and Post-Meroitic Periods

EA 719: S.E. Chapman and D. Dunham, *The Royal Cemeteries of Kush* III, Boston, MA, 1952, pl. 7b. Meroitic texts: F.Ll. Griffith, *Meroitic Inscriptions* I, London, 1912, 75; *Répertoire d'épigraphie Méroïtique* I, Paris, 2000, 104–5 (0052). The pyramid and the finds are described in D. Dunham, *The Royal Cemeteries of Kush* IV, Boston, 1957, 72–4.

EA 1650: See T. Eide, T. Hägg, R.H. Pierce and L. Török (eds), *Fontes Historiae Nubiorum. Textual Sources for the History of the Middle Nile Region* II, Bergen, 1994, 719–23.

EA 51500/51615: See D.A. Welsby, *The Kingdom of Kush*, London, 1996 for background, and S. Wenig, *Africa in Antiquity* II, Brooklyn, NY, 1978, 91–9 for Meroitic ceramics.

EA 51500: F.Ll. Griffith, *Liverpool Annals* 11 (1924), 160, pl. XLVIII (6).

EA 51615: F.Ll. Griffith, *Liverpool Annals* 11 (1924), 161, pl. L (9).

X-Group bronzes: EA 66576: A.J. Mills, *The Cemeteries of Qasr Ibrîm*, London, 1982, 19 (32), pls XXI, LXXXVI.4; D.M. Bailey, *A Catalogue of the Lamps in the British Museum* IV, London, 1996, 41, pl. 48 (Q3672) with references.

EA 67163: Unpublished. For the context see W.C. Frend, *JEA* 60 (1974), 39, 52 (45). Comparable objects are discussed in J.H. Taylor, *Sudan Archaeological Research Society Newsletter* 5 (2003), 27–30.

Coptic/Byzantine Period & Later

EA 73139: O.M. Dalton, *JEA* 3 (1916), 35–7, with a note on the text in W.E. Crum and H.I. Bell, *Wadi Sarga: Coptic and Greek Texts from the Excavations Undertaken by the Byzantine Research Account*, Hauniae, 1922, 13, pp 1–13 introduces the site and the monastic community.

EA 73196: Unpublished. An introduction to Coptic ceramics may be found in A.S. Atiya, *The Coptic Encyclopedia*, New York, 1991, II, 480–504. See also EA 73139 above.

EA 71005: H. Behlmer and A. Alcock, *A Piece of Shenoutiana from the Department of Egyptian Antiquities (EA 71005)*, London, 1996. See also F.D. Friedman, *Beyond the Pharaohs*, Providence, RI, 1989, 235. For sheet 3, see Parkinson, *Cracking Codes*, 104.

EA 618: H.R. Hall, *Coptic and Greek Texts of the Christian Period from Ostraka, Stelae, etc., in the British Museum*, London, 1905, 133, pl. 92. See T.K. Thomas, *Late Antique Egyptian Funerary Sculpture*, Princeton, NJ, 2000 for more information on such objects.

EA 71304: J.M. Plumley and G.M. Browne, *Old Nubian Texts from Qasr Ibrîm* I, London, 1988. EA 71304 is also discussed in *Sudan Texts Bulletin* IV, 1–10. See D.A. Welsby, *The Medieval Kingdoms of Nubia*, London, 2002, 236–41 for a survey of languages used in Nubia.

EA 71955: See J.M. Plumley, *The Scrolls of Bishop Timotheus*, London, 1975 for the texts. Aspects of the context and the historical background appear in a review of Plumley, *op. cit.*, by W.H.C. Frend in *Zeitschrift für Kirchengeschichte* (1978), 190-1. See D.A. Welsby, *Medieval Kingdoms of Nubia*, London, 2002, chap. 10 for the historical background.

Index of British Museum numbers

EA number	Page number	EA number	Page number	EA number	Page number	EA number	Page number	EA number	Page number
2	158	684	90	6706	310	32191	120	52831	124
3	152	691	46	6707	308	32650	38	54412	280
5	152	705	212	7876	110	32751	26	54460	97
7	154	708	136	8446	296	35502	28	54678	100
8	248	719	316	9524	84	35571	44	55193	182
10	288	828	88	9736	296	35572	44	55424	116
12	132	871	114	9999	226	35597	42	55722	62
15	160	919	150	10037	296	37097	105	56929	140
17	266	920	148	10054	233	37976	174	56930	140
19	202	922	148	10057	118	37977	170	57399	180
22	282	935	178	10058	118	37978	174	58323	279
24	298	941	292	10059	198	37979	174	58892	98
26	224	947	210	10068	234	37981	172	59194	96
32	276	963	76	10221	232	37982	176	59648	24
36	192	1001	168	10375	238	37983	176	60006	200
38	162	1013	284	10470	218	37984	172	61283	188
43	144	1063	92	10472	236	37986	172	64391	290
48	134	1103	138	10474	240	37987	146	64564	142
57	156	1134	300	10610	102	37991	148	64659	280
62	156	1147	78	10735	60	37996	36	65346	312
75	184	1150	78	10752–72	102	40915	72	66576	322
76	156	1162	270	10800	246	41544	216	67153	40
80	156	1181	52	15655	258	41545	216	67163	322
81	222	1203	68	16518	269	41546	216	68512	32
93	128	1239	58	16672	244	41547	216	68868	272
101	94	1324	56	20639	280	41548	216	69014	50
111	274	1650	318	20717	314	41603	250	69015	50
117	204	1770	262	20763	278	41668	70	71005	328
140	228	1785	106	20791	34	41748	108	71304	332
147	302	1848	64	20865	190	43071	208	71955	334
171	48	2472	196	20868	236	48001	214	73139	324
174	130	2560	194	21810	304	50699	188	73196	326
480	166	5620	230	22542	242	50702	188		
498	260	5634	206	24656	273	50703	188		
523	286	6459	74	27332	256	51157	30		
524	286	6647	264	27735	258	51168	30		
551	186	6652	112	29476	306	51220	66		
579	86	6660	252	29770	122	51225	66		
618	330	6677	296	29996	268	51245	66		
657	164	6678	294	30720	254	51500	320		
682	54	6704	311	30838	81	51615	320		
683	126	6705	308	30839	81	51813	214		

Index of Egyptian names

Seqenenre 112
Sethnakht 226
Sety I 204, 235
Sety II 224
Shabaka 260
Shanakdakhete 316
Shenoute 328
Shepseskaf 54
Sheshonq 248, 270, 272

Sheshonq II 248
Sitamun 128
Sneferu 36, 50, 56
Sneferuser 86
Soter 308

Taharqa 262, 334
Taimhotep 302
Takelot III 254

Tashebenneith 274
Thutmose I 130
Thutmose II 130
Thutmose III 130, 132, 142, 160
Thutmose IV 142, 144, 146
Timotheus 334
Tiye 180
Tjanefer 234

Tjezemy 60
Tutankhamun 158, 184, 186, 188, 262, 278
Userkaf 54
Userwer 86

Wahibre 274

Zanakht 46

Index of place names